Best Bike Rides
Los Angeles

The Greatest Recreational Rides
in the Metro Area

WAYNE D. COTTRELL

FALCONGUIDES

GUILFORD, CONNECTICUT
HELENA, MONTANA

FALCONGUIDES®

An imprint of Rowman & Littlefield.
Falcon, FalconGuides, and Outfit Your Mind are registered trademarks of Rowman & Littlefield.

Distributed by NATIONAL BOOK NETWORK

Copyright © 2015 by Rowman & Littlefield
Photos: Wayne D. Cottrell unless otherwise noted.
Maps: DesignMaps Inc. © Rowman & Littlefield

British Library Cataloguing-in-Publication Information available.

Library of Congress Cataloging-in-Publication Data

Cottrell, Wayne D.
  Best bike rides Los Angeles : the greatest recreational rides in the metro area / Wayne D. Cottrell.
    pages cm
  Includes bibliographical references.
  ISBN 978-1-4930-0384-6 (pbk. : alk. paper) -- ISBN 978-1-4930-1471-2 (e-book) 1. Cycling--California--Los Angeles Metropolitan Area--Guidebooks. 2. Bicycle trails--California--Los Angeles Metropolitan Area--Guidebooks. 3. Bicycle touring--California--Los Angeles Metropolitan Area--Guidebooks. 4. Los Angeles Metropolitan Area (Calif.)--Guidebooks. I. Title.
  GV1045.5.C22L6746 2015
  796.609794'94--dc23
                    2015011766

♾™ The paper used in this publication meets the minimum requirements of American National Standard for Information Sciences—Permanence of Paper for Printed Library Materials, ANSI/NISO Z39.48-1992.

To my son, Tyler; my dear Nancy;
and the memories of my mother, Barbara,
and grandmother, Louella

Help Us Keep This Guide Up to Date

Every effort has been made by the authors and editors to make this guide as accurate and useful as possible. However, many things can change after a guide is published—roads are detoured or under repair, facilities come under new management, phone numbers change, and so forth.

We welcome your comments concerning your experiences with this guide and how you feel it could be improved and kept up to date. While we may not be able to respond to all comments and suggestions, we'll take them to heart, and we'll also make certain to share them with the author. Please send your comments and suggestions to the following address:

FalconGuides
Reader Response/Editorial Department
246 Goose Lane
Guilford, CT 06437

Or you may e-mail us at:
editorial@falcon.com

Thanks for your input, and happy riding!

Contents

Introduction 1

How to Use This Guide 7

Ride Finder 10

Map Legend 12

Best Central and Southeast L.A. Region Rides 13

  1. Ernest Debs MASH Ride 14

  2. Hollywood Ride of Fame 21

  3. L.A. River Ramble & Echo Park Challenge 29

  4. OC North Coast Promenade 37

  5. South Central Urban Experience 43

  6. Tour of the Lower San Gabriel River Valley 52

  7. Vuelta Tres Rios de Los Angeles 60

  8. Whittier–Workman Hill Workout 68

Best North and Northwest L.A. Region Rides 74

  9. Big Tujunga Canyon Epic 75

10. Cheeseboro-Comado Canyons Chug 82

11. Circuito de Calabasas 88

12. Josephine Peak Hill Climb 94

13. Mission Point: Weldon Canyon 98

14. The Oliver Twist 104

15. Ride Up over Mulholland 110

16. Ruta del Placerita Tujunga 116

17. Verdugo Mountains Panorama Ride 122

18. Verdugo Mountains Perimeter Ride 127

19. Way of the Wilson and May Canyons 133

Best Northeast L.A. Region Rides: San Gabriel

Valley and Mountains 139

20. Ahwingna Pahe Mahar 140

21. Azusadora 39 Classic 145

Overview

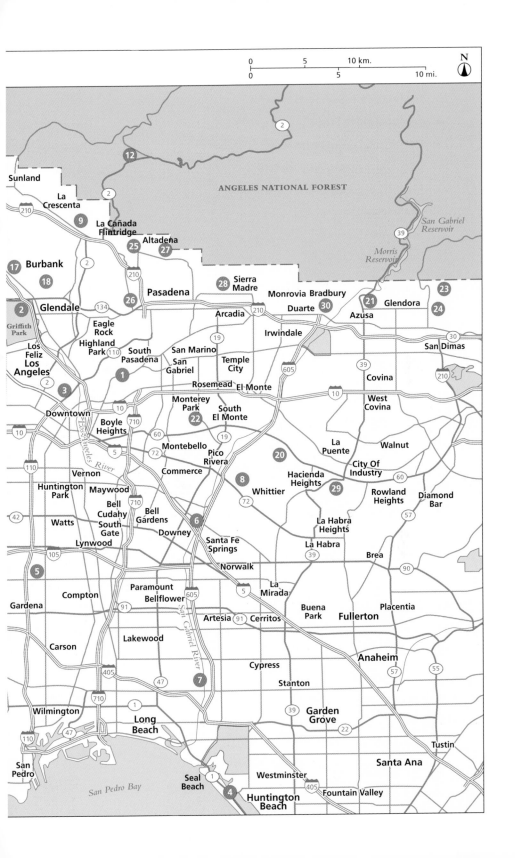

22. Emerald Necklace Cruise. 151

23. Glendora Mountain Trails Traverse 159

24. Glendora Ridge Stage 164

25. Hahamongna Watershed Shred 170

26. Little Old Ride through Pasadena 175

27. Mounts Lowe and Wilson Expedition. 182

28. Santa Anita Canyon Call 190

29. Schabarum Scramble. 195

30. White Saddle Challenge 201

Best West and Southwest L.A. Region Rides 207

31. Baldwin Hills Hahn-wind. 209

32. Beverly Hills Brevet 215

33. Crankin' Franklin Canyon 221

34. Malibulldog MASH 4077 Tour. 226

35. Passeio de Palos Verdes 232

36. Rambla Piuma Pacifico 239

37. Rondo Redondo Beach. 245

38. South Bay Beach–Ballona Bike Tour. 250

39. Topanga Puku Pawahe. 258

40. Topanga to Tuna to Tide 265

41. Zoom Dume Zuma 272

42. Zuma Trancas Calayas 278

Best Catalina Island Rides. 283

43. Catalina East End Eco-Ride 285

44. In & Around Avalon Road Tour 291

45. Middle Catalina Traverse. 297

Ride Log 303

References 305

About the Author 312

Introduction

The Los Angeles region had a population of 15 million in 2013—18 million including its satellite urban areas—making it the second largest in the United States and one of the largest in the world. It is considered to be the most densely populated urban conglomeration in the United States, suggesting that the built-up environment is extensive and deep. A local website, humorously titled "Nobody Hikes in L.A.," is a testament to the prevailing perception that the region is overwhelmed by freeways, streets, and an endless number of motor vehicles and trucks. Where can one go to ride a bicycle? Well, the "Nobody Hikes" website is a great resource for hikers and, to a certain extent, mountain bikers, suggesting that there are some nearby getaways—one just needs to know where to find them. Similarly, there is plenty of good cycling in L.A.—one simply needs to know the right roads, areas, trails, paths, and parks.

From the context of cycling as a sport, the L.A. region is ideal for riding. Although the region, somewhat embarrassingly, did not have a professional football team as of this writing, the area does have three pro basketball teams, two pro baseball teams, two pro ice hockey teams, and two pro soccer teams. Two Summer Olympic Games (1932 and 1984) have been held here as well. In part because of excellent year-round weather, the L.A. region has hosted countless championship-level competitions in sports ranging from archery to weightlifting.

Best Bike Rides Los Angeles offers descriptions of forty-five rides in the L.A. region, including twenty-three for road bikes and twenty-two for mountain bikes. The area of coverage is a rough 25-mile radius around central (downtown) L.A., skewed a bit toward the west. Because of its heavy urbanization, L.A. lacks distinct geographic regions. There are rivers, valleys, hills, mountains, and other enclaves; but the extensive development has led them to effectively merge into one another, or be "paved over." Using area codes, this guide divides L.A. into four regions: central and southeast, north and northwest, northeast, and west and southwest. A fifth region, Catalina Island, is included to ensure that cyclists know about this nearby escape and where to ride on this offshore gem. All the rides are located in Los Angeles County, including Catalina, although a couple cross the border into neighboring Orange and Ventura Counties. Road rides range in length from 4 to 50 miles, while mountain bike ride distances range from 3 to 25 miles. Routes range in altitude from just above sea level, along the beaches, to over 5,600 feet for one of the rides that ascends to a peak in the San Gabriel Mountains. The difference in elevations is one of the widest in the country, making this collection of rides unique.

Encompassing nearly 5,000 square miles, the Los Angeles urbanized area can be overwhelming to the uninformed cyclist. This book uniquely divides the region into a grid and then features up to one road and one mountain bike ride from each cell within the five subregions described above. In comparison, most other cycling books focus on specific roads, paths, or parks. To orient the user, the GPS coordinates of each start-finish point are included. Information on climb lengths and gradients are included as well, including one optional doozy that tilts upward at 32%!

ABOUT THIS GUIDE

This book offers rides of various lengths and terrain to cover a wide range of cycling abilities. Just over half the forty-five rides are for road bikes, and just under half are for mountain bikes. The shortest, flattest rides are for beginners and families; the longest, hilliest rides are for experienced riders. Most of the rides, however, are for recreational and even competitive cyclists looking for a variety of riding routes in the Los Angeles area. Given the large size of the region, it is likely that even riders who are native to the area will not be familiar with all the routes in this book.

Accompanying the maps are specifications (start point, length, traffic volume, trail conditions, etc.) and a text description of each ride. In addition to describing the ride itself, the ride narrative also explores the history, folklore, special events, culture, flora, and fauna along the way so that the rider knows what to expect—and look forward to. The descriptions give each route character, helping the rider to perhaps relive and retrace milestones in the region's history. Not to ignore current conditions, the descriptions also discuss demographics, urban issues, and transportation infrastructure as needed to keep the rider in the present.

GPS coordinates for each ride's starting point are included to help you find your way.

ABOUT LOS ANGELES

As recently as 1840, author Richard Henry Dana, in his book *Two Years Before the Mast*, wrote "....what a country this might be" about Los Angeles. In just 175 years, the undeveloped, quiet, and pristine valleys and mountains of the Los Angeles region have been transformed into a thriving metropolis that is America's second largest and most densely populated. The region's Mediterranean climate has historically been its prime attraction, along with some 74 miles of coastline. During Richard Dana's era, Los Angeles was comparatively inaccessible: For example, the city's residents did not learn about California statehood until over a month after the Compromise of 1850 was legislated by the US Congress. Being hemmed in by deserts and mountains, the ocean offered the best access route. Consequently, growth was slow. The completion of the Transcontinental Railroad in 1869 dramatically improved access to California and fueled a population boom. Although the growth was initially focused on San Francisco, by 1920 Los Angeles had surpassed S.F. as California's most populous city. By this time, Los Angeles was facing its next major challenge: water. Being situated in a relatively dry climate, there was not enough water to support a large population. And, when the rains did come, there were occasional, catastrophic floods that wiped out parts of the valley. A series of civil engineering works during the twentieth century, fostered by forward-thinkers such as William Mulholland, resulted in an extensive collection of dams and channels that tamed L.A.'s waters and provided for millions. Despite the extensive hydro-infrastructure, the quest for water to serve an ever-surging population continues even today.

As of this writing, Los Angeles' population had surpassed 4 million. While the city is definitely a behemoth, many of its satellite cities are large and unique in their own right, including Long Beach (population nearly one-half million), Glendale, Pasadena, and many others. Los Angeles County, in fact, features eighty-eight incorporated cities, of which about half have a population of 50,000 or more. The combined populations of the cities put L.A. County at just over the 10 million mark. Most of the cities are contiguous, meaning that one can travel from one to the next, often hardly noticing that a boundary has been crossed. A number of the L.A. region's cities are discussed in the book, particularly those having their own riveting stories to tell. There are an additional 8 million folks in the surrounding urbanized counties of Ventura, Orange, Riverside, and San Bernardino.

The region is served by a very extensive freeway network, and the large population inevitably produces motor vehicle traffic congestion that delays travelers. Today, travelers can arrive in L.A. on: I-5 from points to the north, such as the San Francisco Bay Area; I-15 from points to the northeast, such as Las Vegas; and I-10 and I-8 from points to the east, such as Phoenix. San Diego is a little over 100 miles to the south, via I-5. Travelers also come to L.A. by aircraft: The Los Angeles International Airport was the second-busiest in the nation as of this writing. Folks also arrive in L.A. by train: Amtrak and regional express commuter trains rumble in and out of the centrally located Union Station regularly. Still others come to L.A. by bus and boat. When I asked an airport worker for directions once, he pointed toward the taxi cabs. When I cautioned him that I was looking to catch a connecting flight at another terminal, he remarked, "Oh—sorry—Los Angeles is home to everybody!"

The success of Los Angeles can be traced, in part, to the diverse array of industries that have found a home in the region. These include oil, first discovered here in 1891, aerospace systems, business, education, fashion, medicine, research, sports, science and technology, and, of course, entertainment. There is also a luxury market here that includes numerous expensive houses—often with eye-popping designs, high-price clothing and jewelry, priceless memorabilia, and other high-end offerings, intended for the wealthy, who have a comfortable niche in L.A. Los Angeles brims with superlatives: More actors, artists, dancers, musicians, and writers live here than in any other place in the world; the city is the most ethnically diverse in the country; the city's economy is the third most powerful of any city in the world (after New York City and Tokyo); and on and on. L.A.'s many landmarks include the La Brea Tar Pits, the John Paul Getty Museum and Villa, Walt Disney Concert Hall, Angels Flight, the Watts Towers, L.A. Live, Staples Center, Dodger Stadium, Griffith Park and Observatory, and, of course, Hollywood (Hollywood Bowl, Graumann's Chinese Theater, Dolby Theater, etc.), not to mention miles and miles of glorious beaches. L.A. also has plenty of "scenes" that simply must be experienced—these include Venice Beach, Sunset Boulevard, Wilshire Boulevard's Miracle Mile, Santa Monica Pier, and many others. Because L.A. is the capital of the motion picture industry, plenty of filming occurs in and around L.A., simply by convenience of location. As you move around the city, certain scenes, viewpoints, and perspectives might seem eerily familiar; chances are, you have "been to this place before" in a TV show or film. Color photographs from the rides in this book should further entice the reader to get out there and see these sites personally.

As for Los Angeles' suitability for extensive cycling, the city's reputation as a "car capital" is debunked in the form of forty-five awesome road and mountain bike rides in the region. The surge in the popularity of bicycling in the United States, particularly in urban regions, is reflected in the extensive bike paths, lanes, and signage in the L.A. area. Many of the rides in this guide take advantage of these assets. Mountain and island escapes are described, indicating that despite L.A.'s high urban density, there are plenty of opportunities to ride away from the noise and intensity. L.A.'s reputation as a "smog capital" is also debunked, as the smog alerts of the 1970s have nearly been eradicated, giving way to the stunning color photos in the book and the bounty of healthy riding.

RESOURCES

Hidden behind the glut of cars, trucks, freeways, congestion, traffic signals, and noise for which Los Angeles is known is a thriving bicycling community. Bicycling in the Los Angeles region is promoted, supported, and improved by a variety of organizations, clubs, websites, and media. The key organizations are the Los Angeles Department of Transportation (100 South Main St., 9th Floor, Los Angeles; 213-972-4972; http://bicyclela.org) and the Los Angeles County Bicycle Coalition (634 South Spring St., Suite 821, Los Angeles; 213-629-2142; http://la-bike.org). Notable social media sites include C.I.C.L.E. (Cyclists Inciting Change thru LIVE Exchange; www.cicle.org) and Biking in L.A. (http://bikinginla.com). The Los Angeles Bike Paths website (www.labike paths.com) provides information on the region's bikeway network, while the SoCalCycling website (http://socalcycling.com) has information on racing, clubs, bike shops, products, events, and other resources. The region is home to a host of bicycling clubs, ranging from recreational riders to serious racing teams; an excellent list is provided at http://socalcycling.com/clubs-teams/. Bicycle shops are also great resources; a fine list is available at http://socal cycling.com/bike-shops/. In addition, each ride in this book is followed by information about one or more nearby bike shops.

SAFETY AND EQUIPMENT

For most of the road routes described in this book, traffic ranges from minimal to medium heavy. In some places the amount of traffic will depend on the time of day and day of the week you are riding. Quiet suburban roads sometimes get swamped with traffic during the afternoon commute. In other places, traffic jams can occur on Saturday afternoon.

To be safe, it is paramount to be predictable. This means that when motorists have a good sense of what to expect from you, you'll be safer on the road. Riding with traffic, signaling turns, and generally obeying the same rules that apply to motor traffic are great habits to take up. For the novice, riding through congestion in Los Angeles will be easier than you think. Part of the reason for this is that drivers are accustomed to sharing the road with you.

Being predictable and eliminating your own bad cycling habits will go a long way in helping you minimize the chances of a collision. Still, your good habits won't prevent you from the being on the receiving end of the foolishness of others. Avoiding troubles caused by the ineptitude and carelessness of drivers means being able to anticipate potential problems before they happen. A couple of the biggest dangers to watch for are drivers opening car doors and drivers making left turns. The door zone—the area where car doors swing open—should be avoided like the plague, even if that requires you to ride farther into the traffic lane than some motorists would like. Let them honk. Better to quietly endure a car horn than get doored. Similarly, when avoiding potholes or other obstacles on the roadside, you have the right to take the lane. Again, some drivers will honk. Your job is to keep a level head and move back to the right side of the road when your pathway is clear.

Seasoned cyclists (those who have had some scrapes of their own) know that one of the most common types of collisions occurs when oncoming cars turn left. A lawyer friend who represents cyclists and pedestrians says this type of crash accounts for about half of his cases involving cyclists. Bikers are advised to use special caution around these problem areas; this means not assuming that drivers see you—and not assuming drivers will stop for you.

In some cases, drivers present less of a problem than do pedestrians and other cyclists. Busier local trails—such as the Marvin Braude Bike Trail and the Los Angeles River Bikeway—can be just as hazardous as the road. While you may be tempted to abandon your laser-like focus while pedaling along a trail, don't. Be prepared to act quickly when stray children, dim-witted Chihuahuas, and disco-dancing in-line skaters suddenly appear in front of you. As pocket-size electronic doodads multiply, cyclists must be even more watchful for squirrelly behavior among those they encounter on the road and on the trail.

If you're just learning the ropes of riding in traffic, a bike safety class can offer a big leg up. Beginners will become more self-assured if they know basic skills such as riding predictably, being visible, and keeping a safe distance from parked cars. People who participate in a good bike safety class consistently express how much safer and more comfortable they feel riding in a variety of traffic conditions. Cycling courses also typically touch upon other topics essential for novices, such as bike selection and fit, basics of bike handling, and maintenance.

So what should you bring on your ride? This list varies a great deal depending on the season, ride length, and how prepared you like to be. First, pack a pump and spare tube or patch kit. A small multi-tool will help with adjustments and minor repairs. Bring lights for front and back if there is even a slight chance that you'll be riding after dusk. Bring water, something to snack on, and one more layer than you think you'll need. Cell phones have proven to be handy in case help is needed; a few dollars stuffed in your pocket will score you some freshly baked cookies along the way to replenish your burned calories.

The weather in the Los Angeles area is perfect year-round for cycling. The higher elevations in the mountains may be the only place you'll find truly cool temperatures, even some snowfall. Most often, a light layer of nylon or fleece is all you'll need in cooler weather; a jacket, light gloves, a thin cap, and comfortable pants will do the trick. If it's a long ride, take an extra layer. In warm weather dress lightly and carry plenty of fluids.

How to Use This Guide

When choosing rides in this book, observe both the length and the net elevation difference, as well as the range of ride times. The length will give you an idea of how long and doable a ride may be for you. Similarly, the net elevation difference will indicate the amount of climbing, although the indication is not exact—additional climbing can be concentrated between the two extremes of the net elevation differential. Road rides range from 3.9 to 49.9 miles, with equal proportions in the 15-to-25-mile and 30-to-40-mile ranges. The easiest rides have an elevation differential of less than 500 feet—these are found along the coast and in flatter inland areas. The Los Angeles region is hilly, though—downright mountainous, in fact—so flat rides are the exception rather than the rule. Only seven rides in this guide have an elevation differential of less than 500 feet; most of them exceed 500 feet of net climbing, while more than 40% feature a net differential of 1,000 feet or more. Mountain bike rides range in length from 3.35 to 24.7 miles, and there is some climbing in each of them. More than half have an elevation differential of over 1,000 feet; well, these *are* "mountain" bike rides!

The Ride Log in the back of the book shows the distribution of ride distances and elevation changes. The easiest rides, and perhaps the best ones to do with children, use bike paths, have no more than a few hundred feet of elevation change, and are in the shorter distance range. Note that rides can be improvised by turning around early on an out-and-back segment or by concentrating on the bike path segments only. Also, longer rides can be created simply by doing two laps of a route rather than one.

UTM coordinates: Readers who use either a handheld or car-mounted GPS unit can punch in the Universal Transverse Mercator (UTM) coordinates for each starting point and have the GPS lead the way. The UTM coordinates are to be used with NAD 27 datums (rather than WGS83 or WGS84). Along with the UTM coordinates, the zone is also given. All coordinates were generated using mapping software rather than taking readings "in the field."

Mileage markers on the map: Do not be alarmed if the distances provided in this book do not match up with distances provided by existing trail maps or your own bike odometer. If you're using a bike odometer, keep in mind that they have to be calibrated carefully; just changing to a larger tire can make a noticeable difference. While GPS devices are generally accurate, they too can lead you astray. If you backtrack or pursue a side trip and forget to subtract this distance from the total mileage covered, it will create a different mileage reading than given in this book. Use the mileage markers on the maps in this book as a rough guide that provides you with a close—but not exact—determination of distance traveled.

HIGHWAY, STREET, PATH, AND TRAIL NAMES

Highway and street names are taken from street maps and signs. State highways can be abbreviated "SR," for "State Route." One SR in particular, SR 1 (Pacific Coast Highway), is commonly referred to as the PCH by locals. Path names are not always evident, but many of the L.A. region bike path names are painted onto the path at spaced intervals. Overpasses are often indicated by an overhead sign. Without these it can be difficult to tell exactly where you are relative to the outside world when on an exclusive bike path (bicyclists, pedestrians, runners, but no motorized vehicles). Trails in the region are, admittedly, not as well marked as in some other regions, such as the San Francisco Bay area. Trails within the Santa Monica Mountains National Recreation Area tend to have good signing, as do those within state parks. Trails in the Angeles National Forest have sporadic signing, and sometimes the marker is that of an USDA Forest Service road rather than what might be indicated on a map. In other areas, such as the Puente Hills, trail markers are sporadic. The mileage logs and text descriptions attempt to convey, as well as possible, proper directions to help you keep on course.

ROAD SURFACE, SHOULDER, PATH, AND TRAIL CONDITIONS

In general, road surfaces in the L.A. region are in good condition unless otherwise noted. Similarly, shoulder widths are adequate unless otherwise noted. Many of the mountain bike rides take advantage of fire roads, which are generally wide and graded. All dirt roads and trails in the L.A. region are, however, subject to rocky terrain. Also, erosion can occur over time, as well as fissures that are akin to small canyons on the trails. Challenging surface conditions can occur after heavy rains, rockslides, and even minor earth movements. Also, some trails feature deep, loose sand in spots—this can be caused by equestrian use as well as by trucks. In some locations the sand is placed deliberately as a means of slowing heavy vehicles on steep grades and in advance of tight curves. It may take a good pair of strong legs, or at least a good line, to negotiate sandy stretches.

Traffic volumes are provided for many of the roads that are used in the routes. The volume provided is typically a 24-hour value from a busy weekday. In general, the most recent traffic volume data are given. In some cases, the data may date from more than ten years ago. The values are nonetheless current, however, given that traffic volumes in built-up areas have tended to stabilize over the last ten years. The stabilization has resulted from the offset of population growth and surges in motor vehicle use, by a slower economy, higher gasoline prices, improvements in public transportation, and improvements to cycling facilities. A guideline is that fewer than 1,500 vehicles per day is very light (rural, country feel); 1,500 to 7,500 vehicles per day is low; 7,500 to 17,500 vehicles per day is medium; and over 17,500 vehicles per day is heavy. The rides tend to avoid heavily trafficked roads, unless there are no other feasible or convenient options.

HOW TO USE THE MAPS

Each ride map illustrates the given cycling route and start-end point against a backdrop of important roads, geographical features, communities, and landmarks. The maps include a limited amount of information, by intention, to emphasize the given route. Selected mile markers, along with the recommended direction of travel, are included on each map. For out-and-back segments, the mile markers generally pertain to the outbound direction of travel. The total length of the ride is listed adjacent to the start-end point. Note that the scale of each map may be different. If you need more detailed map information, please refer to the "Map" entry in each ride's at-a-glance section.

Ride Finder

	Miles	Bike	Main Feature
Central & Southeast Los Angeles			
Ernest Debs MASH Ride*	8.0	mountain	Arroyo Seco Parkway
Hollywood Ride of Fame	20.8	road	Hollywood Boulevard
L.A. River Ramble & Echo Park Challenge*	17.6	road	Optional 32% climb
OC North Coast Promenade*	19.0	road	Huntington bike path
South Central Urban Experience	23.1	road	Watts Towers
Tour of the Lower San Gabriel River Valley*	39.0	road	San Gabriel River
Vuelta Tres Rios de Los Angeles*	49.9	road	L.A. River Bikeway
Whittier–Workman Hill Workout	9.85	mountain	Puente Hills trails
North & Northwest Los Angeles			
Big Tujunga Canyon Epic	36.2	road	Angeles Crest Highway
Cheeseboro-Comado Canyons Chug*	10.7	mountain	Palo Comado Canyon
Circuito de Calabasas	23.6	road	Mulholland Highway
Josephine Peak Hill Climb	8.0	mountain	Peak altitude 5,516 ft
Mission Point: Weldon Canyon	11.2	mountain	Saugus-to-Sea Road
The Oliver Twist	8.4	mountain	Oliver Canyon Road
Ride Up over Mulholland*	17.3	mountain	"Dirt Mulholland"
Ruta del Placerita Tujunga	31.95	road	Placerita Canyon
Verdugo Mountains Panorama Ride	13.8	mountain	View from Verdugos
Verdugo Mountains Perimeter Ride	21.7	road	La Tuna Canyon Road
Way of the Wilson and May Canyons	15.2	mountain	May Canyon trail
Northeast of Los Angeles			
Ahwingna Pahe Mahar*	3.65	mountain	Puente Hills trails
Azusadora 39 Classic	32.7	road	San Gabriel Canyon

	Miles	Bike	Main Feature
Emerald Necklace Cruise*	35.5	road	Rio Hondo Bikeway
Glendora Mountain Trails Traverse	6.3	mountain	Lower Monroe trail
Glendora Ridge Stage	39.4	road	Glendora Ridge Road
Hahamongna Watershed Shred	8.7	mountain	Brown Mountain trails
Little Old Ride through Pasadena	17.5	road	Chevy Chase Drive
Mounts Lowe and Wilson Expedition	24.7	mountain	Mount Wilson Toll Road
Santa Anita Canyon Call	9.4	road	Santa Anita Canyon
Schabarum Scramble*	9.5	mountain	Schabarum Trail
White Saddle Challenge*	17.0	mountain	Monrovia Canyon
West & Southwest of Los Angeles			
Baldwin Hills Hahn-wind*	3.35	mountain	Kenneth Hahn Park
Beverly Hills Brevet	11.3	road	Benedict Canyon Drive
Crankin' Franklin Canyon*	6.05	mountain	Franklin Canyon Park
Malibulldog MASH 4077 Tour*	16.65	mountain	M*A*S*H TV show site
Passeio de Palos Verdes	26.8	road	Palos Verdes Drives
Rambla Piuma Pacifico	18.7	road	Rambla Pacifico road
Rondo Redondo Beach*	3.9	road	Marvin Braude path
South Bay Beach–Ballona Bike Tour*	30.7	road	Marvin Braude path
Topanga Puku Pawahe	16.75	mountain	Topanga Canyon Park
Topanga to Tuna to Tide*	38.2	road	Topanga Canyon Road
Zoom Dume Zuma	33.1	road	Pacific Coast Highway
Zuma Trancas Calayas	12.85	mountain	Zuma Canyon
Santa Catalina Island			
Catalina East End Eco-Ride	13.3	mountain	East End Road
In & Around Avalon Road Tour*	10.6	road	Tour of Avalon
Middle Catalina Traverse	20.0	mountain	Middle Ranch Road

Portions of the routes marked with an asterisk feature paved bicycle paths or easy trails that would be appropriate for riders with children.

Map Legend

Transportation

Interstate/Divided Highway	═══════
Featured US Highway	═══════
US Highway	═══════
Featured State Highway	▬▬▬▬▬
Featured County or Local Road	──────
Primary Highway	──────
County/Local Road	──────
Featured Bike Route	▪▪▪▪▪▪▪▪▪
Bike Route	▪▪▪▪▪▪▪▪▪
Trail/Dirt Road	─ ─ ─ ─

Hydrology

Reservoir/Lake	⬭
River/Creek	∿

Land Use

State/Local Park	⬓

Symbols

Interstate	⑤
US Highway	〔101〕
State Highway	①
County/Forest Road	2N64
Trailhead (Start)	❶
Mileage Marker	17.1◆──
Visitor Center	❓
Point of Interest	■
Parking	🅿
Airport	✈
University/College	🎓
Direction Arrow	→
Gate	⌁
Stairs	▥

Best Central and Southeast L.A. Region Rides

The Central/Southeast region of Los Angeles includes cities and communities surrounding the lower Los Angeles and San Gabriel Rivers. The region stretches from the Los Angeles communities of Eagle Rock, Hollywood, and Silver Lake in the north, along with South Pasadena, to Long Beach and Seal Beach in the south. These cities and communities are served by the 213, 323, and 562 area codes. If freeways are used as the boundary indicators—as seems appropriate in a region that is so dependent on freeway travel—these routes would be I-110, I-105, and I-710 in the west; I-605 in the east; and SR 2, SR 134, SR 110, and I-10 in the north. (The southern boundary is the ocean.)

With a population of 2.75 million spread over an area of 304 square miles, the population density is high—about 9,000 per square mile. The biggest cities in the region are Los Angeles (not the entire city—about 0.5 million of the city's residents live in the contiguous communities) and Long Beach, with a population of 462,257 in 2010 but nearly 0.5 million as of this writing. Running a distant third, fourth, and fifth are the unincorporated community of East Los Angeles (126,496 in 2010) and the cities of Downey (111,772) and Norwalk (105,549).

Because of the high urban density, there are limited off-road cycling opportunities in this region. However, Ernest E. Debs Regional Park, to the north of downtown, and the western edge of the Puente Hills near Whittier offer some great riding. The roads tend to be crowded with motor vehicles, but fortunately an excellent bicycle path network provides some outstanding road riding. In fact, it is very likely that a cyclist can get around the city faster on the paths than a driver can on city streets (and even on the freeways during periods of heavy traffic congestion).

The rivers that define the region run dry most of the time because of the urbanization. The natural environment seems to be limited to the parks, although some of these, such as Griffith Park, are magnificent. The region includes some of the Los Angeles region's most illustrious communities, including Hollywood, Compton, and Watts, as well as communities that have had their share of infamy, including Bell, East Los Angeles, Signal Hill, and Sunset Beach. Regarding the latter, most of the region is within Los Angeles County except for a few communities in far western Orange County.

This guide features six road bike and two mountain bike rides within the Central/Southeast region. The road rides range in length from 17.6 to 49.9 miles, the latter being the longest ride in this book. The mountain bike rides are 8.0 and 9.85 miles in length, respectively, with the latter featuring a shorter 5.85-mile option.

Ernest Debs MASH Ride

Start: Ernest E. Debs Regional Park, central parking lot accessed from Monterey Road

Length: 8.0 miles (clockwise loop plus an out-and-back)

Riding time: 40 minutes to 2 hours (my time: 55:36)

Terrain and surface: 70% paved; 30% dirt trails (wide, occasionally bumpy fire roads)

Elevation: Low: 423 feet along Arroyo Seco Parkway; high: 882 feet in Ernest Debs Regional Park

Traffic and hazards: 70% of the ride on car-free paths and trails; 30% on public roads. Griffin Avenue carried 7,100 vehicles per day in 2004; Mercury Avenue carried 3,900 vehicles per day in 2009.

Map: *The Thomas Guide—Street Guide: Los Angeles and Orange Counties* (any recent year), page 595

Getting there: By car—From central Los Angeles, head northeast on SR 110 / Arroyo Seco Parkway (formerly Pasadena Freeway). Exit at Marmion Way and turn right onto Marmion. Turn right onto Arroyo Verde Road and then right again at Monterey Road. Head south on Monterey, passing through the Hermon neighborhood and into the community of Monterey Hills. After a climb through and passage by an architecturally significant retaining wall, look for the entrance to the park on the right, on the descent. The road into the park features numerous speed bumps. *Note:* This route requires that you pass the park on its west side prior to exiting the freeway; then a reversal of direction, on city streets, returns you to the park's east side.

    By public transit—Hop on the Metro Gold Line (light-rail transit) at any of several central Los Angeles stations and head north, toward Pasadena. Exit at Highland Park station and head toward the southwest on your bike. Turn left onto Avenue 57 and continue across Figueroa Street. At Via Marisol, turn left and cross over SR 110 and the Arroyo Seco. Continue to Monterey Road; turn right here and head south. After a brisk climb (see above) and descent, turn right to enter Ernest E. Debs

Regional Park. The park access road is uphill. At this writing, the Gold Line was running every 6 to 20 minutes seven days a week.

Starting point coordinates: N34.091492° / W118.193561°

THE RIDE

The Ernest Debs MASH Ride starts and finishes in Ernest E. Debs Regional Park, which is located north-northeast of central Los Angeles. The route covers trails and roads in the park, the adjacent Montecito Heights neighborhood, and the Arroyo Seco Parkway bike path. Many of the parks in Los Angeles' core area do not allow mountain bikes. This regional park does, however, in part because the trails are wide fire roads and are easily shared with hikers and runners. The fire roads are bumpy, but technical skills are not required. The ride title is merely a combination of the areas featured in the ride: E. E. Debs, short for Ernest Eugene Debs (1904–2002), former Los Angeles County elected official, is the park's namesake. "MASH" is an abbreviation, with the letters a little out of order, for Montecito Heights and Arroyo Seco.

Although 70% of the ride is on paved roads and paths, the 30% on trails makes a mountain bike the best choice for the excursion. The 8.0-mile round-trip is executed via a (recommended) clockwise loop, although there is a 1.25-mile out-and-back segment along the Arroyo Seco Parkway. The 400-plus-foot differential suggests that there is a decent amount of climbing (and descending) in this relatively short ride!

Start the ride in Ernest E. Debs Regional Park, in the parking lot located at the end of the access road from Monterey Road (east side of the park). Mr. Debs served in various elected capacities in the county for thirty-two years, 1942–1974. He came to California at age 20 in a boxcar, intending to break into the motion picture industry as a dancer. While doing other things, he made a slow, gradual transition into politics, and the rest is history. The park is considered to be one of Los Angeles' "peaceful places" and has been highly recommended for an urban escape. The park features habitats for California walnut and oak.

Bike Shops

Gabe's Bike Shop, 5346 Huntington Dr. S., Los Angeles; (323) 226-1921
Raffi's Bicycles, 5509 N. Figueroa St., Los Angeles; (323) 474-6430; http://raffisbike shop.com
Lincoln Heights Cyclery, 3422 N. Broadway, Los Angeles; (323) 221-2670
T.V. Bikes, 3410 N. Broadway, Los Angeles; (323) 350-4238

Looking toward downtown L.A. from Walnut Forest Trail in Ernest E. Debs Regional Park

Head toward Monterey Road, either within the lot or the parallel access road. At the edge of the lot, bear right (navigate the gate) onto the rudimentary trail. Skirt the edge of the picnic area; at the Y junction, bear right and head downhill. The bumpy trail curves to the right before making a sharp left and emptying out onto a paved park road. Continue along this road, navigating another gate and passing the athletic fields of Rose Hill Park (which borders Debs Regional Park). You are now on Boundary Road.

At the stop sign turn right onto Mercury Avenue, making a brisk climb at a 9% grade into the Montecito Heights neighborhood. This Los Angeles community, which commands some of the best views of the city, was a center of the Arts and Crafts movement of the late nineteenth century. The area was also the residence of abstract expressionist artist Jackson Pollock during his teenage years.

At the stop sign turn right onto Reynolds Avenue and—shifting into your lowest gear—gasp at the 21% grade in front of you. This is a quiet residential street, so you might be able to use the whole street to "paperboy" (i.e., zigzag) your way to the top. If you elect to do the paperboy switchback, be alert to the occasional motor vehicle. Halfway up, a possibly distracting sign marks your formal entrance into Montecito Heights. Although there are some steep hills within the regional park, this will be the steepest by far. Once at the top, the road curves 90 degrees to the left, becoming Roberta Street. At the *second* intersection with Montecito Drive, turn right (the first leads to a dead end). This pleasant residential street winds and descends through the Montecito Heights neighborhood. I would rank this as one of the most exhilarating road descents around—not too steep, only a couple of stop signs, and plenty of curves to test your bike-handling skills. As always, be ever watchful of motor vehicle traffic.

After whooping your way to the bottom of Montecito Drive, turn right onto Griffin Avenue. As the road hugs the Montecito Heights Recreation Center, to your left, look for an unmarked access road. Turn left here and then make an immediate right onto the access path for the Arroyo Seco Parkway. Turn right onto the parkway and head northeast. "Arroyo Seco" is Spanish for "dry stream," and you will notice that you are essentially riding in the stream-bed! El Arroyo Seco is not actually dry, but it tends to have a low flow. Its waters replenish a basin that provides half the city of Pasadena's supply. The

The California Cycleway

The Arroyo Seco carves its way to the northeast of Los Angeles between Mount Washington and the San Rafael Hills on the west and the Monterey Hills to the east. Because it is a natural corridor, the Arroyo has always played a significant role in regional transportation. In the late nineteenth century, the Santa Fe Railroad traveled through the corridor, heading to either central Los Angeles or points east. Later, the Pacific Electric Railway operated electric streetcars between Los Angeles, Pasadena, and the San Gabriel Valley. Today the Pasadena Freeway (SR 110), also known as the Arroyo Seco Parkway, snakes its way adjacent to the river.

Most significant for bicyclists, though, is that Horace Dobbins, mayor of Pasadena in the late 1890s, built what was known as the California Cycleway in the Arroyo Seco corridor, along what is now Edmondson Alley. The Cycleway was an elevated structure made of Oregon pine that provided a grade-separated route for cyclists (primarily to avoid railroad and streetcar crossings) between Los Angeles and Pasadena. A total of 1.3 miles of the proposed 9.0-mile route were constructed, and the structure reached a maximum height of 50 feet. A 10-cent toll was charged for a one-way trip; 15 cents for a round-trip. The ambitious project failed to turn a profit, however, and the turn-of-the-twentieth-century cycling craze faded against competition from motor vehicles and public transit. The structure has long been dismantled, but the Arroyo Seco Parkway represents a revival of sorts.

stream merges with the Los Angeles River southwest of here (see the sidebar). Continue on the path to its endpoint at aptly-named Arroyo Seco Park.

"End of path" marks the turnaround. Return the way you came, and look very carefully to your left for the ramp that leads to Hermon Park. Note that there are very few access points to the path; this will be the first one after the turnaround, located under the Avenue 60 bridge. Make a sharp left and head up the ramp into the Hermon Park parking area.

Turn right at the top of the ramp and ride through the long linear parking area. There are frequent speed bumps. Upon exiting the park, carefully cross Via Marisol. Enter Debs Regional Park via Seco View Trail, navigating the gate (you may have to dismount to get past the V channel). Remount and climb the dirt trail up into the park (11% grade). Please note that although the trails in the park are named, there are no markers. After 0.45 mile the trail intersects the Walnut Forest Trail, which merges from the left. Keep straight here; you are now on Walnut Forest Trail. At the junction with Sycamore Trail at 0.75 mile, stay to the left, remaining on Walnut Forest. At the junction with Scrubjay Trail at 0.85 mile, keep climbing, remaining on Walnut Forest. At the 1.05-mile mark, a breathtaking vista of Mount Washington (to your right) and downtown Los Angeles (straight ahead) warrants a stop. You may find others gathered up here to take in the fantastic view. Execute the hairpin turn adjacent the bench to remain on Walnut Forest Trail. This is not the high point of the park or the ride, so be prepared for a short descent followed by more climbing.

After 1.5 miles of trail riding, hang a sharp right onto Summit View Trail (also called Summit Ridge Trail), a paved road that serves the interior of the park. There may be maintenance vehicles here (I encountered a Los Angeles police car cruising the trails below), but the road should be otherwise traffic-free, although popular with hikers. The road finally reaches the crest and high point (882 feet) before making a gradual descent. (There is a circle of benches here at what was once a gazebo, damaged as of this writing, just off the road to your right.) Bear left at the junction and then left again to stay on Summit View Trail (also referred to as Valley View Trail), and begin a steep descent (200-foot drop at a 13% grade). The ride ends at the bottom of the descent.

MILES AND DIRECTIONS

0.0   Start in the central parking lot of Ernest E. Debs Regional Park, located at the end of the access road from Monterey Road. Head toward Monterey Road.

0.1   Turn right at the gate onto trail that skirts the edge of the picnic area.

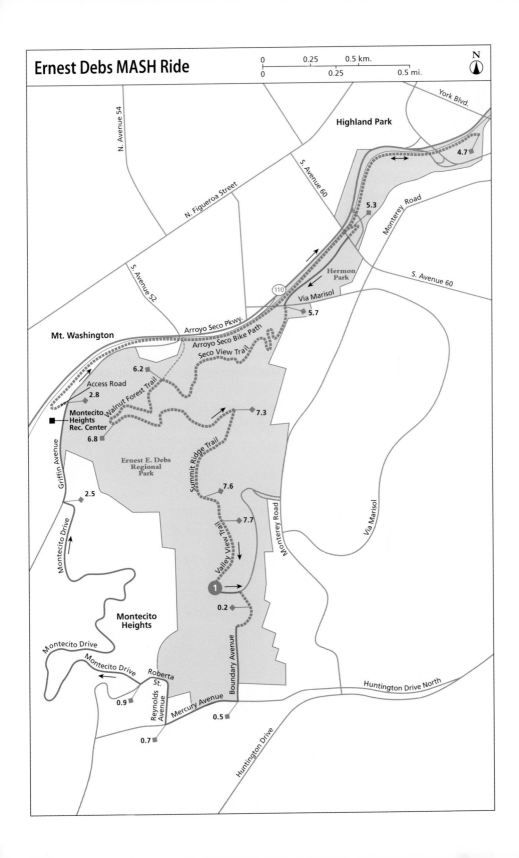

Ernest Debs MASH Ride

| 0 | 0.25 | 0.5 km. |
| 0 | 0.25 | 0.5 mi. |

N

York Blvd.

Highland Park

N. Avenue 54

N. Figueroa Street

S. Avenue 60

Monterey Road

4.7

5.3

S. Avenue 52

Arroyo Seco Pkwy.

110

Via Marisol

5.7

Hermon Park

S. Avenue 60

Mt. Washington

Arroyo Seco Bike Path

Seco View Trail

Walnut Forest Trail

6.2

Access Road

2.8

Montecito Heights Rec. Center

6.8

7.3

Ernest E. Debs Regional Park

Summit Ridge Trail

7.6

7.7

Griffin Avenue

2.5

Montecito Drive

Via Marisol

Monterey Road

Valley View Trail

1

0.2

Montecito Heights

Montecito Drive

Montecito Drive

Roberta St.

Boundary Avenue

Huntington Drive North

0.9

Reynolds Avenue

Mercury Avenue

0.5

0.7

Huntington Drive

0.2 Bear right at the Y junction and head downhill.

0.4 Exit the park, continuing straight onto Boundary Avenue.

0.5 Turn right at the stop sign onto Mercury Avenue.

0.7 Turn right at the stop sign onto Reynolds Avenue—a steep climb (21% grade).

0.8 Road bends 90 degrees to the left, becoming Roberta Street.

0.9 Turn right at the stop sign onto Montecito Drive. (**Note:** This is the second Montecito intersection.)

2.5 Turn right at the stop sign onto Griffin Avenue.

2.8 Turn left onto the unnamed access road at the north end of Montecito Heights Recreation Center; immediately bear right onto the path accessing the Arroyo Seco Parkway then turn right onto the parkway.

4.7 Reach end of the bike path at top of ramp; turn around and return along Arroyo Seco Parkway.

5.3 Hang a sharp left onto the ramp and climb up to Hermon Park (parking area); turn right and ride through the parking lot (multiple speed humps).

5.7 Exit Hermon Park; cross Via Marisol and enter Ernest Debs Regional Park via the Seco View Trail (gate, followed by climb at 11% grade).

6.2 Reach a junction, now on Walnut Forest Trail (unmarked; keep straight).

6.5 Stay left at junction with Sycamore Trail.

6.6 Continue climbing (keep straight) at junction with Scrubjay Trail.

6.8 Come to vista point; trail bends to the left 180 degrees (still on Walnut Forest Trail).

7.3 Top of trail; turn right onto paved Summit View Trail (also called Summit Ridge Trail).

7.6 Bear left where the park road splits (still on Summit View/ Summit Ridge Trail).

7.7 Turn left and begin steep (13%) descent (still on Summit View Trail; also called Valley View Trail).

8.0 End the ride at bottom of the hill, adjacent to the parking lot.

Hollywood Ride of Fame

Start: Griffith Park, along Crystal Springs Drive north of Los Feliz Boulevard

Length: 20.8 miles (clockwise loop)

Riding time: 1.25 to 4 hours (my time: 1H52:19)

Terrain and surface: Paved roads, including some park roads

Elevation: Low: 397 feet at Griffith Park Drive and Los Feliz Boulevard; high: 1,212 feet at Mulholland Drive and Runyon Canyon Road

Traffic and hazards: Daily traffic volumes range from just 840 vehicles on Nichols Canyon Road to 34,770 on Los Feliz Boulevard west of Griffith Park Drive. High volumes are also found on Barham Boulevard (28,750 per day in 2005) and on one-way Cahuenga Boulevard (26,400 per day in 2005). Hollywood Boulevard carried "only" 15,300 vehicles daily near Vine Street in 2003; this is the most *congested* road, though, with heavy tourist and public bus movements, stopped vehicles (often for entertainment), and high pedestrian volumes.

Map: *The Thomas Guide—Street Guide: Los Angeles and Orange Counties* (any recent year), page 593

Getting there: By car—From central Los Angeles, head north on the I-5 freeway. Take either the Los Feliz Boulevard or Griffith Park exit. From the former, turn left onto Los Feliz and then right onto Crystal Springs Drive, entering Griffith Park. Look for parking on the right. From the latter, look for openings in the median to head south on Griffith Park Drive and then north on Crystal Springs Drive; look for parking on the right.

By public transit—L.A. Metro bus route 96 runs from downtown Los Angeles to Griffith Park via Riverside Drive and Crystal Springs Drive every 30 to 40 minutes on weekdays, every 50 minutes on Saturday, and every hour on Sunday and holidays.

Starting point coordinates: N34.119072° / W118.273256°

Similar to other rides in the Central/Southeast Los Angeles region, the Hollywood Ride of Fame is truly an "urban" ride. Expect there to be plenty of traffic signals, motor vehicles, pedestrians, buses, and roadside distractions. Avoid doing this ride for time or speed; instead enjoy the scenery and attractions along the way. The featured segment of the route is Hollywood Boulevard, taking you right into the heart of the famed strip. Please note that the street is periodically closed for special events; when I encountered one of these, I simply dismounted and walked through. Despite the casual nature of the Hollywood portion of the ride, most of the route is in the Hollywood Hills and the hills of Griffith Park, where some stretches of road are steep and arduous. Be prepared for some climbing and descending, and always be cautious of heavy motor vehicle traffic.

Start the ride in Griffith Park, in the southeast corner of this renowned urban landscape. (Please see sidebar for commentary on the park's use in filming.) Immediately exit the park and turn right onto Los Feliz Boulevard. This is one of the busiest stretches of the entire ride, with traffic volumes reaching 35,000 per day. There are three lanes westbound along here, but the outermost lane is used for parking—actually a plus for cyclists, as the buffer between parked cars and the middle lane serves as a de facto bike lane. After waking your legs up with some climbing up Los Feliz, look for Hillhurst Avenue. Turn right here; this is your gateway to the central area of Griffith Park. The road climbs steeply as its name changes to Vermont Avenue and then to Vermont Canyon Road, entering the park. As you enter the park, there is a golf course on the right and the Greek Theatre on the left. This is just a taste—Griffith Park is a busy place! Continue climbing; just before the tunnel portal, which is for motor vehicles, turn left onto Observatory Drive to make the final ascent to the Griffith Observatory.

Bike Shop

Safety Cycle, 1018 N. Western Ave., Los Angeles; (323) 464-5765; www.safetycycle.com

The Art Deco exterior of the Griffith Observatory should be immediately recognizable, given its frequent appearance in film and television. The observatory's proximity to Hollywood certainly has something to do with its affinity for the camera. *Beverly Hills 90210, CHiPs, Dragnet, MacGyver, Melrose Place, Mission: Impossible, Remington Steele,* and *The Terminator* are just a few of the television shows or films that have shot the observatory in one or more episodes. There is a planetarium, exhibits, theater, and cafe, making this a worthwhile stop. Continue pedaling slowly past the observatory (slowly

A cyclist searches for . . . something . . . in his jersey while approaching the Griffith Observatory.

because the area is typically busy with pedestrians), beyond the barrier, and into the parking lot. At the base of the hill, turn left to descend on Western Canyon Road. Note that overflow parking for the observatory is along this road, so anticipate heavy motor vehicle flows and parking movements (and plenty of folks on foot). The road changes its name to Fern Dell Drive as it exits the park. At the end of Fern Dell, turn right onto Los Feliz.

Los Feliz bends to the left, becoming Western Avenue. Watch your speed on the descent, being aware of the motor vehicle traffic. At the second traffic signal, turn right onto Hollywood Boulevard. This segment of the ride is a smorgasbord of sights, especially after crossing US 101. Among the many well-known venues are the Pantages, Kodak, and Grauman's Chinese Theaters on the right and the Guinness World Record and Ripley's Believe It or Not! Museums on the left. The famous Walk of Fame, featuring more than 2,500 stars on the walkway, begins at Gower Street and continues to La Brea Avenue. Stars also continue on Vine Street, which is a cross-street, in case you want to take a detour. In addition to these iconic sites, you will also see well-known restaurants, street performers, and eerily familiar look-alikes in

Hollywood Boulevard and Griffith Park

The one-time Prospect Avenue was renamed Hollywood Boulevard in 1910, when the city of Hollywood was annexed by Los Angeles because of the need for L.A.'s water supply and sewer system. The motion picture industry, and to a certain extent television, thrived in Hollywood throughout the better part of the twentieth century. The cylindrical Capitol Records Tower, built in 1956, marked the beginning of an era of architectural standouts. The Hollywood Walk of Fame opened in 1960 and has continued to expand with the addition of stars (over 2,500 and counting!). The Hollywood Boulevard Commercial and Entertainment District, on the National Register of Historic Places, was established in 1985. The district extends from Vine Street to Highland Avenue, although the Walk of Fame is actually longer, stretching from Gower Street to La Brea Avenue.

Despite the apparent growth of the Hollywood Boulevard corridor, the area actually fell into serious decline during the 1980s. Many of the film and TV studios and radio stations had moved out of the area (generally to elsewhere in the Los Angeles region) by then. Revitalization began in earnest during the mid-1990s. The Hollywood extension of the Metro Red Line subway was opened in 1999 (entrances to the stations can be seen at various points along Hollywood Boulevard). The Kodak Theater (since renamed the Dolby Theater), at Hollywood Boulevard and Highland Avenue, opened in 2001 and became the permanent home of the annual Academy Awards broadcast in 2002. Hollywood Boulevard closes for this occasion, as well as for parades and even filming. As noted in the ride description, this is not necessarily the best place for a bike ride—but who would want to miss the experience?

Just to the northeast of Hollywood Boulevard, and visited as part of this ride, is Griffith Park. Other than being the eleventh-largest urban park in the United States and being home to numerous attractions, the park is a major filming destination. In fact, nearly every day of the year is a production day somewhere in the park. Some landmarks have been filmed multiple times and appear in numerous movies and TV shows but do not always look the same because of different camera perspectives. Iconic films such as *Rebel Without a Cause, The Terminator, Back to the Future, Who Framed Roger Rabbit?, The Searchers*, and *Invasion of the Body Snatchers* (1956 original version), along with a number of TV shows and music videos, have been shot in the park. While Griffith Observatory may be the most recognizable backdrop, a tunnel near the observatory, Bronson Caves, and, of course, the Hollywood Sign, are all familiar film and TV settings.

costume. Even the intersections are famous (e.g., Hollywood & Vine, Hollywood & Highland).

Once you're beyond La Brea, the hubbub settles down and things return to normal. Time to get on with the ride! After continuing on Hollywood Boulevard for a stretch beyond Hollywood, turn right onto Nichols Canyon Road. You are now heading up into the Hollywood Hills. The elevation gain, at a fairly consistent grade, is from 417 feet at Hollywood Boulevard to 1,021 feet at Woodrow Wilson Drive. Turn right here and—whoa!—this is the steepest climb of the ride. The road climbs 94 feet over the next 0.15 mile, for a gradient of 12%. Turn right at the top onto Mulholland Drive. After a bit more climbing, Mulholland begins a long, twisty descent to the US 101 corridor. Mulholland was very bumpy when I rode it, with plenty of road damage, so it was not possible to let loose on the descent. At the bottom, turn right onto an unnamed bridge and cross over the freeway. Turn left onto Lakeridge Place on the opposite side and descend to Cahuenga Boulevard East. Turn right and ride parallel to US 101. At Barham Boulevard, signs direct travelers to Universal Studios, which is straight ahead. Although the theme park and studios are a highly recommended visit, you are not going there today; turn right onto Barham.

After a gradual climb, Barham begins the speediest descent of the ride. The road is fairly wide here and mostly straight, so it is possible to tuck and enjoy the downhill. Turn right onto Forest Lawn Drive at the bottom of the descent and head east. On your right will be one of several Forest Lawn Memorial Parks found in the Los Angeles region. One article referred to Forest Lawn as a "theme park necropolis"; despite the joke, quite a few notable personalities are interred at these cemeteries. Also, the Hollywood Hills location (this one) offers ceremonies that are attended by VIPs. Uniformed attendants stand guard at the entrance, adding to the impressiveness of the place. Among the many famous personalities buried here are actor-comedian Morey Amsterdam, actor-musician Scatman Crothers, composer Ken Darby, actress Bette Davis, police brutality victim Rodney King, and songstress Nicolette Larson.

Continue past Forest Lawn and turn right onto Zoo Drive—this is the official re-entrance into Griffith Park. Bear right again, onto Griffith Park Drive, and enjoy the ensuing climb and descent. There are several inviting trailheads along this road, but unfortunately bicycles are not allowed on the trails inside the park. To your right, on the climb, is Mount Hollywood (1,625 feet). Out of view from here is the HOLLYWOOD sign, which is actually on the south face of Mount Lee, to the west of Mount Hollywood. The road continues past the old zoo (see "L.A. River Ramble & Echo Hills Challenge" for a discussion of the zoo). Watch out for road damage on the descent. At the bottom of the descent keep right, remaining on Griffith Park Drive. The ride ends adjacent to the parking areas located along the northbound side of the road as you head south. There is limited access across the median strip; you may have to pass your starting point before crossing the median and returning.

MILES AND DIRECTIONS

0.0 Start from the parking areas located adjacent to Crystal Springs Drive, on the southeast side of Griffith Park. Look for an opening in the median and head south, along Griffith Park Drive.

0.2 Traffic signal at Los Feliz Boulevard; turn right.

1.2 Traffic signal at Hillhurst Avenue; turn right (begin climbing).

1.4 Stop sign at road merging from the left. Keep straight, now on Vermont Avenue.

1.8 Enter Griffith Park, now on Vermont Canyon Road.

2.5 Turn left onto East Observatory Drive, just upstream of the tunnel. A traffic control officer may be present. Ride up the hill to the Griffith Observatory.

3.2 Exit the Griffith Observatory area and turn left onto Western Canyon Road. Watch for motor vehicle and pedestrian traffic along the road.

4.8 Exit Griffith Park, now on Fern Dell Drive.

5.1 Traffic signal at Los Feliz Boulevard; turn right.

5.3 Road bends 90 degrees to the left, now on Western Avenue. Begin descent.

5.7 Traffic signal at Hollywood Boulevard; turn right.

8.4 Traffic signal at Nichols Canyon Road; turn right and begin climb.

11.1 Stop sign at Woodrow Wilson Drive; turn right and begin climb at 12% grade.

11.3 Stop sign at Mulholland Drive; turn right. (**Warning:** rough road.)

13.3 Turn right onto unnamed bridge; cross over US 101.

13.4 Stop sign at Lakeridge Place; turn left.

13.5 Stop sign at Cahuenga Boulevard East; turn right—watch for motor vehicles.

13.9 Traffic signal at Barham Boulevard; turn right. Gradual climb, followed by long descent.

14.9 Traffic signal at Forest Lawn Drive; turn right and head east. Forest Lawn Memorial Park is on the right.

Hollywood Ride of Fame

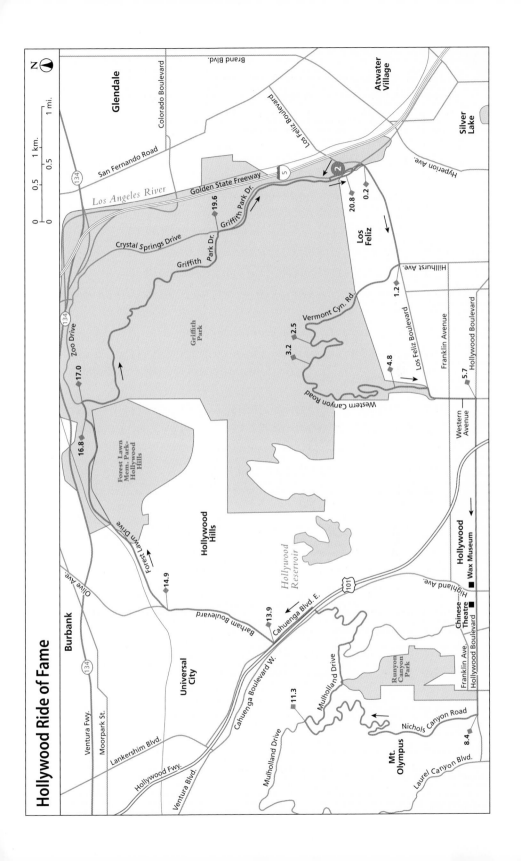

16.8 Traffic signal at Zoo Drive; turn right.

17.0 Stop sign at Griffith Park Drive; turn right. Begin climb.

19.6 Stop sign at Griffith Park Drive/Crystal Springs Drive; turn right.

20.8 End the ride adjacent to the parking area on the northbound side of the road. (Cross the road at a designated opening in the median.)

L.A. River Ramble & Echo Park Challenge

Start: Elysian Park, near Dodger Stadium in central Los Angeles; Chavez Ravine parking area just north of Academy Road

Length: 17.6 miles (counterclockwise loop; 16.8-mile loop without "Challenge")

Riding time: 1 to 2.5 hours (my time: 1H19:11)

Terrain and surface: Paved roads and one riverside path, passing through parks and neighborhoods

Elevation: Low: 323 feet on the Los Angeles River Bike Path; high: 738 feet on Park Drive south of Avon Park Terrace

Traffic and hazards: 35% of ride is on a car-free path. The busiest roads used by the route are Riverside Drive (23,100 vehicles per day between Los Feliz Boulevard and Allesandro Street in 2007), Stadium Way (12,600 vehicles per day at Academy Drive in 2007), and Griffith Park and Zoo Drives in Griffith Park (9,500 vehicles per day in the late 2000s). Traffic on Stadium Way surges during events at Dodger Stadium.

Map: *The Thomas Guide—Street Guide: Los Angeles and Orange Counties* (any recent year), page 595.

Getting there: By car—From central Los Angeles, head west on Cesar Chavez Avenue, which becomes Sunset Boulevard west of the downtown district and I-110. Turn right onto Echo Park Avenue. Stay to the right at the Y junction onto Morton Avenue. Turn right onto Academy Road and enter Elysian Park. Turn left onto Chavez Ravine Road and park in a designated spot.

By public transit—Dodger Stadium and Elysian Park are close enough to central Los Angeles to simply ride there. Follow the motor vehicle route; or, to enter the park from its east side, head north on Broadway to Bishops Road. Turn left here and then right onto Stadium Way. Follow this road as its winds over (and under!) I-110 and then heads along the south and west sides of the fringes of Dodger Stadium, eventually entering Elysian Park. Turn left onto Academy Road and then right onto Chavez Ravine Road to reach the start-finish area. ***Note:***

Traffic may be heavy in the vicinity of the Dodger Stadium during games and special events, such as an outdoor ice hockey match between the Kings and the Ducks.

Starting point coordinates: N34.080956° / W118.247194°

THE RIDE

The L.A. River Ramble & Echo Park Challenge starts and finishes in the Chavez Ravine parking area of Elysian Park, which is located near Dodger Stadium, immediately north-northwest of downtown Los Angeles. The ride opens with a leisurely, nearly flat ride along the Los Angeles River and returns through Griffith Park. The ride concludes, however, with a jaunt through the Echo Park neighborhood that incorporates a series of very steep climbs and descents. A "flatter" option (eliminating the Echo Park Challenge) is available for those who do not wish to tackle Baxter.

The ride is a 17.6-mile counterclockwise (recommended direction) loop. Start by heading south on Chavez Ravine Road to the mouth of the parking area and turning left onto Academy Road. Chavez Ravine Road is the remnant of the once-thriving community of Chavez Ravine. This predominantly Mexican-American community—later adding other ethnic groups—was established in the 1840s. The community was sustained for about one hundred years, until the City of Los Angeles started to covet the area. Ultimately, eminent domain prevailed, and the city claimed the community and eventually sold the land for construction of Dodger Stadium and the large, surrounding parking lot. (Just for the record, the Dodgers moved to Los Angeles from Brooklyn in 1958.) Chavez Ravine has been memorialized in albums, movies, stage shows, and television.

Follow Stadium Way as it climbs and then descends, exiting Elysian Park. This six-lane road carries heavy traffic during games and special events at Dodger Stadium. Otherwise, the traffic volumes are quite light for a six-lane road. At the traffic signal at the bottom of the descent, make a sharp right onto Riverside Drive. The turn is followed by an unsettlingly dark underpass (I-110) that is thankfully short. Riverside is a four-lane road. My experience was to play hopscotch with a city transit bus in the outer lane; motor vehicles can otherwise easily pass in the inner lane. As you head south, watch closely for the Los Angeles River on the left. Where the river comes roadside, turn left and enter the L.A. River Bike Path.

You are now heading toward the northwest, riding parallel to the Los Angeles River. But where is the water? At one time the river truly flowed,

Albeit low, the L.A. River's flow is a welcome sight to this rider along the L.A. River Bike Path.

frequently flooding the plains between Los Angeles and Long Beach. Because the river's course was unpredictable, the US Army Corps of Engineers tamed it by encasing nearly its entire length—from the San Fernando Valley to its mouth at the Pacific Ocean in Long Beach—in concrete. Today the river is primarily a flood-control channel. In fact, the wide and frequently dry channel is perhaps more well known as a movie setting (e.g., *Chinatown, Grease, Point Blank, Terminator 2: Judgment Day*) than for its hydrology. Nonetheless, the bike path is a pleasant respite from L.A.'s hubbub, with 7.2 miles of car-free, grade-separated travel. Sights along the path—well, it is primarily a transportation corridor—include a busy set of railroad tracks on the opposite side of the river, to your right, and I-5, immediately to your left.

The nearly flat path curves toward the left and heads west as it rounds the northeastern end of Griffith Park and the Santa Monica Mountains. Plans are to extend the path for a total of 51 miles. But currently this segment of the path ends at Victory Drive. Turn left here—you may as well stay on the sidewalk—and ride along Victory Drive (very short segment). At the Zoo Drive traffic signal, cross the street, turn left, and head southeast on Zoo. You are now entering Griffith Park on its eastern side. Zoo Drive curves to the right, with the Los Angeles Zoo and Botanical Gardens to your right. The 133-acre zoo is known for its escaping animals, including antelope, chimpanzees, kangaroos, zebras, a wolf (Virginia), and even a gorilla (Evelyn). As of this writing, a mountain lion—not a resident of the zoo—was known to be living in Griffith Park.

Presuming that you have not had an impromptu wildlife encounter, Zoo Drive becomes Crystal Springs Drive as it rounds a left-hand curve. Although the park is surprisingly wild for its urban location, this side of the park is generally tame. You may sense an eerie familiarity as you ride through the park, as though you have been here. Perhaps you have—numerous locations in Griffith Park have been incorporated into well-known films, television shows, and music videos. (See sidebar for Hollywood Ride of Fame.) Tempting stops as you ride through the park include the Griffith Park Merry-Go-Round, on your right, and the Griffith Park & Southern Railroad (miniature train ride), on your left. Crystal Springs Drive undulates with moderate rises and descents along the east side of the park. Exit the park by continuing straight at the busy Los Feliz Boulevard intersection. You are now on Riverside Drive.

Bike Shop

Spokes N Stuff, 4400 Crystal Springs Dr., Los Angeles (in Griffith Park); (323) 662-6573; www.spokes-n-stuff.com

Just beyond Los Feliz, on the right, is the William Mulholland Memorial (fountain, sculpture, and plantings), which was dedicated in 1940. Mulholland (1855–1935) is recognized as the "father" of the Los Angeles region's water system, having supervised the construction of the 233-mile-long Los Angeles Aqueduct. This water supply was vital in enabling Los Angeles to grow into the super-mega-metropolis it is today. Mulholland's career was marred, however, by the collapse of the St. Francis Dam (located up San Francisquito Canyon, north of Los Angeles) in 1928, just 12 hours after he and others performed a safety inspection. The resultant flood caused more than 600 deaths and is considered to be the worst civil engineering disaster of the twentieth century.

Continue heading southward on Riverside Drive, with noisy and busy I-5 running parallel to your left. After passing under the Glendale Freeway structure (SR 2), it is time to make a decision.

To take the Echo Park Challenge, turn right onto Allesandro Street, located immediately beyond the Glendale Freeway structure. It is a gentle climb into the Echo Park neighborhood. Continue along Allesandro to Baxter Street then shift to your lowest gear, turn left, and whoa! Where is the ladder? This monstrosity of a hill climbs at a 32% gradient, making it one of the steepest streets

The World's Steepest Streets

With a 32% gradient, Baxter Street (in a tie with Fargo Street) is the fourth-steepest street in the world and the second-steepest in Los Angeles. Eldred Street, located in the Highland Park neighborhood, is the steepest in L.A., with a 33% gradient. The rankings exclude streets with very short, steep pitches, such as 28th Street in San Pedro in extreme southern L.A. (33.3%) and Honakaa-Waipio Road (45%) in Waipio, Hawaii. Since 1950 the city of Los Angeles has limited street gradients to 15%.

One reason L.A. and other cities built super-steep roads is that the original surveyors' lines emphasized grid patterns laid over the land, regardless of the topography. Hence, some cities—notably San Francisco—have extensive grid patterns with several parallel steep streets. Los Angeles has just a handful of these, steeper than San Francisco's steepest, with Baxter Street being the longest—and with its roller-coaster combination of climbs and descents, the most fun!

in the world (see sidebar). The challenge is to conquer Baxter and keep riding without stopping—or tipping over. Thankfully, this is a reasonably quiet residential street, so you should be able to execute paperboy switchbacks (i.e., zigzag). There are plenty of curiosity-seekers around, though, including folks who drive the street just for fun. When I rode this (made it to the top!), a driver asked if I had ever ridden the street before. My response was incoherent. The Fargo Street Hill Climb, which is 1 block away and is parallel to Baxter, is staged every year by the Los Angeles Wheelmen. Some ride it fast, some ride it for the achievement, and others ride it multiple times—just because it's there.

Why ride Baxter instead of Fargo? The two streets have the same gradient, but Baxter continues for several blocks, while Fargo stops after one, steep block (it picks up later). Once you crest Baxter at Alvarado Street, the descent down the back side is nearly as steep. In fact, drivers have been known to panic at the crest because they cannot see the street over their car hoods—giving the sensation of driving off a cliff. With your bike's brakes squeezed, take on the descent. You might want to let it fly toward the bottom, as the subsequent climb is also very steep (23%). Once past Lemoyne Street, the Baxter gradient eases greatly as the street descends and climbs to the bench on the west side of Elysian Park.

Follow the road as it curves to the left, becoming Avon Street. Watch carefully for Avon Park Terrace (*not* Avon Terrace) and turn right. Be careful to turn right onto the leftmost side of the street, which is two-way, rather than the right side, which leads to a dead end. Compared to Baxter Street, the 15% grade might seem to be for novices. As Avon Park Terrace crests, follow the road as it curves to the right, becoming Park Drive. The street is a hidden jewel, hugging Elysian Park on your left, with residences on your right. The street generally descends. At mile 17.3 the road makes a sharp right turn, becoming Morton Place, and descends steeply (15%). Hit the brakes as you near the base of the descent and, carefully watching for traffic to the left, right, and behind you, execute a 180-degree turn to put you on Academy Road heading eastward into Elysian Park. Academy climbs at a 13% grade to enter the park. Continue to Chavez Ravine; turn left here to conclude the ride.

For the easier option (avoiding the Echo Park Challenge), at Allesandro Street keep straight on Riverside Drive. Turn right onto Stadium Way, making a brisk climb back into Elysian Park. Turn right at Academy Road and then make an immediate right onto Chavez Ravine Road to conclude the ride.

MILES AND DIRECTIONS

0.0 Start in Elysian Park, along Chavez Ravine Road, to the north of Academy Road. Head south and turn left onto Academy Road.

0.1 Stop sign at Stadium Way; turn left and head north, leaving the park.

1.3 Traffic signal at Riverside Drive; turn right and proceed through the dark underpass.

2.6 Look for access to the Los Angeles River Bike Path on the left; carefully cross Riverside and ride onto the path. The path curves to the left and heads northwestward.

9.8 Reach the end of the bike path. Turn left onto the sidewalk adjacent to Victory Boulevard; cross over the freeway.

9.9 Cross Zoo Drive at the traffic signal; once across, turn left and head east and then south on Zoo Drive, entering Griffith Park.

11.0 Zoo Drive becomes Crystal Springs Drive within Griffith Park.

11.8 Crystal Springs Drive splits; head south on Griffith Park Drive. (The northbound side of the road is Crystal Springs Drive.)

13.3 Traffic signal at Los Feliz Boulevard; continue straight, now on Riverside Drive.

15.1 Traffic signal at Alessandro Street; turn right. (**Option:** Keep straight to bypass Echo Hills Challenge.)

15.8 Turn left onto Baxter Street. Begin steep (32%) climb, followed by steep descent, followed by steep (23%) climb, followed by steep descent. Baxter Street is the Echo Hills Challenge!

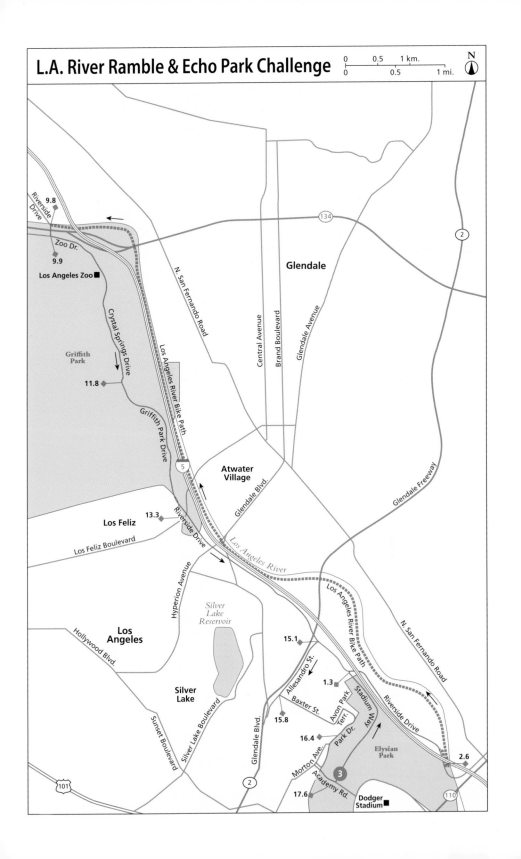

16.4 The road bears left, becoming Avon Street.

16.5 Turn right onto Avon Park Terrace (*not* Avon Terrace); ride on the left-side road, not the right-side road. Begin steep (15%) climb.

16.7 Avon Park Terrace curves to the right, becoming Park Drive. Elysian Park is to the left. Begin a swift descent.

17.3 Park Drive bears right, becoming Morton Place. Descend steeply (15% grade) to Morton Avenue.

17.4 Turn left at bottom of hill and then make an immediate left onto Academy Road. Watch for motor vehicle traffic when making these turns. Begin 13% climb into Elysian Park.

17.6 End the ride at Chavez Ravine Road.

OC North Coast Promenade

Start: Parking area for Sunset County Beach; Warner Avenue and Pacific Avenue, Sunset Beach

Length: 19.0 miles ("skinny" clockwise loop)

Riding time: 45 minutes to 2 hours (my time: 1H01:12)

Terrain and surface: Paved roads and path

Elevation: Low: 9 feet in Sunset Beach; high: 37 feet on SR 1 southeast of Seapoint Drive

Traffic and hazards: 44% of the ride is on a car-free path. SR 1 carried an average of 37,500 motor vehicles per day through Huntington Beach in 2012, with some weekend variations.

Map: *The Thomas Guide—Street Guide: Los Angeles and Orange Counties* (any recent year), page 827.

Getting there: By car—From central Los Angeles, head south on I-5, turning onto I-605 South and then I-405 South. Exit at Bolsa Chica Road and head south. Turn right at Warner Avenue. Once across SR 1 (Pacific Coast Highway/PCH), turn right onto North Pacific Avenue and then left into the Sunset Beach parking area.

    By public transit—From central Los Angeles, take the Metro Blue Line to downtown Long Beach (end of the line). Transfer to Long Beach Transit route 91, 92, 93, 94, or 96 to California State University, Long Beach. Transfer here at the Veterans Affairs Medical Center, which is immediately adjacent the campus, to Orange County Transit Authority (OCTA) route 1. This bus heads north–south along SR 1. Exit at Warner Avenue (Sunset Beach) and head over to the ride's starting point.

Starting point coordinates: N33.711836° / W118.063817°

THE RIDE

The OC North Coast Promenade, with OC standing for Orange County, is a flat and potentially fast jaunt up and down the Huntington Beach coast. This is the flattest ride in this book, with only a 28-foot differential between the low and high elevations. The route uses the shoulder of famous SR 1 outbound and a beachside bike path for the return ride. Serious cyclists use the highway exclusively, staying off the path. However, the path is recommended for its beachside atmosphere, as well as the opportunity to enjoy car-free vistas of the surf.

Start the ride in the parking area for Sunset County Beach, located at the Warner Avenue and Pacific Avenue intersection in Sunset Beach. Warner Avenue comes to a dead end adjacent to the parking area, just west of SR 1, so it

Four bikes, one in motion, on the Huntington Beach Bike Trail near Huntington Beach Pier

is easy to find. Until 2011, Sunset Beach was an independent community, with a population of just under 1,000. Despite resistance from the residents, Sunset Beach was annexed by the city of Huntington Beach in August 2011. Huntington Beach is a behemoth, with an estimated population of 189,707 in 2012 and an area of 32 square miles, including 9.5 miles of beachfront. The city is referred to as—and even fought for the title of—"Surf City USA" because of its world-renowned breaks and surfing competitions. Even Dean Torrence, of legendary surf-rock duo Jan and Dean, admitted that Huntington Beach embodies the subject of the equally legendary song "Surf City."

Start the ride with a true promenade through Sunset Beach by heading north on North Pacific Avenue. This is a leisurely start, as the road is a low-speed jaunt through the community, with frequent traffic controls at cross-streets. Turn left at Anderson Street and then left again onto South Pacific Avenue for the return trip. To the north of Anderson is the gated community of Surfside.

As you near the parking area, where you started, cross back over to North Pacific Avenue and continue heading southward. Turn left onto Warner Avenue and then right onto SR 1 at the traffic signal. Pick up speed here—do not be surprised if there are other cyclists, including small pelotons, zooming along the shoulder of the highway. The large habitat to the left is Bolsa Chica Ecological Reserve. This large (nearly 1,000-acre) protected wetland is home to multiple species of fish, as well as numerous migratory and nonmigratory birds. Bicycles are not allowed within the reserve, but hiking is a popular activity.

Once beyond Bolsa Chica and Seapoint Avenue, SR 1 makes a noticeable climb to enter the busy beachside waterfront of Huntington Beach. Watch for slowing and turning motor vehicles. There should be plenty of folks in beachwear and carrying beach gear. Starting at Goldenwest Street, there are traffic signals every 0.25 to 0.5 mile for the next few miles. Be observant, be cautious, and keep hauling on through. As you near the Huntington Beach city limit, which is at the Santa Ana River, veer off SR 1. Turn right onto a short connector path and then right again onto the Huntington Beach Bike Trail. You are now heading northwest on the beach bike path. The path continues for some 9.5 miles, all the way to Sunset Beach. The width of the path varies, although it is

Bike Shops

Jax Bicycle Center, 401 Main St., Huntington Beach; (714) 969-8684; http://jaxbicycles.com
Livery Design Gruppe (designer bicycles), 220 Walnut Ave., Huntington Beach; (714) 374-0900; http://liverydesigngruppe.com
Wheel Fun Rentals, 21100 Pacific Coast Hwy., Huntington Beach; (714) 845-8000 or (714) 536-4863; http://wheelfunrentals.com

4

Huntington Beach Pier

As is the case in many beachfront communities, the local pier tends to take on a life all its own. Huntington Beach's pier is no exception. First, please note that bicycles are not allowed on the pier, so either lock it or walk it. The pier is strategically located as a direct extension of the city's Main Street, although it is not made for vehicular traffic of any kind.

Construction on the first, all-wooden pier began in 1903. The original pier extended 1,000 feet into the ocean until a strong 1912 storm sent part of the pier plunging into the ocean. The pier was rebuilt in 1914 to 1,350 feet and then extended by another 500 feet in 1930. The famous magnitude 6.4 Long Beach earthquake of 1933 severed that pier. After yet another rebuild, the pier was hit by a hurricane(!) in 1939 that destroyed the extension. The US military took over the pier in 1941, positioning a heavy-caliber machine gun at its end along with a lookout post. Four decades of peace followed World War II, with the pier remaining fully intact. Storms hit the pier in 1983 and 1988, however, calling for further reconstructions. A sturdy concrete pier reinforced with steel and coated with epoxy was finally built in 1992 and was extended out to 1,856 feet, making it one of the longest piers on the West Coast.

If you venture out to the end of the pier, you will find a Ruby's Diner waiting for you. Also, if you are camera-shy, be aware that pier scenes are broadcast in real time to the more than 500 Hollister stores in the United States and Canada. Although the cameras are primarily a promotional gimmick for the chain of teen apparel stores, they also serve a serious marine safety purpose and are used by local lifeguards. The pier has appeared in films and on television, including *Betty White's Off Their Rockers, Beverly Hills 90210,* and *The Real Housewives of Orange County.*

generally wide. The path is busiest near the Huntington Beach Pier, so expect to ride slowly in that vicinity. Huntington State Beach transitions into Bolsa Chica State Beach; together, the two run essentially the entire length of the path on your left. (From the northern end of Bolsa Chica, Sunset Beach continues the uninterrupted stretch of sand.)

Past (northwest of) the Huntington Beach Pier, the path jogs left and then right before coming to a fork—take either path (they merge downstream of here). The left path tends to be quieter than the right, or upper, one. The key feature of the right path is its elevation: The path is higher than the beach,

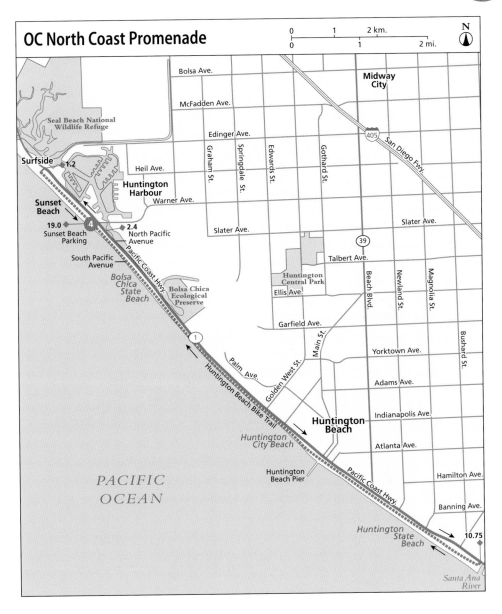

OC North Coast Promenade

0 — 1 — 2 km.
0 — 1 — 2 mi.

N

Bolsa Ave.

Midway City

McFadden Ave.

Seal Beach National Wildlife Refuge

Edinger Ave.

405 San Diego Fwy.

Surfside 1.2

Heil Ave.

Graham St.

Springdale St.

Edwards St.

Gothard St.

Huntington Harbour

Warner Ave.

Sunset Beach

19.0 4 2.4

Sunset Beach Parking

North Pacific Avenue

Slater Ave.

Slater Ave.

39

South Pacific Avenue

Pacific Coast Hwy.

Talbert Ave.

Beach Blvd.

Newland St.

Magnolia St.

Bolsa Chica State Beach

Bolsa Chica Ecological Preserve

Huntington Central Park

Ellis Ave.

Garfield Ave.

Bushard St.

1

Palm Ave.

Golden West St.

Main St.

Yorktown Ave.

Huntington Beach Bike Trail

Adams Ave.

Huntington Beach

Indianapolis Ave.

PACIFIC OCEAN

Huntington City Beach

Atlanta Ave.

Huntington Beach Pier

Pacific Coast Hwy.

Hamilton Ave.

Banning Ave.

Huntington State Beach

10.75

Santa Ana River

enabling a nice view of the ocean and the breaks in the tidal action. The beach tends to be obscured by the short but steep cliffs. Huntington Beach is famous for its breaks. The location is ideally situated for a merger between swells from the northern Pacific Ocean in winter and the remnants of surges from storms in the southern Pacific in summer. Throw in the effects of wave redirection caused by distant Catalina Island, and the result is one of the most consistently dynamic surfing spots in the world.

After a pleasant stretch with Dog Beach on your left and oil drilling and energy works to your right, the path crosses a bridge over an inlet to the Bolsa Chica wetlands. The inlet marks the northern boundary of Huntington State Beach and the southern boundary of Bolsa Chica State Beach. Here the path is level with the beach. You will see intermittent restrooms, refreshment outlets, and parking lots along this stretch. In the parking lots you can see surfers prepping themselves and their boards for the waves.

The Huntington Beach Bike Trail ends at Warner Avenue, just downstream of the parking area where you started the ride. Navigate the traffic circle, bearing either to the left or the right, to return to the lot and conclude the ride.

MILES AND DIRECTIONS

0.0 Start at Sunset Beach parking lot, at the corner of Warner and North Pacific Avenues in Huntington Beach. Head north on North Pacific.

1.2 Turn left at Anderson Street and immediately turn left again onto South Pacific Avenue.

2.3 Cross over the gap in the median strip to North Pacific Avenue; continue heading south.

2.4 End of North Pacific Avenue; turn left onto Warner Avenue.

2.45 Traffic signal at SR 1; turn right and head southeast.

10.7 Just upstream of the bridge over the Santa Ana River inlet, veer off SR 1 and onto the bike path.

10.75 Turn right onto the Huntington Beach Bike Trail, now heading northwest.

19.0 End the ride at the end of the bike trail at Warner Avenue.

South Central Urban Experience

Start: Earvin "Magic" Johnson County Recreation Area, 905 East El Segundo Blvd., Los Angeles (Willowbrook)

Length: 23.1 miles (clockwise loop)

Riding time: 1.25 to 3.5 hours (my time: 1H37:08)

Terrain and surface: 57% of the ride on paved roads, 41% on paved bike paths, and 2% on a concrete park path

Elevation: Low: 57 feet along the Compton Creek bike path just north of Greenleaf Boulevard in Compton; high: 153 feet at Otis Avenue and Randolph Street in Bell

Traffic and hazards: El Segundo Boulevard was carrying 20,450 vehicles per day at Central Avenue in 2011; Graham Avenue carried 2,040 daily vehicles south of East 103rd Street in Watts in 2001; East 92nd Street was carrying 14,090 vehicles per day at Wilmington Avenue in 2006.

Map: *The Thomas Guide—Street Guide: Los Angeles and Orange Counties* (any recent year), pages 704 and 734.

Getting there: By car—From central Los Angeles, head south on I-110 or I-105 East. Exit at Central Avenue and head south. Turn right at El Segundo Boulevard and head west. Turn right at Wadsworth Avenue and enter Earvin "Magic" Johnson County Recreation Area. Turn left at the first road and park in the lot.

    By public transit—From central Los Angeles, head south on the Metro Blue Line. Exit at the Imperial Highway/ Metro Green Line transfer station. Head west from the station to Wilmington Avenue and then turn south on Wilmington. Turn left onto El Segundo Boulevard and look for Earvin "Magic" Johnson County Recreation Area, on the right. Turn right onto Wadsworth Avenue and then left into the parking lot. Start the ride from the opposite end of the lot.

Starting point coordinates: N33.917786° / W118.260544°

Although South Central L.A. has received its share of negative publicity over the years, this subregion remains a viable community with plenty of heart and soul. Violence and, possibly to an even greater extent, corruption are real here, although the latter has been more prominent of late. One oddly positive product of South Central has been its music: Gangs beget gangster activity, which begets gangster rap, ultimately providing some of music's, even film's, biggest stars. Some of those stars, including Ice-T (Tracy Morrow, from Crenshaw), Snoop Dogg (Calvin Broadus, from Long Beach), Dr. Dre (Andre Young, from Compton), and Ice Cube (O'Shea Jackson, from South Central L.A.), all grew up in or near this subregion.

South Central L.A. became internationally famous in 1992, when riots following an acquittal of L.A. policemen in their handling of Rodney King plunged the community into chaos. The riots seemed to have started at the intersection of Florence and Normandie Avenues, in the heart of South Central, spreading wildly from there. The fifty-three fatalities and over 2,000 injuries nearly doubled those of the infamous 1965 Watts riots. The latter was a key event in the 1960s civil rights movement. This ride actually begins right in the heart of Watts, which today has a much more modern-day feel. The

Earvin "Magic" Johnson

The South Central Urban Experience starts and ends at the Earvin "Magic" Johnson County Recreation Area in Willowbrook. Despite being born and raised in Lansing, Michigan, "Magic" is strongly linked with the Los Angeles region, having played for the National Basketball Association's Los Angeles Lakers for thirteen years. He retired in 1991 after testing positive for HIV, although he returned for the 1992 NBA all-star game, as well as an additional thirty-two regular season games for the Lakers in 1996. Among his "hoop" accolades were three NBA Most Valuable Player awards, nine trips to the NBA finals, twelve trips to the NBA all-star game, an Olympic gold medal (in 1992 as a member of the "Dream Team"), election to the Basketball Hall of Fame, and honors as one of the fifty greatest players in NBA history.

Since retiring from pro hoops, Magic has developed numerous business interests, including several very prominent investments. As of this writing, he was part owner of the Los Angeles Dodgers, Los Angeles Sparks (women's pro basketball), and a movie theater complex in Baldwin Hills, as well as a sponsor of the park that serves as the staging point for this ride.

A small group of cyclists chills under the trees adjacent to Simon Rodia's Watts Towers.

ride starts in the Earvin "Magic" Johnson County Recreation Area at revamped facilities that existed only as the scaled-down Willowbrook Park in the days of the Watts and South Central L.A. riots.

Despite the historically notorious gangland presence, I guarantee that you will not be dodging bullets or drive-bys during this ride. The area has a surprisingly strong community feel, not to disregard the occasionally gritty, inner urban atmosphere. The ride is nearly flat, with less than a 90-foot difference between the route's high and low points.

From the Earvin "Magic" Johnson County Recreation Area, head to the north side of the park along a concrete path. The path circumnavigates a fishing lake. On the opposite side of the lake, head toward the small parking lot. Ride through and then exit the lot, turning right onto East 120th Street. Although you have entered Watts, the road reenters Willowbrook just past Central Avenue. This unique ride takes you through seven different communities in addition to several that you "bypass" while riding along the Los Angeles River. All the communities are densely populated, so expect plenty of street and traffic activity. Willowbrook, which is unincorporated, had a population of

35,983 in 2010. The community is home to the Charles R. Drew University of Medicine and Science, as well as the Martin Luther King Jr.–Harbor Hospital.

Turn left onto Compton Avenue at the traffic signal and head north. After crossing the Imperial Highway, welcome to Watts! Once a separate city, the community was annexed by L.A. in 1926. Watts's population is about the same as that of Willowbrook. In addition to the aforementioned riots and the Watts Towers (see sidebar), Watts is the birthplace of several notorious street gangs, including various factions of the Bloods and the Crips. Perhaps not so well known is that Watts is predominantly Hispanic (62% as of 2010) and has the youngest median age of any Los Angeles community (21).

Turn right onto East 108th Street, crossing some railroad tracks along the way. At Wilmington Avenue turn left; stay in the left lane for an immediate left turn onto Santa Avenue. On your left, 1 block up the road, are the Watts Towers. (You probably noticed them on your left as you rode along East 108th Street.)

After taking a good, long look at this fine example of urban Italian "naive" art, continue heading northwest on Santa Ana Avenue. Turn right onto Graham Avenue (notice the bike path running parallel to the adjacent light rail tracks). Turn right onto East 103rd Street, followed by a left turn onto Beach Street. This residential street curves to the left and then to the right to continue northward. Turn right at East 92nd Street and head east. After crossing Alameda Street, and some more railroad tracks, the road name changes to Southern Avenue and you enter the city of South Gate. South Gate had a population of 94,396 in 2010 and was about 94% Hispanic. Despite tying for having the highest sales tax rate in California (10.25%), this city and the surrounding cities have faced some serious financial troubles. South Gate was nicknamed "Azalea City" in 1965 after adopting the flowering shrub. Notable South Gate natives, representing the city's diversity, include pioneering West Coast rap group Cypress Hill and Nobel Prize winner Glenn Seaborg (for whom the element seaborgium is named).

Bike Shop

Watts Cyclery, 11202 Wilmington Ave., Los Angeles; (323) 563-6604

Turn left onto Otis Street and head north. Otis is admittedly not the best street for cycling, with four lanes, medium traffic, and not a lot of room for bikes. Enter the city of Huntington Park after crossing Santa Ana Street. Huntington Park had a population of 58,114 in 2010 and was about 97% Hispanic. Thrash metal band Slayer originated in Huntington Park. Enter the city of Cudahy upon crossing Salt Lake Avenue and some more railroad tracks. Otis Street becomes Otis Avenue. Cudahy covers just 1 square mile, making it one of the smallest cities in Southern California but with one of the highest population densities (23,805 residents in 2010). About 96% of the residents at that time were Hispanic. Cudahy made headlines in 2012 when a former mayor and a former city manager were indicted on bribery and corruption charges.

Enter the city of Bell at Florence Avenue. In 2010 Bell's population (35,477) was roughly equivalent to that of Willowbrook and Watts. The corruption in Bell is well-known and might even be an attraction to visitors.

Watts Towers

Seemingly out-of-place, out-of-the-blue, and out-of-nowhere, the Watts Towers were designed and constructed by Italian immigrant Sabato "Simon" Rodia. His boundless folk-art project was started in 1921 and abandoned in 1954. Reaching as high as 99 feet, the towers are a blend of steel reinforcing bars and Rodia's own mixture of concrete, embedded with pieces of porcelain, tile, and glass, and decorated with "found" objects. Upon closer look, one can see bottles (many of which have historic logos), broken pieces of pottery, ceramic tiles, figurines, mirrors, sea shells, and other scraps. Even the steel rebar was scrap—Rodia walked up to 20 miles up and down nearby railroad tracks searching for discarded material. Rodia actually lived in a bungalow underneath the structure, so the entire project was constructed on his own property. He abandoned the site in 1955, however, to avoid further dealings with the City of Los Angeles and to secure his own future as he aged. (Born in 1879, he was in his mid-70s at the time.) He passed away ten years later in Martinez, in Northern California.

By 1959 the City of Los Angeles had condemned the structure and was planning to demolish it. However, opposition, international in scope, and a couple of benefactors were able to preserve it. The structure passed a "topple test," in which a steel cable was attached to it and pulled with a force of 10,000 pounds.

Today the towers are a National Historic Landmark, on the National Register of Historic Places, and a California Historical Landmark—surprisingly, these designations did not occur until 1990. Upon visiting the towers (highly recommended), you will find that they are protected by fencing. Access inside the compound is only available during specially guided tours. In any case, be sure to get off your bicycle and take some time to gaze at this marvel of vernacular architecture.

Follow Otis as it narrows to two lanes, and gets quieter, past Gage Avenue. At Otis's end, turn right onto Randolph Street and head east. As you near the Los Angeles River, look for a connector path on your left. Enter the path and ride up the short ramp to the L.A. River Bikeway. Turn right and head south on the concrete path. (For a discussion of the L.A. River, see the L.A. River Ramble & Echo Park Challenge.) You are not likely to see any water in the river—nearly all of it has been diverted well north of here to serve the needs of L.A.'s sprawling population. You will see some graffiti on the path, and well as some poorly kept segments (overgrown weeds, surface damage, trash) and a few transients (particularly under the bridges). On the plus side, there are no cars along here, and there are several appealing stretches.

Be sure to use the underpasses at all street crossings for continuous, non-stop riding. The path crosses the L.A. River, to follow its eastern bank, at Imperial Highway. Follow the signs—there are several tight turns. After returning to South Gate for a stretch, the path heads along the edge of the city of Paramount. Watch closely for the Alondra Boulevard overpass—this is where you leave the path. Street names are written on most of the overpasses, although some are missing. Two useful benchmarks are the Compton West Golf Course, and Dominguez High School, which are both to your left just before the Alondra overpass. Exit to the left, along a connector path, to Alondra. Get into the street and turn right. The return to shared roads is punctuated by a freeway interchange. Use caution as you ride across. Welcome to Compton! Move to the left, and then turn left onto Atlantic Street.

Once you are heading south on Atlantic Avenue, veer right onto South Atlantic Drive. This street through one of Compton's neighborhoods is decidedly quieter than Atlantic Avenue. Compton had a population of 97,559 in 2012, about 65% Hispanic. Compton is well known for its hip-hop culture, with the city's streets serving as the proving ground for such acts as N.W.A. ("Straight Outta' Compton"), The Game, and Kendrick Lamar, among others. Do not be surprised, however, if no one is rapping as you ride past. The city is actually quite diverse; it's even home to America's only all-USA exhibition cricket team. South Atlantic bends to the right, becoming Greenleaf Avenue.

After crossing the light-rail tracks at Willowbrook Avenue, look for the Compton Creek bike path on the right. Although some maps suggest that the path continues southeast of here, I was unable to find a continuous stretch. Turn right and head northeast along the path. Compton Creek is one of several Los Angeles River "feeders" when there is an ample flow of water. This bike path is quite different from the L.A. River Bikeway in that street crossings are not grade separated. The path is diagonal relative to the streets it crosses. The lack of curb cuts and median breaks at some crossings makes travel along this path difficult. Uninterrupted riding is not possible, but the stretches between the streets are generally peaceful and pleasant. The path ends at El Segundo Boulevard. Carefully cross El Segundo, turn left, and head west. Centennial High School will be on your left. Reenter Willowbrook after crossing Central Avenue. Turn right and enter the Earvin "Magic" Johnson County Recreation Area at Wadsworth Avenue. Turn left and enter the parking area to conclude the ride.

MILES AND DIRECTIONS

0.0 Start from the parking area on the south side of Earvin "Magic" Johnson County Recreation Area, in the Willowbrook community of Los Angeles. Head north through park on paths.

0.6 Exit the recreation area on the north side of the parking lot; turn right onto East 120th Street.

1.25 Traffic signal at Compton Avenue; turn left.

1.65 Traffic signal at Imperial Highway; keep straight and enter the community of Watts.

2.2 Traffic signal at East 108th Street; turn right.

2.6 Traffic signal at Wilmington Avenue; turn left—stay in the left lane.

2.65 Traffic signal at Santa Ana Boulevard; turn left. Simon Rodia's Watts Towers will be on the left.

2.9 Stop sign at Graham Avenue; turn right.

3.1 Traffic signal at East 103rd Street; turn right.

3.2 Turn left onto Beach Street; the road bends left and then right to continue northward.

3.95 Stop sign at East 92nd Street; turn right.

4.65 Cross railroad tracks at Alameda Street and enter the city of South Gate, now on Southern Avenue.

6.55 Traffic signal at Otis Street; turn left.

7.35 Traffic signal at Santa Ana Street; keep straight and enter city of Huntington Park.

7.5 Cross Salt Lake Avenue and enter city of Cudahy, now on Otis Avenue.

7.95 Enter city of Bell at Walnut Street.

8.55 Traffic signal at Gage Avenue; jog right and then left to continue on Otis Avenue.

8.75 End of Otis Avenue (stop sign) at Randolph Street; turn right.

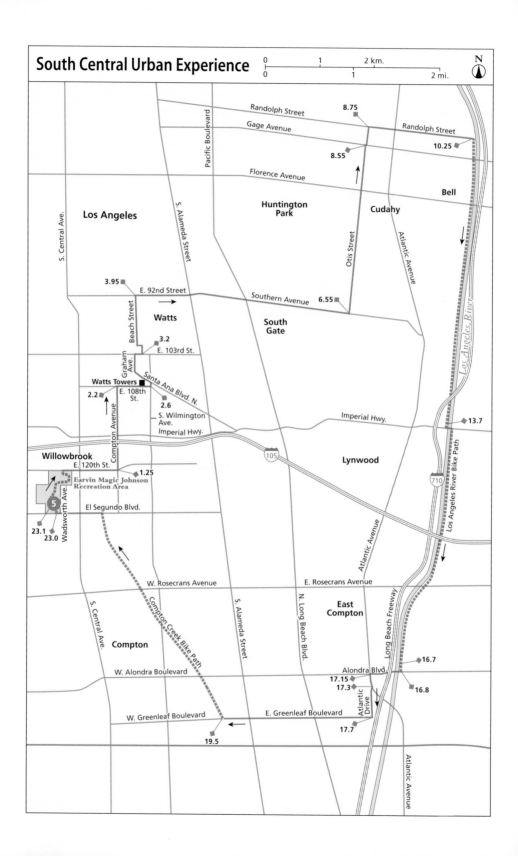

South Central Urban Experience

0   1   2 km.

0   1   2 mi.

N

Randolph Street

Gage Avenue

8.75

Randolph Street

10.25

Pacific Boulevard

8.55

Florence Avenue

Bell

Los Angeles

S. Alameda Street

Huntington
Park

Cudahy

S. Central Ave.

Otis Street

Atlantic Avenue

3.95

E. 92nd Street

Southern Avenue

6.55

Los Angeles River

Watts

Beach Street

South
Gate

3.2

E. 103rd St.

Graham Ave.

Watts Towers

Santa Ana Blvd. N.

2.2

E. 108th
St.

2.6

Imperial Hwy.

13.7

S. Wilmington
Ave.

Imperial Hwy.

105

Los Angeles River Bike Path

Compton Avenue

Willowbrook

Lynwood

E. 120th St.

1.25

710

Earvin Magic Johnson
Recreation Area

5

El Segundo Blvd.

23.1

Wadsworth Ave.

23.0

W. Rosecrans Avenue

E. Rosecrans Avenue

Atlantic Avenue

S. Central Ave.

Compton Creek Bike Path

S. Alameda Street

N. Long Beach Blvd.

East
Compton

Long Beach Freeway

Compton

16.7

W. Alondra Boulevard

Alondra Blvd.

17.15

16.8

17.3

Atlantic Drive

W. Greenleaf Boulevard

E. Greenleaf Boulevard

19.5

17.7

Atlantic Avenue

10.25 Enter Los Angeles River Bikeway on the left; head up the connector path.

10.3 Turn right and head south on Los Angeles River Bikeway.

13.7 Cross over the L.A. River at Imperial Highway.

16.7 Exit bike path to the left at Alondra Boulevard, along the path connector.

16.8 Turn right onto Alondra (ride in the street). Cross over I-710, now in the city of Compton.

17.15 Traffic signal at Atlantic Avenue; turn left.

17.3 Bear right onto South Atlantic Drive.

17.7 Road bends 90 degrees to the right, becoming Greenleaf Boulevard.

19.5 Turn right onto Compton Creek bike path, just downstream of railroad crossing at Willowbrook Avenue.

19.95 Stop at Oleander Avenue; path continues on opposite side of Oleander—carefully cross the street.

20.1 Alondra Boulevard crossing; path continues on opposite side of street.

20.75 Compton Boulevard crossing; path continues on opposite side of street.

20.9 Wilmington Avenue crossing; path continues on opposite side of street. Diagonal crossing—exercise caution.

21.4 Rosecrans Avenue crossing; path continues on opposite side of street.

22.4 End of Compton Creek bike path at El Segundo Boulevard. Cross road and turn left onto El Segundo.

22.7 Traffic signal at S. Central Avenue; keep straight. Leave Compton and enter Willowbrook.

23.0 Turn right at Wadsworth Avenue and enter Earvin "Magic" Johnson County Recreation Area.

23.1 Turn left to enter the south parking lot and conclude the ride.

Tour of the Lower San Gabriel River Valley

Start: Santa Fe Springs Park, 10068 Cedardale Dr., Santa Fe Springs

Length: 39.0 miles (clockwise loop)

Riding time: 2 to 5 hours (my time: 2H35:23)

Terrain and surface: 40% on paved roads; 60% on paved bike paths

Elevation: Low: 22 feet, along the San Gabriel River Trail adjacent to El Dorado Park East in Long Beach; high: 1,026 feet near the intersection of Turnbull Canyon Road and Skyline Drive in Hacienda Heights

Traffic and hazards: With 60% of the ride on exclusive paths, only 40% is shared with motor vehicles. Turnbull Canyon Road was carrying 1,280 vehicles per day in 2009; Colima Road was carrying 37,200 vehicles per day south of Camino del Sur in 2010; Valley View Avenue was carrying between 30,000 and 40,000 vehicles per day in La Mirada in 2009.

Map: *The Thomas Guide—Street Guide: Los Angeles and Orange Counties* (any recent year), page 706

Getting there: By car—From central Los Angeles, head south on I-5 and turn onto I-605 northbound. Exit at Telegraph Avenue; turn right and head east. Turn right onto Orr and Day Road and head south. Turn right onto Davenrich Street. After passing under I-605, watch for signs directing you to Santa Fe Springs Park. Turn right onto Cedardale Drive and enter the park.

   By public transit—From central Los Angeles, ride the Metro Blue Line to the Imperial Highway station. Transfer to the Metro Green Line and head east to the end of the line (Norwalk). From the Norwalk station, head south (by bicycle) to Foster Street. Turn right onto Foster Street and head west to the end of the street. Continue onto the access path to the San Gabriel River Bikeway. Turn right to start the ride (or head north to Santa Fe Springs Park).

Starting point coordinates: N33.946203° / W118.096383°

THE RIDE

The Tour of the Lower San Gabriel Valley takes advantage of the San Gabriel River and Coyote Creek bicycle paths, filling the gaps in between with city streets, including an exhilarating climb up Turnbull Canyon Road in Hacienda Heights. The 39.0-mile ride starts and finishes at Santa Fe Springs Park in the city of Santa Fe Springs. The city had a population of 16,223 in 2010. Santa Fe Springs' legacy is in the automobile industry; it's home to a maker of Cadillac engine parts and the original home of the Shelby Cobra (1960s-era hot rod). Exit Santa Fe Springs Park and head west toward the San Gabriel River on the paved path. At the San Gabriel River Trail, turn right and head north. Similar to many other Los Angeles–region riverside bikeways, there are no at-grade crossings, making for uninterrupted riding. Also as with the other bikeways, there will likely be very little water in the river (see "San Gabriel River" sidebar). **Note:** Along this segment, you are riding in the opposite direction of the Vuelta Tres Rios de Los Angeles route.

After 3.15 miles, exit the bike path to the right via an unnamed connector. The connector is not marked; the best way to identify it may be according to the distance that you have traveled since leaving the park. Continue through the opening in the fence and over the railroad tracks; the connector empties out onto Dunlap Crossing Road (paved street). You are now in West Whittier–Los Nietos, an unincorporated community of 25,540 (as of 2010). Pass under I-605. Cross Norwalk Boulevard; you are now on Mines Boulevard. Turn left onto Glengarry Avenue; at Hadley Street turn right.

Enter the city of Whittier after crossing Whittier Boulevard, remaining on Hadley Street. The road begins to climb gradually. Whittier had a population of 85,331 in 2010, with about 66% Hispanic. The Whittier Narrows earthquake struck in 1987; the magnitude 5.9 quake and strong 5.2 aftershock resulted in eight fatalities in the city and the destruction or demolition of a number of buildings. Whittier High School is on the right just past Gregory Avenue. Film buffs might recognize the campus as the setting for fictional Hill Valley High School in the *Back to the Future* movies. Turn left onto Painter Avenue and continue climbing, now at a 4% grade. The 2007 film *Disturbia* was shot along Painter. This area of the city is known as "uptown" Whittier, with a mixture of historical and pricey homes. Turn right onto Beverly Boulevard; as you leave Whittier and enter Turnbull Canyon, the road name changes to Turnbull Canyon Road. (See the Whittier–Workman Hill Workout for a discussion of Turnbull Canyon.) The 1994 film *Roadracers* was shot in uptown Whittier and Turnbull Canyon. The director was searching for a "1950s look" and was content with Whittier.

Two riders on Turnbull Canyon Road discuss how they will catch that rider up ahead.

Turnbull Canyon Road, the featured climb of this ride, is a popular training ground for local cyclists. From Painter Avenue it is 2.5 miles and 544 feet to the crest, at Skyline Drive. Although the average gradient is 4%, the road gets steeper as you penetrate the canyon, complete with hairpin turns. (**Caution:** Be sure to not cross the centerline.) There is minimal development along Turnbull Canyon Road, making it seem as though you are worlds away from the L.A. bustle. Beyond the crest at Skyline Drive, enter the community of Hacienda Heights. Many of the homes up here have tremendous vistas. The road makes a quick, twisting descent. The road name changes to Las Lomitas Drive beyond a T intersection at which Turnbull Canyon Road turns to the left. Keep straight here on Las Lomitas then turn right onto Vallecito Drive.

Hacienda Heights is a relatively upscale residential community with a 2010 population of 54,038. At that time 82% of the residents were of either Hispanic or Oriental heritage. Among the community's current and/or part-time residents were Fergie (R&B-pop group Black-Eyed Peas) and Jill Sterkel (two-time Olympic swimming gold medalist).

Turn left onto Camino del Sur and begin a brisk climb. The road crests and then descends to the Colima Road intersection. Turn right here for a 0.5-mile climb at a 5% grade. Colima reenters Whittier about halfway up the climb. After cresting at a 791-foot elevation, Colima begins a rapid descent into the city. Watch for turning motor vehicle traffic, and control your speed. I found myself moving nearly as fast as the cars along some of Colima's segments. Leave Whittier and enter the unincorporated community of South Whittier (population of 57,156 in 2010) after crossing Lambert Road. Just beyond Lambert, Colima curves to the left, becoming La Mirada Boulevard. Bear right here to remain on Colima (most of the motor vehicle traffic will follow La Mirada).

Bike Shops

Karina Pro Bicycles, 13101 Whittier Blvd., Whittier; (562) 693-8073

Pioneer Bicycles, 8015 Pioneer Blvd., Whittier; (562) 692-6470

Continue on Colima across Leffingwell Road, turning right onto Tedford Drive. Turn left onto Valley View Avenue and then right onto Foster Road. After crossing the bridge over Coyote Creek, turn left to enter the Coyote Creek Bikeway. *Note:* As of this writing, the bikeway was scheduled to be closed until mid-May 2015 because of construction along I-5. Certain segments of the bikeway may be open while others are closed (hopefully with clear detour signs). I rode the bikeway all the way through during a time when it was supposed to be closed, so check with the California Department of Transportation (Caltrans), local municipalities, local publications, and the Internet, as well as local riders, for the latest information.

The Coyote Creek Bikeway is a pleasant, gradually downhill paved bike path that parallels the creek for 9.5 miles until the creek merges with the San Gabriel River. One reference described the bikeway as "devoid of all scenery." True, most of the bikeway passes by industrial uses, but Cerritos Regional Park is accessible and Cypress's Forest Lawn Cemetery can be viewed from the path. After leaving Santa Fe Springs, the path passes through the cities of Cerritos, La Palma, Lakewood, Hawaiian Gardens, Cypress, and Los Alamitos before finally entering Long Beach. The bike path also ducks in and out of Orange County along the way before finally returning to Los Angeles County for good.

Cross over Coyote Creek at Lincoln Avenue in Cypress to ride along its eastern bank. At the end of the bikeway, where Coyote Creek meets the San Gabriel River, turn right to cross back over the creek; then turn right again and head north on the San Gabriel River Trail. Please note that there are stories of unsuspecting cyclists missing the bridge at the end of the Coyote Creek Bikeway, heading down the steep embankment out of control, and crashing

San Gabriel River

The once-mighty San Gabriel River, which flooded heavily in 1862 and again in 1938, today is little more than a trickle along its lower reaches. What happened to all the water? Southern California was experiencing a serious drought as of this writing, and one's first thought is that the lack of water is a direct outcome of the drought. Logical, but not quite true.

Actually, the danger of flooding led the US Army Corps of Engineers to dam the river in a couple of places well upstream of its lower reaches. The dams also help control the river flow, enabling its waters to be used as a regional resource. With an estimated 2 million persons living within the river's floodplain, substantially more than during the great floods of the nineteenth and twentieth centuries, there was little choice but to tame the river.

Before the era of modern-day floods, the San Gabriel River was the site of an important battle in the Mexican-American War. The Battle of the Rio San Gabriel occurred January 8, 1847, at the juncture between present-day Whittier, Pico Rivera, and Montebello. On that day, General Stephen W. Kearny and Commodore Robert F. Stockton joined forces to confront General Jose Maria Flores of Mexico. Although the Commodore and General were initially in dispute as to the right of command, Stockton had more men and a potentially better strategy. After scouts discovered Flores' position at a key ford along the river, Stockton's men launched a river crossing. Flores' attacks on the front lines proved ineffective, and the US's 600 or so men ultimately overwhelmed Flores' 350. Flores' troops retreated and were defeated at the Battle of La Mesa the next day. A total of two men were killed on each side, and nine were wounded on each side, an even exchange of injuries and deaths for a critical US victory.

Today's concerns are the environmental degradation and loss of ecological and riparian habitats associated with the damming and "paving over" of the river and riverbed. The upper portions of the San Gabriel River, which begins in the Santa Monica Mountains, still flow. But the river has been converted into a flood control channel along its lower portions to protect the huge population of the San Gabriel Valley from Mother Nature's unpredictability while fulfilling some municipal water needs.

into the (usually dry) channel below! Use caution here—there is no guardrail at the sharp right-hand turn onto the bridge.

From the Coyote Creek–San Gabriel River Trail junction, it is a 10.8-mile trip back to Santa Fe Springs. (**Note:** Along here you are riding in the opposite direction of the Vuelta Tres Rios ride.) The low point of the route, at just 22 feet above sea level, comes adjacent to El Dorado Park East in Long Beach. The path continues through or along the edges of Long Beach, Lakewood, Cerritos, Bellflower, Norwalk, and Downey before finally returning to Santa Fe Springs. I-605 is parallel to the bike path during the entire trip along the river, often seemingly within arm's reach. Despite the freeway noise, there are numerous scenic stretches along the path. Several parks afford direct access to the path, including El Dorado Park in Long Beach, Rynerson Park in Lakewood, Liberty Park in Cerritos, and Wilderness Park in Downey. Look for the turnoff into Santa Fe Springs Park just beyond the I-5 underpass, on your right.

MILES AND DIRECTIONS

0.0   Start at Santa Fe Springs Park in Santa Fe Springs. Exit the park and head west along a connector path toward the San Gabriel River.

0.05 Turn right onto the San Gabriel River Trail (paved bike path).

3.15 Leave the path and turn right onto unnamed connector; cross railroad tracks and join Dunlap Crossing Road.

3.2   Continue along Dunlap Crossing Road (paved street); enter West Whittier–Los Nietos.

3.5   Traffic signal at Norwalk Boulevard; keep straight, now on Mines Boulevard.

3.75 Turn left onto Glengarry Avenue.

4.0   Turn right onto Hadley Street and head east.

4.7   Traffic signal at Whittier Boulevard (SR 72); keep straight and enter the city of Whittier.

5.9   Traffic signal at Painter Avenue; turn left.

6.25 Stop sign at Beverly Boulevard; turn right.

6.6   Leave city of Whittier and enter Turnbull Canyon, now on Turnbull Canyon Road in the community of Hacienda Heights.

6.8   Pass the Turnbull Canyon Trail trailhead on the left.

8.8   Reach crest of Turnbull Canyon Road at Skyline Drive intersection (Skyline Trail on the right).

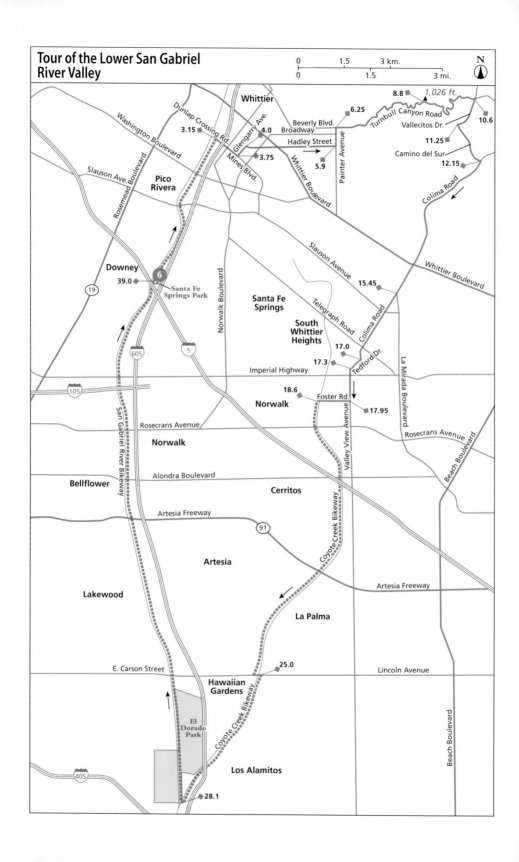

10.5 Keep straight at T intersection, now on Las Lomitas Drive.

10.6 Stop sign at Vallecitos Drive; turn right.

11.25 Stop sign at Camino del Sur; turn left.

12.15 Traffic signal at Colima Road; turn right.

12.4 Reenter the city of Whittier; keep straight on Colima Road.

15.3 Traffic signal at Lambert Road; keep straight. Leave Whittier and enter the community of South Whittier.

15.45 Bear right where the road curves to the left and becomes La Mirada Boulevard, still on Colima.

17.0 Stop sign at Tedford Drive; turn right.

17.3 Stop sign at Valley View Avenue; turn left.

17.95 Traffic signal at Foster Road; turn right.

18.6 Turn left onto Coyote Creek Bikeway, just after crossing bridge over Coyote Creek. Enter the city of Santa Fe Springs.

25.0 Cross over Coyote Creek on bike path at Lincoln Avenue; continue south on bikeway.

28.1 End of Coyote Creek Bikeway; turn right to cross bridge over Coyote Creek. Turn right onto San Gabriel River Bikeway and head north.

38.95 Leave the bike path; turn right onto unnamed connector path to return to Santa Fe Springs Park.

39.0 End the ride at the end of the connector path in Santa Fe Springs Park.

Start: El Dorado East Regional Park, 7550 East Spring St., Long Beach

Length: 49.85 miles (clockwise loop)

Riding time: 2.5 to 6.5 hours (my time: 3H06:54)

Terrain and surface: 92% on paved bike paths; 8% on paved roads

Elevation: Low: 11 feet, along the Long Beach Shoreline bike path in Long Beach; high: 240 feet atop the Whittier Narrows Dam along the Rio Hondo Bikeway in Montebello (on the dam's west side) and along the San Gabriel River Bikeway in Pico Rivera (on the dam's east side)

Traffic and hazards: The heaviest traffic volumes of the ride by far are on East Second Street in Long Beach. Shoreline Drive in the Long Beach's Shoreline Village area is occasionally closed for special events, such as the annual Toyota Grand Prix of Long Beach.

Map: *The Thomas Guide—Street Guide: Los Angeles and Orange Counties* (any recent year), page 796

Getting there: By car—From central Los Angeles, head south on I-5 and turn onto I-605 southbound. Exit at Spring Street; turn right and head west. Turn right to enter El Dorado Regional Park. Pay the entrance fee; turn right and follow the park road. (**Note:** There may be a high water crossing.) Continue through the underpass under Wardlow Road to access El Dorado Park East. Turn left at the next road and then right into the parking area. This has been a popular staging area for Tuesday-evening bicycle races.

    By public transit—From central Los Angeles, ride the Metro Blue Line to downtown Long Beach. Exit at Willow Street. Transfer to Long Beach Transit bus route 102 or 104 and ride eastward to El Dorado Park (exit along Spring Street). Each bus runs hourly on weekdays, providing half-hour headways to the park; no service on weekends and holidays.

Starting point coordinates: N33.820783° / W118.089761°

THE RIDE

The Vuelta Tres Rios de Los Angeles may be the "mother of all bike rides" in the Los Angeles region, taking full advantage of several of the area's lengthy riverside bikeways and a shoreline path to make a loop that is almost exclusively on bike paths. A few gaps exist in the loop, but they are reasonably short. The ride can be started from a number of places; Veterans Memorial Park, along the Rio Hondo in the city of Commerce, is probably the closest point along the route to central Los Angeles. However, I have chosen El Dorado Park in Long Beach as the staging area, in part because Long Beach is a featured city along the route. Also, El Dorado Park has traditionally been the scene of weekly "Tuesday Night World Championship" bicycle races. This route begins in Long Beach and passes either through or along the edges of Paramount, South Gate, Downey, Bell Gardens, Commerce, Montebello, Pico Rivera, South Whittier, Santa Fe Springs, Norwalk, Cerritos, and Lakewood. Do not be dissuaded by the distance—this may be one of the fastest urban 50-mile rides you have ever done! In fact, I would argue that this ride can be completed in a time faster than a motorist could drive 50 miles on L.A.'s city streets.

Leave the parking area at El Dorado Park East and head southwest toward the Wardlow Road underpass. Before ducking under the road, hang a left and head south on the San Gabriel River Trail (paved bicycle path). Continue straight onto the bike path, heading south as it cruises along the western border of El Dorado Park. After leaving the park, the path moves back to the "banks" of the San Gabriel River, continuing southward. Beyond the park, at the merger with Coyote Creek, the path crosses a bridge, turns right, and continues southward. The path effectively continues all the way to the Pacific Ocean. There is no connection from there, however, so leave the path at Second Street, taking the connector path on your left. (When I rode this route, there were no signs at the connector.) Turn right onto Second Street and head into Long Beach. Although it may seem to be merely a stepsister of Los Angeles, Long Beach is a large city in its own right, with a population of 462,257 in 2010 (seventh-largest in California). Among the city's notables are aircraft manufacturer Boeing (formerly McDonnell-Douglas), Daugherty Field (major international airport), and the Port of Long Beach (second-busiest container port in the United States). The city is also home to the *Queen Mary* (all-time record holder for the greatest number of passengers ever transported by ship: 16,082). A magnitude 6.4 earthquake hit Long Beach in 1933, causing widespread destruction and forcing extensive rebuilding (and new seismic building codes).

After crossing SR 1, in the Marina-Pacifica area of Long Beach, Second Street lifts up and over Marine Stadium. This was the site of the rowing events during the 1932 Summer Olympic Games and is now a California Historical Landmark. Enter the Long Beach community of Naples. Although it is barely detectable from here, Naples is situated on three islands that are interlaced with canals. The "Venice of America" design was the product of the Mayberry & Parker firm. Cross over Alamitos Bay, leaving Naples. Move into the left turn lane as you cross the bridge and turn left onto Bay Shore Avenue immediately after crossing the bay. Welcome to the Belmont Shore neighborhood of Long Beach!

Notice the inland beach on your left as you ride along Bay Shore Avenue. Follow Bay Shore as it curves to the left, with Alamitos Bay on your left. At Ocean Boulevard cross the street and head directly onto the Shoreline Bike Path. On this featured segment of the route, you ride parallel to the coastal beach of Belmont Shore for about 3 miles, heading westward. A breakwater

A rider approaches the Whittier Narrows Dam along the Rio Hondo Bikeway.

keeps the waters calm along this beach, so you will not see a surfing crowd here. Island Chaffee is visible in the bay, one of the four man-made THUMS (Texaco, Humble [now Exxon], Union, Mobil, Shell) islands. Each island is actually a disguised oil drilling platform, built during the mid-1960s and decorated with trees, waterfalls, and other landscaping. The islands are also known as the Astronaut Islands, with each one bearing the name of an Apollo 1 or related-mission astronaut. The path jogs right and then left as it passes Belmont Veterans Memorial Pier. The pier was competed in 1915 and updated in 1967. The pier is 1,620 feet in length and made of concrete (the original pier, 975 feet in length, was wooden). Cars used to be able to drive to the end of the pier, but today's version is for fishing and strolling only.

Beyond and west of the pier, Junipero Beach is to your left, followed by Alamitos Beach. As you near the marina (recognizable by the many boats moored in the waters), the path bends to the left. After a sharp left-hand turn followed by a right-hand turn, the path is immediately adjacent to the marina. Island Grissom (another THUMS island) is in the bay, just outside the marina area. This island features waterfalls and sculptured screens, the latter serving as both a decoration and a deterrent to swimmers. If you look across Queensway Bay, you can see the *Queen Mary*, the legendary ocean vessel. After traveling adjacent to the boats for a stretch, look for Shoreline Village Drive to your right. Exit the path here and move into the road. At the traffic signal, turn left onto Shoreline Drive. (**Note:** This road is occasionally closed for special events, such as the annual Toyota Grand Prix of Long Beach.) Turn right onto Pine Avenue and then left onto Seaside Way. Follow this road to Golden Shore Avenue and turn left, heading back toward Queensway Bay.

Look for the entrance to the Los Angeles River Bikeway to the right. Entering the path requires a right, followed by a quick left and then a quick right. You are now riding along the eastern bank of the Los Angeles River, essentially a dry riverbed, heading north. This is the southern, longer section of the L.A. River Bikeway, locally referred to as LARIO. (A ride along one of the northern segments is described in the L.A. River Ramble.) The bikeway is speedy, with grade-separated crossings allowing for nonstop, continuous travel. Also note that the bikeway passes through some of the "most dangerous sections in the greater L.A. area" (quoting a Wikipedia article). There is minimal evidence of this along the bikeway, with the exception of some graffiti, a few transients, and the occasional under-bridge enclaves. You are not likely to see much activity out here because of the path's openness, but it is probably just as well to keep moving. The path takes you through the community of North Long Beach (part of Long Beach), Paramount, and South Gate before diverging onto the Rio Hondo Bikeway. The transition between the two bikeways

Los Angeles Region Bike Paths

The Los Angeles region had, as of this writing, about 350 miles of exclusive bike paths, with plans to expand to 1,600 miles. Many of the paths take advantage of the area's "rivers," although most of these are dry concrete channels. These channels were generally products of US Army Corps of Engineers' work in the mid-twentieth century—to both provide water and control it.

Following the history of bike path development in L.A. is a challenge, however, partly because of the multiple players, jurisdictions, and funding sources involved. At most, a bike path is developed in a piecemeal fashion, with new segments extending old segments. For example, the Los Angeles River Bikeway alone involved, at various times in its history, the Santa Monica Mountains Conservancy, Friends of the Los Angeles River, the city of Los Angeles, the county of Los Angeles, advisory committees and task forces, the Los Angeles city council, various state propositions (generally serving as funding sources) and the U.S Army Corps of Engineers. These entities worked either together or in sequence to build the still-expanding bikeway.

The evolution of the region's bikeways can be traced back to the decision to "pave" the various riverbeds and line their embankments with concrete. The creation of these corridors attracted the railroads and, ultimately, the freeway system. A latter-day thought was to add bicycle paths to these corridors—and the rest is history!

is seamless. (Continuing northward on the L.A. River Bikeway requires a river crossover at Imperial Highway in South Gate.)

The Rio Hondo Bikeway parallels the Rio Hondo, which means "deep river." Wondering where the water is, you may think that it is a misnomer. As with other L.A. rivers, nearly all the water is captured upstream at dams and diversions, in part to serve the region's water needs and in part to control flooding. The Rio Hondo was actually created by the 1867 floods, when the San Gabriel River changed its course. Today the two riverbeds parallel each other for a stretch, separated by no more than 2 or 3 miles. After following the eastern bank of the Rio for 1.75 miles, the path crosses a bridge to continue along its western bank. From here you will ride along the borders of Bell Gardens and Montebello. The Washington Boulevard crossing in Montebello is notable as the site of the Battle of Rio San Gabriel (see sidebar in the previous ride, Tour of the Lower San Gabriel River Valley).

At the Whittier Narrows Dam, the Rio Hondo Bikeway bends to the left for a 7.5% climb (for about 500 feet) to the top of the dam. This is really the only climb of the entire ride, so I encourage you to dig deep and attack this one. Once atop the dam, the path curves toward the right before making a gradual descent adjacent to the "spreading grounds" of the Rio Hondo upriver of the dam. Actually, there is usually very little water here. This is a decidedly different segment of the bikeway, with Lincoln Avenue to your left and greenery and vegetation to your right. The bikeway curves to the left as it comes to an end at the intersection of San Gabriel Boulevard and Lincoln Avenue.

Turn right onto San Gabriel Boulevard and head east. After crossing Rosemead Boulevard (signalized and busy), veer off the street and onto the bike path. The path leaves the hectic pace of the city streets behind and heads off into the surprisingly lush environment of the Whittier Narrows. The path on which you are riding is otherwise known as Siphon Road. Watch for the T junction with the San Gabriel River Bikeway; there is a sign here. Turn right and head south. I-605 roars to your left, although the bike path is worlds away. Negotiate a series of switchbacks as the path makes its way back to the top of Whittier Narrows Dam. Continue south on the bikeway from here. At mile 36.25 the bikeway moves from the west to the east bank of the San Gabriel River at San Gabriel Parkway. From here it is an enjoyable, car-free 13.6 miles back to El Dorado East Regional Park.

MILES AND DIRECTIONS

0.0 Start at El Dorado East Regional Park in Long Beach, in the far northern quadrant of the park (north of Wardlow Road). Head toward the San Gabriel River on a connector path.

0.1 Turn left onto the San Gabriel River Bikeway and head south.

1.8 Turn left onto the bridge; cross over Coyote Creek and turn right at end of bridge to continue heading south on San Gabriel River Bikeway.

4.3 Leave bikeway via connector path to East Second Street (there may not be a sign).

4.35 End of connector path; turn right onto East Second Street.

5.3 Bridge over Marine Stadium; enter Naples.

6.55 After crossing second bridge, turn left at traffic signal onto Bay Shore Avenue.

6.65 Stop sign at 54th Place; bear left to continue on Bay Shore Avenue.

6.7 Stop sign at Ocean Avenue; keep straight onto Shoreline Bike Path.

7.75 Pass Belmont Veterans Memorial Pier.

9.9 Path jogs left and then right, adjacent to Shoreline Marina.

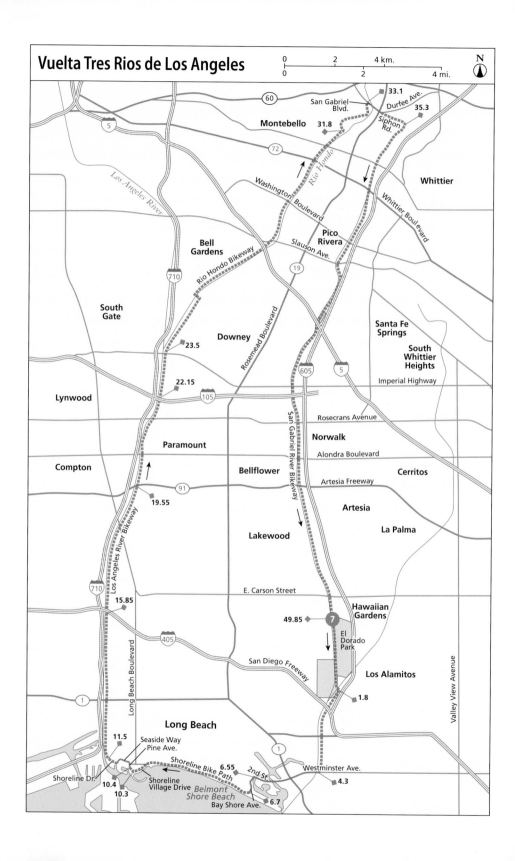

Vuelta Tres Rios de Los Angeles

0   2   4 km.
0   2   4 mi.

N

60

San Gabriel Blvd.

33.1

Durfee Ave.

35.3

Montebello   31.8

Siphon Rd.

5

72

Rio Hondo

Whittier

Los Angeles River

Washington Boulevard

Whittier Boulevard

Bell Gardens

Pico Rivera

Slauson Ave.

Rio Hondo Bikeway

710

Santa Fe Springs

19

South Gate

Downey

South Whittier Heights

Rosemead Boulevard

23.5

605

5

Imperial Highway

22.15

105

Lynwood

Rosecrans Avenue

San Gabriel River Bikeway

Norwalk

Paramount

Alondra Boulevard

Compton

Bellflower

Cerritos

91

Artesia Freeway

19.55

Artesia

La Palma

Los Angeles River Bikeway

Lakewood

E. Carson Street

710

15.85

Hawaiian Gardens

49.85   7

Long Beach Boulevard

405

El Dorado Park

Los Alamitos

San Diego Freeway

1

1.8

Valley View Avenue

Long Beach

11.5

Seaside Way
Pine Ave.

1

Shoreline Bike Path

6.55   2nd St.

Westminster Ave.

4.3

Shoreline Dr.

10.4

Shoreline Village Drive

10.3

Belmont Shore Beach

6.7

Bay Shore Ave.

10.3 Leave Shoreline Bike Path at Shoreline Village Drive; ride along the path and then move to the street.

10.4 Traffic signal at Shoreline Drive; turn left.

10.65 Traffic signal at Pine Ave; turn right.

10.85 Traffic signal at Seaside Way; turn left.

11.4 Stop sign at Golden Shore Avenue; turn left.

11.5 Turn right to enter parking area; make an immediate left and then an immediate right onto Los Angeles River Bikeway.

15.85 I-405 underpass.

19.55 SR 91 underpass.

22.15 I-105 underpass.

23.5 Keep straight onto Rio Hondo Bikeway.

25.25 Turn left to cross bridge; turn right to continue riding on west bank of Rio Hondo.

31.8 Bikeway curves left to climb Whittier Narrows Dam (7.5% grade).

31.9 Bikeway merges with dam access road and then diverges.

33.1 End of Rio Hondo Bikeway (south section) at San Gabriel Boulevard; turn right onto San Gabriel.

34.6 Cross Rosemead Boulevard and enter bike path (Siphon Road).

35.3 Turn right onto San Gabriel River Bikeway.

35.45 Bikeway negotiates switchbacks adjacent to San Gabriel River Dam.

36.25 Cross over San Gabriel River at San Gabriel Parkway; follow signs to continue on San Gabriel River Bikeway.

49.75 Exit bikeway at El Dorado East Regional Park; turn left onto connector path.

49.85 End ride at end of connector path in El Dorado East Regional Park.

Whittier–Workman Hill Workout (with Bailout Option)

Start: Hellman Wilderness Park, 5700 Greenleaf Ave., Whittier

Length: 9.85 miles (two loops or figure 8); 5.85-mile loop for bailout

Riding time: 1 to 4 hours (my time: 1H30:00)

Terrain and surface: 85% on dirt trails; 15% on paved roads

Elevation: Low: 386 feet at Beverly Boulevard and Greenleaf Avenue in Whittier; high: 1,353 feet on Skyline Trail near the junction with Workman Ridge Trail, near the peak of Workman Hill

Traffic and hazards: 1.0 mile of the ride uses Turnbull Canyon Road and Beverly Boulevard in Whittier.

Map: *The Thomas Guide—Street Guide: Los Angeles and Orange Counties* (any recent year), page 677

Getting there: By car—From central Los Angeles, head east on SR 60 and turn onto I-605 southbound. Exit at Beverly Boulevard and head east into Whittier. Turn left onto Greenleaf Avenue and climb 2 blocks. The entrance to Hellman Wilderness Park is on the right; park here.

   By public transit—From central L.A., ride Metro's Silver Line (light-rail transit; not the Silver Streak) to the El Monte Station. Transfer to Metro bus route 270 heading south, toward Whittier. Exit at Beverly Boulevard and Greenleaf Avenue. Ride north (uphill) on Greenleaf Avenue to Hellman Wilderness Park. Route 270 runs every 55 to 65 minutes on weekdays, and every 60 minutes on Saturday. There is no service along this route Sunday and holidays.

Starting point coordinates: N33.990742° / W118.037275°

THE RIDE

The Whittier–Workman Hill Workout is a challenging mountain bike ride that features steep climbs, long climbs, rapid descents, a rough descent, and a few narrow trails that may test your bike-handling skills. The ride consists of two loops that converge at the crest of Turnbull Canyon Road, east of Whittier,

Peppergrass Trail, approaching Mariposa Trail (hmmm, left or right?) in the Puente Hills

in the community of Hacienda Heights. The ride can be ridden as a figure 8, with a clockwise loop (partial) followed by a counterclockwise loop and then the completion of the clockwise loop. The Whittier–Workman Hill Bailout is a shorter option that eliminates the second loop. Please note that trail markers exist along this ride, but they are sporadic and limited. Be sure to stay on the main trail (i.e., avoid making any sharp turns onto trails at junctions), and pay attention to the markings that do exist. Good, comprehensive maps of the trails in the area are limited.

Begin the ride from the parking lot for Hellman Wilderness Park, located along Greenleaf Avenue, north of Beverly Boulevard, in Whittier. The park and environs feature abundant coastal oak and sage scrub. Head east onto Peppergrass Trail and—hello!—immediately begin a steep climb at an average 15% gradient. The trail reaches a false crest and dips slightly just upstream of the junction with Mariposa Trail. Either trail can be taken from here. Mariposa's grade is gentler than Peppergrass's, which continues at 15%. However, Peppergrass is wider than Mariposa. Plus, Mariposa skirts a bench along the ridge that you are climbing, so there is a drop-off to your left. For those of us who are right-eye dominant, a drop-off on the left can be a bit unsettling. Take your pick. The trails merge up ahead, on the ridge of the Rose Hills, which are essentially a subrange of the Puente Hills. Hellman Wilderness Park extends only part of the way up the climb, although the transition to the Puente Hills Native Habitat Preservation Authority is imperceptible.

At the top the trail enters a false flat segment before curving to the left to navigate a brisk climb around a knoll. Note that there are trail junctions along here; stay on the main fire road. To your left, on the opposite side of Sycamore Canyon, is the stately Hsi Lai Temple—the largest Buddhist temple and monastery in the Western Hemisphere and considered to be one of the great Buddhist wonders of the world. The temple can only be viewed from a distance from your vantage point and must be accessed from the other side of the canyon. Continue to the end of the fire road; turn right at the junction with Skyline Trail (also known as Skyline Fire Road). For a short distance you will be riding in the opposite direction of the Ahwingna Pahe Mahar ride.

Skyline Trail, or Skyline Fire Road, is part of the Juan Bautista de Anza National Historic Trail. Skyline makes a gradual climb to over 1,200 feet in elevation before descending into a Hacienda Heights hilltop community. After negotiating a gate, you come to a paved road (Skyline Road) as you return to civilization. At the Eldridge Drive intersection down the street, turn right to continue on Skyline Road. Turnbull Canyon, where you will eventually wind up in this ride, is to your right. At Turnbull Canyon Road, stop and turn right; then immediately cross the road to continue on Skyline Trail. (If you opt for the Bailout route, turn right onto Turnbull Canyon Road.)

Bike Shops

GS Cyclery and Wheels, 6713 Greenleaf Ave., Whittier; (562) 698-9426; http://gscyclery.blogspot.com
Delgado Repair Bike, 12608 Penn St., Whittier; (562) 789-8238

Although Skyline Trail initially seems uninviting after you cross Turnbull Canyon Road, with a gate and corrugated metal mat (the latter being there when I did this ride), the trail is open for public use. With a steep dirt embankment on either side of the gate, it was necessary to dismount and walk around it (while hanging onto the gate posts to keep from sliding down the embankment). Once around the gate, once again enter the grounds of the Puente Hills Habitat Preservation Authority. From here it is a 0.3-mile climb at a 12% grade to the Workman Ridge Trail junction. The crest of Workman Hill, the highest point in the Puente Hills, is to your left. You will return to this point after completing a counterclockwise loop. Turn right onto Workman Ridge Trail. After a tame start the trail descends rapidly. The houses in the distance get closer as you descend toward one of Whittier's neighborhoods. Just when

Puente Hills Landfill

To the north of Hellman Wilderness Park and the Rose Hills, on the northern slopes of the Puente Hills, is the massive Puente Hills Landfill. Glimpses of the landfill might be caught from this ride's Rattlesnake Ridge Trail, as well as from vantage points in the Ahwingna Pahe Mahar ride. The landfill is the largest in the United States, climbing to a height of 500 feet and covering 700 acres. The landfill was moving toward closure and extinction as of 2013, when it stopped accepting new refuse. The current focus is on recycling and on converting waste to "green" uses, such as electricity generation. The Puente Hills Habitat Preservation Authority is overseeing the gradual conversion of the landfill into restorative and recreational uses.

In case you are interested in seeing "Garbage Mountain," as it was referred to in the documentary series *Megastructures*, tours are conducted.

it appears as though you might plunge into someone's backyard, the trail makes an abrupt 90-degree bend to the left. Workman Ridge Trail ends here and Worsham Canyon Trail begins.

Worsham Canyon Trail is narrow, slightly wider than singletrack. The trail is a featured segment of this ride in part because of its seclusion. The trail rolls initially before starting an extended ascent. There are numerous switchbacks as the trail navigates the canyon. The canyon is typically dry, with a semiarid appearance that is evident in the brittle, crackly plant growth. The trail ends at the Skyline Trail (Skyline Fire Road). The final 0.3 mile of the trail climbs out of Worsham Canyon at a 14% grade, with an even steeper pitch toward the end. Turn left onto Skyline Trail. The trail continues to climb as it makes its way around Workman Hill. The landscape is open and barren up here, with only an easement to entertain your eyes. The trail peaks at 1,353 feet near the end of the loop, near the Workman Ridge Trail junction. Turn right here and negotiate the rapid descent to Turnbull Canyon Road. **Note:** The tricky gate described above must be negotiated again.

Once on Turnbull Canyon Road, turn left. You may see some speedy road cyclists here, perhaps feeling a bit slow on your mountain bike. No worries, though—leave the road just downhill from Skyline Trail on an unnamed trail, on your right, that heads into Turnbull Canyon. The trail begins steeply and then eases. The trail was heavily eroded when I rode it, with a number of loose rocks and a few fissures, so use caution during the descent. The trail makes a few switchbacks before straightening out. Turnbull Canyon is surprisingly lush compared to the rest of the ride. Turnbull Canyon is also rumored to have had a "dark" past, dating all the way back to the days of the Gabrielinos (original Native American inhabitants), who considered the canyon unhallowed ground. According to legend, accidental deaths, incidental deaths, satanic cults, baby selling, ghosts, witches, and even an insane asylum are part of the canyon's storied past.

Turnbull Canyon Trail makes a sharp right-hand bend just prior to a junction; turn left at this junction to continue on the trail. The gradual descent continues to the end of the trail at a popular trailhead along Turnbull Canyon Road. Turn right here to continue along the road. Enter "uptown Whittier." After a short but quick descent and several stop signs, turn right onto Greenleaf Avenue. The ride ends at Hellman Wilderness Park, just 1.5 blocks up Greenleaf after a brisk climb at a 7% grade.

MILES AND DIRECTIONS

0.0 Start at Hellman Wilderness Park parking lot in Whittier. Exit toward the east on Peppergrass Trail (also referred to as Side Fire Road) and begin a steep climb.

0.4 Bear left onto Mariposa Trail. (Staying right will keep you on Peppergrass Trail, but the climb is much steeper.)

1.0 Keep straight at trail junction, now back on Peppergrass Trail (aka Side Fire Road).

1.3 End of Peppergrass Trail; turn right onto Rattlesnake Ridge Trail (aka Tank Fire Road).

1.5 Stay to the left where the trail splits, still on Rattlesnake Ridge Trail (aka Rose Hills No. 1 Fire Road).

2.2 Bear right onto Skyline Trail (aka Skyline Fire Road).

2.7 Gate; keep straight onto Skyline Drive (paved).

2.9 Road turns right at Eldridge Drive intersection; stay on Skyline Drive.

3.1 Stop sign at Turnbull Canyon Road; continue across road and onto Skyline Trail (aka Skyline Fire Road). (**"Bailout" option:** Turn right onto Turnbull Canyon Road and then pick up the route at mile marker 7.1 below.)

3.4 Bear right onto Workman Ridge Trail (marker) (aka Rose Hills No. 2 Fire Road). Begin fast descent and also loop.

4.0 Bear left at junction with Turnbull Canyon Trail (aka Rose Hills No. 2 Fire Road), still on Workman Ridge Trail.

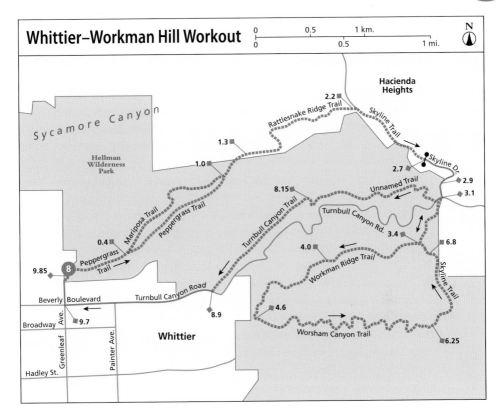

4.6 Trail bends 90 degrees to the left, becoming Worsham Canyon Trail (marker). Trail narrows.

6.25 Turn left onto Skyline Trail (aka Skyline No. 2 Fire Road).

6.8 End of loop; bear right, continuing on Skyline Trail (aka Skyline Fire Road).

7.1 Gate at Turnbull Canyon Road—end of loop. Continue beyond gate and then turn left onto Turnbull Canyon Road.

7.2 Veer off road onto unnamed trail that descends into Turnbull Canyon.

8.15 Turn left onto Turnbull Canyon Trail (aka Rose Hills No. 3 Fire Road).

8.9 End of trail; turn right onto Turnbull Canyon Road.

9.7 Stop sign at Greenleaf Avenue; turn right and begin climb.

9.85 End ride at entrance to Hellman Wilderness Park.

Best North and Northwest L.A. Region Rides

The North/Northwest region of Los Angeles includes communities served by the 818 area code. The San Fernando Valley dominates the region, along with a few satellite cities. The population is 2.2 million, with 85% living in Encino, Granada Hills, Tarzana, Van Nuys, and other Los Angeles communities. That 85% represents almost half of Los Angeles' population, all inhabiting the sprawling valley that stretches from the San Gabriel Mountains in the east to Ventura County in the west and from the Santa Susana Mountains in the north to the Santa Monica Mountains in the south. The other 15% of the region's population lives in the surrounding cities, the largest of which are Glendale (191,719 in 2010) and Burbank (103,340). The entertainment industry has a stronghold in this region, with the headquarters and studios of some major companies (e.g., DreamWorks, Walt Disney) housed in Burbank and, to a certain extent, Glendale. Although much of the San Fernando Valley is working class, there is plenty of wealth on the fringes: The city of Hidden Hills, for example, had an average household income of $290,000 in 2010.

Because the region is effectively surrounded by mountains, there is plenty of access to good, challenging off-road riding. The Santa Monica Mountains Conservancy has worked to preserve much of the Santa Monica and Verdugo Mountains, while the San Gabriel Mountains are within the Angeles National Forest. Road riding in the valley is not great, but a few suitable roads penetrate the mountains. Also, the roads near the Verdugo Mountains, in the southeast corner of the San Fernando Valley, are inviting. This book features four road rides in this subregion, ranging in length from 21.7 to 36.2 miles, and seven mountain bike rides ranging from 8.0 to 17.3 miles. All these rides include at least 900 feet of elevation change, suggesting that, despite the area being dominated by the valley, the best riding is on the valley's fringes.

Big Tujunga Canyon Epic

Start: Two Strike Park, 5107 Rosemont Ave., La Crescenta-Montrose

Length: 36.2 miles (clockwise loop)

Riding time: 2 to 6 hours (my time: 2H42:51)

Terrain and surface: 100% paved roads

Elevation: Low: 1,312 feet at the base of the Angeles Crest Highway (SR 2 and Foothill Boulevard in La Cañada-Flintridge); high: 3,658 feet at the junction between the Angeles Forest Highway (CR N3) and the Angeles Crest Highway (SR 2).

Traffic and hazards: Traffic averaged 3,500 motor vehicles per day on SR 2 at the Angeles National Forest boundary in 2012, with seasonal and day-of-the-week variations; 2,100 vehicles per day on Big Tujunga Canyon Road in 2008 (near Mount Gleason Avenue).

Map: *The Thomas Guide—Street Guide: Los Angeles and Orange Counties* (any recent year), page 504

Getting there: By car—From central Los Angeles, take I-5 north to SR 2 to I-210 West. Exit at Ocean View Avenue and turn right. Turn left at Foothill Boulevard and head northwest. Turn right onto Rosemont Avenue and climb the hill to Two Strike Park.

    By public transit—Ride L.A. Metro bus route 90 or 91 from central (downtown) L.A. to the intersection of Montrose and Rosemont Avenues in La Crescenta-Montrose. Exit here and ride up Rosemont Avenue to Two Strike Park. The buses alternate, running every 12 to 30 minutes on weekdays, every 25 to 50 minutes on Saturday, and every 30 to 60 minutes on Sunday and holidays.

Starting point coordinates: N34.232361° / W118.235078°

THE RIDE

The Big Tujunga Canyon Epic is an exciting ride for which the label "epic" is not an overstatement. The ride features a long climb via the "back way" to Angeles Crest in the San Gabriel Mountains and a rapid descent down the Angeles Crest Highway. These two ride features are connected by a rolling jaunt through communities in La Crescenta, Glendale, and Tujunga (which is part of Los Angeles). It is a loop course, for which the recommended direction is clockwise. The Angeles Crest portion of the route was ridden in a stage of the 2014 Tour of California; retracing the path of some of the world's greatest cyclists is an added bonus!

Start the ride at Two Strike Park on Rosemont Drive in La Crescenta. Despite the baseball-oriented moniker, the park also has a basketball court, picnic tables, and a children's play area in addition to baseball facilities. The park's name was actually the creation of actor Dennis Morgan, who remarked that children with no park in which to play had "two strikes against them."

Leave the park and head downhill on Rosemont Drive through a La Crescenta-Montrose neighborhood. La Crescenta-Montrose is an unincorporated community, with a population of 19,653 in 2010. The median household income is well above the L.A. region's average. As of 2010, the heritage of nearly one-third of the residents was either Korean or Iranian. Rosemont Drive and the surrounding community have featured in some fascinating historical events (see sidebar).

Turn right onto Orange Avenue; the name of the road changes to Santa Carlotta Street shortly after entering the city of Glendale. The city had a population of 191,719 in 2010, down a tad from the year 2000, making it the third-largest city in Los Angeles County (after L.A. and Long Beach). The city is the home of the first Bob's Big Boy restaurant, as well as the first Baskin-Robbins ice-cream parlor. Today the city's most well-known business is probably DreamWorks Animation. One-third of the population is Armenian.

Turn right onto Lowell Street at the end of Santa Carlotta. Lowell curves to the left, becoming Day Street as the road enters the Los Angeles community of Tujunga. Tujunga was incorporated as a city in 1925 and then annexed to L.A. in 1932. The community's relative remoteness compared to the central area of L.A. once made it a haven for persons with respiratory problems. At the end of Day Street, turn right onto Silverton Avenue and then left onto Apperson Street.

Apperson Street heads downhill; watch your speed—and for crossing and turning motor vehicles. Turn right onto Tujunga Canyon Boulevard and continue to descend gradually. The main road curves to the left, becoming Wentworth Street as you enter Sunland. After another brisk descent, turn

A copter chases Tour of California cyclists along the Angeles Crest Highway.

right onto Mount Gleason Avenue. Although the road goes nowhere near it, there is a Mount Gleason in the San Gabriel Mountains that loom ahead. Follow Mount Gleason Avenue until it ends at Big Tujunga Canyon Road; turn right here and enter the canyon. This is where the ride truly begins! Big Tujunga Canyon has a tame beginning, actually sloping downward for a ways before gradually turning upward. Strenuous climbing does not begin until the road crosses Tujunga Wash at the lower crossing (see The Oliver Twist for more information). Pass the Tujunga Little League fields just 0.4 mile up the canyon. The Louis Routh juvenile probation facility is on the right at mile 1.1. Cross over the Tujunga Wash (lower crossing) at mile 2.2 (elevation 1,604 feet). The average gradient on Big Tujunga Canyon Road to this point is 1.5% to 2%. About two-thirds of the entire ride is in the Angeles National Forest, although you will see only a small amount of dense forestation along the way. The route is quite open, leaving one begging for hydration on a warm day.

From here the climbing gets steeper but is broken with occasional down-hill segments. The average gradient is 2.5% to 3% until the Tujunga Wash Bridge (upper crossing), 7.9 miles up the canyon, although the downhill

La Crescenta's Rosemont Avenue

The Big Tujunga Canyon Road Epic starts and finishes on Rosemont Avenue in La Crescenta. This unassuming street has generated its own legacy through the years, perhaps starting with the Great Flood of 1934. In November 1933 wildfires in the San Gabriel Mountains were followed by 12 inches of rain in December. The combination of these events led to massive mudslides on New Year's Day 1934 that sent mud and debris into the communities below as portions of the hillsides above the Crescenta Valley collapsed. Some residents took refuge in American Legion Post No. 288, located near Rosemont and Fairway Avenues; but it, along with other buildings, was destroyed, killing twelve inside. A memorial was later established at the location.

The Kimball Sanitarium was located at the corner of Rosemont Avenue and Foothill Boulevard from the 1920s until the 1960s. Actor Bela Lugosi was a patient as he sought treatment for a morphine addiction. Actress Frances Farmer was also a patient, receiving insulin shock therapy for a misdiagnosed case of paranoid schizophrenia. The sanitarium was eventually closed. During the facility's demolition, padded cells, straitjackets, and other torturous "therapy" devices were discovered. Today the site is occupied by a much-more-docile Ralph's supermarket.

Nearly directly across the street, the La Crescenta Motel has served as a setting of numerous well-known films and television shows, including *Glee* and *Criminal Minds*. The motel opened in 1946, replacing the Silver Gate Inn of the early twentieth century.

interludes mean that the actual gradient of the climbs is steeper. The concrete arch bridge across Tujunga Wash near the Big Tujunga Dam was completed in 1958 and is striking in its setting within the canyon. The best vantage point is on the way to the bridge rather than on the bridge or beyond it. The bridge is at an elevation of 2,153 feet. An access road to the Big Tujunga Dam is 8.3 miles up the canyon, at 2,326 feet, although the dam cannot be seen from here. A better vantage point would be to your left after another 0.5 mile or so. From the bridge, the average gradient of the climb is a steady 6% to 7.5% all the way to the end of Big Tujunga Canyon Road at the Angeles Forest Highway (CR N3). The elevation at the junction is 3,250 feet.

Angeles Forest Highway, built in 1941, offers stunning vistas of this region of the San Gabriel Mountains. Mount Lukens (elevation 5,066 feet) is well off to your right. You can look back and see Big Tujunga Canyon Road snaking its way up the canyon. The low area between Big Tujunga Canyon and

CR N3 is Grizzly Flat. The highway continues to climb, albeit not as steeply, to intersect the Angeles Crest Highway (elevation 3,658 feet—high point of the ride). The Clear Creek Ranger Station is at the intersection; there is water at the station. Turn right here. This is the main highway from L.A. into the San Gabriel Mountains, so you will find heavier traffic volumes along this road than on the comparatively peaceful roads you just climbed.

SR 2 is a USDA Forest Service Scenic Byway, as well as a State Scenic Highway. The scenery is mainly in the vistas from the highway. Although you may be inclined to keep your eyes on the road, an occasional glance into the distance will reveal a spectacular view of the San Gabriel Valley and the Verdugo Mountains. From here it is a rapid descent (5% average grade) over the next 9 miles to Foothill Boulevard in La Cañada-Flintridge. Watch your speed and stay to the right at all times. This segment of the highway has been ridden in the Tour of California professional cycling stage race. The current elevation, which may have taken you two or more hours to gain, may be lost in less than thirty minutes as you plummet into civilization. Note that the highway is heavily used during commute periods as an alternative to the region's busy freeways. Segments of the highway have been closed at times because of fires, mudslides, rockslides, and other events both natural and nonnatural.

Traffic signals and a heightened number of motor vehicles greet you as you plunge down SR 2 and reenter the urban development of the L.A. region. You may still be descending at a high speed, so keep your hands near the brakes and watch for motor vehicles. Cross over I-210 and then turn right onto Foothill Boulevard. This is the low point of the ride (elevation 1,312 feet). As if all that climbing you did earlier to reach the Angeles Crest was not enough, from here it is a net climb to the finish. Foothill climbs at an average 2% grade to Rosemont Avenue (elevation 1,549 feet); turn right here. End the ride with a brisk 300-foot climb at a 7% grade to Two Strike Park.

MILES AND DIRECTIONS

0.0 Start at Two Strike Park in La Crescenta-Montrose; head downhill on Rosemont Avenue.

0.15 Stop sign at Orange Avenue; turn right.

1.1 Stop sign at Pennsylvania Avenue; turn left and then turn right to continue on Orange Avenue.

1.25 Stop sign at Maryland Avenue; keep straight, now on Santa Carlotta Street.

2.35 Stop sign at Lowell Avenue; turn right.

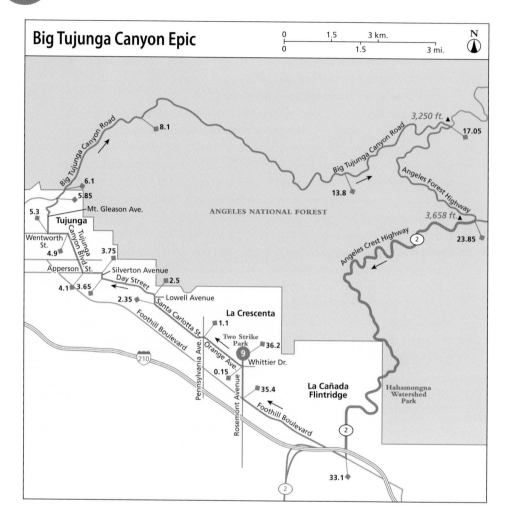

Big Tujunga Canyon Epic

2.5 Stop sign at Y intersection with Markridge Road and Day Street. Turn left onto Day Street and enter city of Los Angeles (Tujunga community).

3.65 Street bears right; you're now on Silverton Avenue.

3.75 Stop sign at Apperson Street; turn left.

4.1 Traffic signal at Tujunga Canyon Boulevard; turn right.

4.9 Stop sign at Wentworth Street; turn left.

5.3 Traffic signal at Mount Gleason Avenue; turn right.

5.85 Stop sign at Big Tujunga Canyon Road; turn right.

6.1 Enter Angeles National Forest.

8.1 Cross Tujunga Wash (lower crossing).

13.8 Cross Tujunga Wash (upper crossing) on concrete arch bridge.

17.05 Stop sign at Angeles Forest Highway (CR N3); turn right.

23.85 Stop sign at Angeles Crest Highway (SR 2); turn right.

30.35 Leave Angeles National Forest.

32.9 Cross over I-210.

33.1 Traffic signal at Foothill Boulevard; turn right.

35.4 Traffic signal at Rosemont Avenue; turn right.

36.2 End ride at Two Strike Park.

Cheeseboro-Comado Canyons Chug

Start: Old Agoura Park, 5301 Chesebro Rd., Agoura Hills

Length: 10.7 miles (counterclockwise loop plus short out-and-back)

Riding time: 45 minutes to 3 hours (my time: 1H16:39)

Terrain and surface: Variable—82% dirt trails; 18% paved road. Trails are mostly wide track, but there are some singletrack segments with some exposed rock.

Elevation: Low: 916 feet at Old Agoura Park; high: 1,728 feet along Sheep Corral Trail

Traffic and hazards: 82% of the ride is on car-free trails; 18% of the ride is on a moderately used residential road.

Map: *The Thomas Guide—Street Guide: Los Angeles and Orange Counties* (any recent year), page 558

Getting there: By car—From central Los Angeles, take US 101 north. Exit at Palo Comado Canyon Road and turn right. Turn right onto Chesebro Road and proceed to Old Agoura Park, on the left.

    By public transit—From central Los Angeles, ride the Metro Red Line (subway) to the North Hollywood station. Transfer to the Orange Line (bus rapid transit) to the Warner Center station. Transfer to Metro bus route 161. Exit at Palo Comado Canyon Road and follow the instructions above to ride to Old Agoura Park.

Starting point coordinates: N34.146308° / W118.738369°

THE RIDE

The Cheeseboro-Comado Canyons Chug is a pleasant off-road ride through picturesque Cheeseboro and Palo Comado Canyons in the Agoura Hills, far western Los Angeles County, and part of Ventura County. Combined, the two canyons are part of the northernmost region of the Santa Monica Mountains National Recreation Area (so claims the National Park Service website, although to me the area does not appear to be any farther north than other areas of the NRA). Cheeseboro Canyon Park is easily accessed from US 101, heading north and west from central L.A. This fairly short ride offers a wide variety of terrain and scenery—you are bound to see other cyclists out here!

Start from Old Agoura Park in Agoura Hills. Although the main entrance to the park is on Colodny Drive, I recommend starting from the eastern, "equestrian," side of the park on Chesebro Road. Park in the large dirt lot. The route can be ridden either clockwise or counterclockwise. I describe the counterclockwise route—this direction may be preferred simply because it will be easier to access the paved Chesebro Road from the Palo Comado trailhead, toward the end of the ride, rather than from the southerly direction at the beginning.

Once on your bike, turn left and head north on Chesebro Road. After a short stretch through a pastoral setting, veer right at the gate onto Cheeseboro

A rider makes a symmetrical passage through the chaparral along Sheep Corral Trail.

Canyon Trail. When I rode this trail, during a serious drought, the surface featured loose, sandy dirt, making pedaling laborious. One hallmark of this ride, however, is the varied surfaces. Just when you may be growing weary of one surface, there is a change! Cheeseboro Canyon Trail curves to the left in advance of its junction with the Palo Comado Connector Trail. Turn right at the junction to continue on Cheeseboro Canyon. The surface changes here as the sandy dirt disappears and the trail becomes more akin to a dirt road.

After a short, steep climb, the trail climbs very gradually through the canyon. Stay to the left at the Canyon View Trail junction to remain in the canyon on Cheeseboro Canyon Trail. The surroundings are mostly open savanna, with a few valley oak and sycamore trees along the way. Stay to the left at the Y junction with Cheeseboro Ridge Trail to remain in the canyon. The trail curves to the left and then to the right, eventually entering a wooded riparian zone of coastal live oaks. The trail narrows, becoming singletrack for a segment before widening again. Do not worry; you are on the right trail—although there is a name change once on the singletrack and you are now on Sulphur Springs Trail. The trail is so named because of the faint sulfur odor emitted by the springs (which I admittedly did not even notice when riding through here, probably being distracted by other things). The open savanna returns as you exit the riparian zone. Baleen Wall is to your right—not an actual wall, but a steep rock formation. The relatively smooth trail is occasionally interrupted by some exposed rock, including two segments that may force all but the most experienced cyclists to dismount.

Bike Shops

JRA Bikes and Brew, 5019 Kanan Rd., Agoura Hills; (818) 991-1572; http://jrabikes andbrew.com

Serious Cycling in Agoura Hills, 29041 Thousand Oaks Blvd., Agoura Hills; (818) 597-8330; www.seriouscycling.com

The trail's surface changes once again as you enter a chaparral "district." Chaparral is an almost exclusively California plant community. You will see a mixture of coastal sage scrub and other shrubs. The chaparral is a product of the region's climate and, surprisingly, the regularity of wildfire. Sulphur Springs Trail ends at Shepherd's Flat, an open area amid the chaparral. Turn left here onto Sheep Corral Trail. There is an old sheep corral on the right along the way (although I admittedly did not see it—perhaps I was not being very observant on this ride). The trail twists its way through. At the Y junction (mile 5.1, shortly after the junction with Sheep Corral Trail), take either route; they will merge just 0.2 mile downstream of here. The right-hand route is considered to be less challenging than the left-hand route. (I took the left-hand, or "southern," route and found it not too technical until the very end, where the final "lip" of the trail was so steep upon returning to the main trail that my back wheel skidded and slid out.) Back on the main trail, Sheep Corral climbs, at times steeply, to the high point of the ride (1,728 feet). From the crest the trail descends swiftly to the Palo Comado Canyon Trail.

Hang a sharp left onto Palo Comado Canyon and begin the long descent to the south side of the park. One website refers to this as a fire road, suggesting that it is wide and not technical. The descent is steep and winding to begin with, before easing off (but still descending). This is the fastest segment of the ride, so let 'er rip, being ever watchful for hikers, runners, and equestrians (and other cyclists!). You may need to check your speed on the opening, steep segment, which featured some loose rock when I rode it. Ignore all connector trails and just keep flying southward on Palo Comado Canyon. (You may want to explore the connectors during another ride, though.) Keep straight at the end of Palo Comado Canyon, although the trail bends sharply to the left, becoming the Palo Comado Connector Trail. The connector would return you to Cheeseboro Canyon Trail, from which a right turn would take you back to the starting point.

For my option, keep straight through the trailhead (ride around the gate) and continue onto the paved Chesebro Road. The road descends gradually, similarly to Palo Comado Canyon Trail, with a few speed humps to slow you down. Some maps indicate that Chesebro Road is private in this area. I did not encounter any barriers when riding through here, but be respectful of the community's exclusivity. It is a speedy 1.7 miles to Old Agoura Park and the end of the ride.

MILES AND DIRECTIONS

0.0 Start at Old Agoura Park in Agoura Hills. Park on the "equestrian" side of the park; exit onto Chesebro Road and turn left.

0.3 Veer right, off the road and onto Cheeseboro Canyon Trail (negotiate a gate).

1.1 Palo Comado Connector Trail junction; bear right to stay on Cheeseboro Canyon.

1.5 Canyon View Trail junction; stay left to remain on Cheeseboro Canyon.

1.9 Enter Ventura County (no sign or marker).

2.15 Y junction; stay left to remain on Cheeseboro Canyon. (Cheeseboro Ridge Connector Trail is to the right.)

Cheeseboro-Comado Canyons Chug

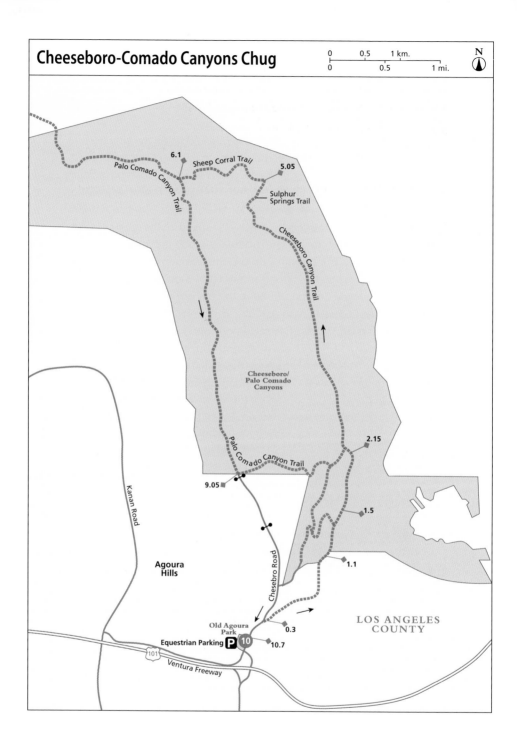

0   0.5   1 km.
0   0.5   1 mi.

N

6.1
Sheep Corral Trail
5.05
Palo Comado Canyon Trail
Sulphur
Springs Trail

Cheeseboro Canyon Trail

Cheeseboro/
Palo Comado
Canyons

2.15

Palo Comado Canyon Trail

9.05

1.5

Kanan Road

Agoura
Hills

Chesebro Road

1.1

LOS ANGELES
COUNTY

Old Agoura
Park
Equestrian Parking **P** **10**   **0.3**

10.7

101

Ventura Freeway

3.65 Enter singletrack segment, dense with oak trees, now on Sulphur Springs Trail.

5.05 Turn left at junction; now on Sheep Corral Trail.

5.9 High point of ride (1,728 feet).

6.1 End of Sheep Corral Trail; make a sharp left onto Palo Comado Canyon Trail.

9.05 End of Palo Comado Canyon Trail; exit at trailhead (narrow passage) onto Chesebro Road. Reenter Los Angeles County.

10.7 End ride at Old Agoura Park.

Circuito de Calabasas

Start: Headwaters Corner, 3815 Old Topanga Canyon Rd., Calabasas; alternative start: Wild Walnut Park, 23050 Mulholland Hwy., Calabasas; secondary alternative start: Calabasas Creekside Park and Community Center, 3655 Old Topanga Canyon Rd., Calabasas

Length: 23.6 miles (clockwise loop)

Riding time: 1.25 to 3.5 hours (my time: 1H36:44)

Terrain and surface: 100% paved roads

Elevation: Low: 546 feet on Mulholland Highway, west of Las Virgenes Road in Malibu Creek State Park; high: 1,459 feet on Mulholland Highway at Dry Canyon Cold Creek Road and Mountain Park Drive

Traffic and hazards: 2,918 vehicles per weekend day in 2010 on Mulholland Highway east of Las Virgenes Road; 1,710 vehicles per weekend day in 2010 on Mulholland Highway east of Cornell Road. Weekend volumes were heavier than weekday volumes.

Map: *The Thomas Guide—Street Guide: Los Angeles and Orange Counties* (any recent year), page 558

Getting there: By car—From central Los Angeles, take US 101 northbound and westbound to Mulholland Drive, near the Los Angeles–Calabasas border. Turn left onto Mulholland Drive and head south. Turn right onto Valmar Road, which becomes Old Topanga Canyon Drive as you enter Calabasas. At Mulholland Highway turn right; the entrance to Headwaters Corner is on the right shortly after the turn.

    By public transit—Ride the Metro Red Line (subway) to the North Hollywood station (end of the line). Transfer to the Metro Orange Line (bus rapid transit) and ride to the Warner Center station (end of the line). Transfer to Metro bus route 169 eastbound, toward Woodland Hills. Exit at Mulholland Drive and Valmar Road. From here ride southward on Valmar Road and follow the above instructions. Bus route 169 runs every 20 to 60 minutes Monday through Friday (no weekend service).

Starting point coordinates: N34.135586° / W118.631103°

THE RIDE

The Circuito de Calabasas, a nifty 23.6-mile loop on the north side of the Santa Monica Mountains, starts and ends in the city of Calabasas. The ride leaves the city and enters an unincorporated area of Los Angeles County; the route also has a short segment in the city of Los Angeles. The highest peak in the Santa Monica Mountains is Sandstone Peak at 3,111 feet, meaning these are not "high" mountains. But the rider can expect a few "rolls," some longer and steeper than others. The longest climbs and descents are on the ocean side of the mountains; this ride stays on the "valley" side. Calabasas (population of 23,058 in 2010), is known as an upscale community of the "rich and famous." If you behave, maybe the citizens will allow you to ride through their posh town. The city's name is a morphed form of the Spanish word for pumpkin or squash. In keeping with this, the city stages a pumpkin festival every October. The notable residents are too many to list here, but they include drummer Rick Allen (Def Leppard), actor Sean Astin, baseball legend Rod Carew, NBA star Lamar Odom, and country songstress LeAnn Rimes.

I identified three different sites, each close to the other, from which this ride could be staged. I started at Headwaters Corner from its small off-street parking lot located along Mulholland Highway, on the right side just south of Old Topanga Canyon Road. Headwaters Corner is a 12-acre site that serves as an environmental and cultural interpretive center for Dry Canyon Creek. The creek is a headwater for the Los Angeles River, which flows through the site. The

> ### Bike Shops
> **Santa Monica Mountains Cyclery,** 21526 Ventura Blvd., Woodland Hills; (818) 456-4105; www.smmcyclery.com
> **Wheel World Cyclery,** 22718 Ventura Blvd., Woodland Hills; (818) 224-2044; http://wheelworld.com

address is on Old Topanga Canyon Road, although the entrance is actually on Mulholland Highway. Alternatively, the ride could be started from Wild Walnut Park, at the small off-street lot on the left side of Mulholland a little farther south from Old Topanga Canyon. As a third alternative, you could begin the ride from Creekside Park, located off Old Topanga Canyon just south of Mulholland. The last site has the largest parking lot, and the only paved one. Reaching the lot does require a short, steep climb, however—you may not care too much for this at the end of the ride! In any case, begin the ride by heading southwestward on Mulholland Highway. **Note:** This is a different road from Mulholland Drive, which you will actually ride later in the route.

From an elevation of 1,050 feet at the beginning of the ride, you immediately begin to climb—gradually at first, and then more steeply. The high

Despite the cracks in the tar, a cyclist enjoys the shoulder along Agoura Road in Agoura Hills.

point of the ride is at mile 1.7 (1,459 feet); the average gradient to get up here is a manageable 4.5%. From here Mulholland Highway makes a long descent into Cold Canyon (elevation 861 feet). After a short climb to 899 feet, Mulholland descends again, eventually reaching the low point of the ride (546 feet) in crossing Liberty Canyon, just beyond Las Virgenes Road. Here Mulholland enters Malibu Creek State Park (see Malibulldog MASH 4077 Tour for more information about the park). The rugged topography you can see from the road is typical of the Santa Monica Mountains, of which the park is a part. After a steady climb to 1,019 feet (and an outstanding vista to your left), the highway descends to 859 feet before climbing again to 946 feet. From here the highway descends to a four-way stop–controlled intersection with Cornell Road (839 feet).

Turn right onto Cornell. Paramount Ranch Park is on the left, just up the road. From 1927 the ranch served as the setting for numerous Paramount Pictures films. Extensive sets were constructed to replicate San Francisco, Tombstone, Dodge City, a Welsh mining village, and other locales. Most of the old sets have been torn down, but a collection of buildings used in Westerns remains for visitors to view. Filming continues; special events are held here as well. Continue along Cornell as it undulates adjacent to the park. At the stop sign turn right onto Kanan Road (CR N9) and enter the city of Agoura Hills.

Agoura Hills is an affluent city with a population of 20,330 as of 2010. Notable residents include writer-activist Erin Brockovich, Olympic marathon medalist Deena Kastor, film director Guillermo del Toro, and rock groups Linkin Park and Incubus, among others. The city's motto is "Gateway to the Santa Monica Mountains." Well, you actually just left the mountains—turn right from Kanan Road (which can be busy) onto Agoura Road and head east. You are now riding parallel to US 101. The road passes residential and retail development, with some light industrial development toward the end of the road. After a 3.9-mile stretch, returning to the city of Calabasas, turn left onto Las Virgenes Road (CR N1). Move away from the shoulder as you prepare to cross over US 101 (this is the hairiest part of the entire ride). Motorists will be entering the freeway here to head east, so be ever watchful of their movements. Once across the freeway, turn right onto Mureau Road. You are still riding parallel to US 101, now on its north side.

Although you have escaped the Santa Monica Mountains, Mureau Road actually presents one of the stiffer climbs of the entire ride. Over the next 2.1 miles Mureau climbs from 792 feet at Las Virgenes to 1,143 feet where it crosses over US 101, becoming Calabasas Road. The average gradient is 3%, but there are some steeper segments. After crossing US 101 and curving to the left to become Calabasas Road, the road heads generally downhill into the city's commercial district. The crosswalks through here are artsy but bumpy, intentionally crafted to slow motor vehicles. Continue to Mulholland Drive; by now you have entered the Woodland Hills community of Los Angeles. Turn right onto Mulholland and head south. At the first signal, turn right onto Valmar Drive, which becomes Old Topanga Canyon Road as you reenter Calabasas. At the traffic signal turn right onto Mulholland Highway. End the ride at Headwaters Corner, which will be on your right (or, alternatively, at Wild Walnut Park, which is just up the road on the left).

MILES AND DIRECTIONS

0.0 Start at either Headwaters Corner or Wild Walnut Park (parking areas) along Mulholland Highway in Calabasas. Head southwest on Mulholland.

0.15 Intersection with Old Topanga Canyon Road (southern part); keep straight on Mulholland.

Circuito de Calabasas

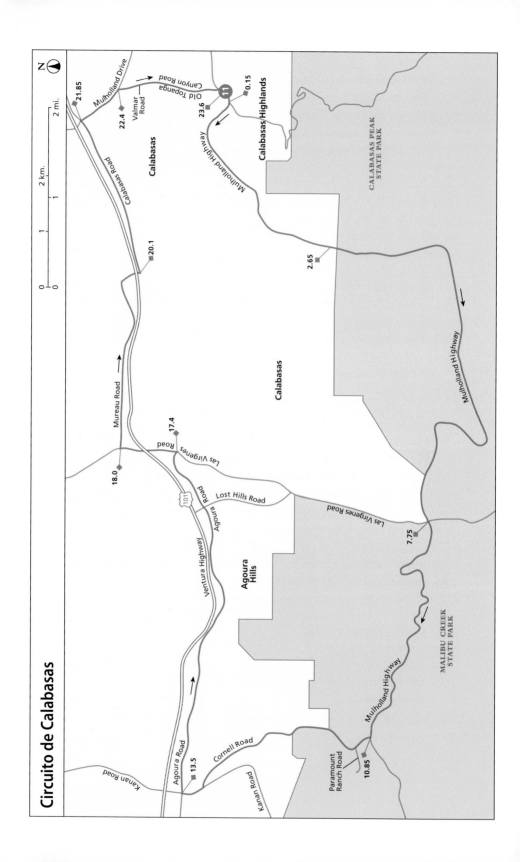

1.7   High point of ride (1,459 feet) at Dry Canyon Cold Creek Road and Mountain Park Drive.

2.65 Leave city of Calabasas; enter Los Angeles County (unincorporated area).

7.75 Traffic signal at Las Virgenes Road (CR N1); keep straight and enter Malibu Creek State Park.

7.85 Low point of ride (546 feet) in Malibu Creek State Park, crossing Liberty Canyon.

10.85 Four-way stop sign at Cornell Road; turn right.

13.25 Stop sign at Kanan Road (CR N9); turn right. Enter city of Agoura Hills.

13.5 Traffic signal at Agoura Road; turn right.

15.65 Leave the city of Agoura Hills at Liberty Canyon Road; enter unincorporated territory.

16.2 Reenter city of Calabasas.

17.4 Traffic signal at Las Virgenes Road (CR N1); turn left and cross over US 101.

18.0 Traffic signal at Mureau Road; turn right, leaving Calabasas for unincorporated area.

20.1 Cross over US 101; road curves to the left, becoming Calabasas Road. Reenter Calabasas.

21.75 Enter the city of Los Angeles (Woodland Hills).

21.85 Traffic signal at Mulholland Drive; turn right.

22.4 Traffic signal at Valmar Road; turn right.

22.55 Enter the city of Calabasas, now on Old Topanga Canyon Road.

23.55 Traffic signal at Mulholland Highway; turn right.

23.6 End ride at Headwaters Corner.

Josephine Peak Hill Climb

Start: Base of Josephine Peak Trail, near Clear Creek Ranger Station

Length: 8.0 miles (out-and-back)

Riding time: 1 to 3.5 hours (my time: 1H33:22)

Terrain and surface: 100% dirt trail

Elevation: Low: 3,649 feet at base of Josephine Peak Road; high: 5,516 feet at Josephine Peak

Traffic and hazards: The ride is entirely off-road (no motor vehicles).

Map: *The Thomas Guide—Street Guide: Los Angeles and Orange Counties* (any recent year), page 505

Getting there: By car—From central Los Angeles, take I-5 freeway to SR 2 and head north.

   By public transit—There is no scheduled public transportation service into the San Gabriel Mountains. Your best bet would be to either bike up the Angeles Crest Highway (SR 2) or drive (see "getting there by car" directions above).

Starting point coordinates: N34.271053° / W118.153742°

THE RIDE

At 5,646 feet, Josephine Peak is not the highest in the San Gabriel Mountains, but along with Mount Wilson, it may be the most accessible by bicycle. The route is quite simple—strictly an out-and-back excursion. The turnaround point is the summit of Josephine Peak, although the actual summit is 130 feet higher than where the trail goes. There is no designated parking near the trail. The Clear Creek Ranger Station has parking only for official vehicles; the adjacent visitor center restricts stays to 15 minutes. There is plenty of parking on the side of the road, though, along the Angeles Forest Highway (CR N3). Continue past the Josephine Peak Road trailhead; there will be pull-off areas on the left. There are also pull-off areas along SR 2, to the northeast of CR N3. Be sure to pull entirely off the road. All vehicles must display a Southern

Long shadows and an evening view from Josephine Peak; the summit is to the right.

California Adventure Pass, since this location is within the boundaries of the Angeles National Forest. Visit www.fs.usda.gov/detailfull/r5/passes-permits/recreation/?cid=stelprdb5208699&width=full for current fees. Although bloggers grumble about the lack of scenery along the trail up to the peak, the views from the trail are fantastic. Strawberry Peak (located due east of Josephine), parts of the Los Angeles area, and even Santa Catalina Island may be seen, particularly from the crest.

I admittedly was fearful of climbing to 5,516 feet, the second-highest elevation of any ride in this book. The starting location spots you 3,649 feet, however, making it just under a 1,867-foot climb. The 4.0-mile distance to the top and the 1,867-foot elevation differential suggest an average gradient of 8.8%. The grade is actually quite steady, so if you can find a rhythm, the climb is quite manageable. It is a fairly wide fire road all the way to the top. The first segment of the climb is on Josephine Peak Road, which features a few switchbacks. It had some erosion (gullies and fissures, mostly small, caused by running water) when I rode it.

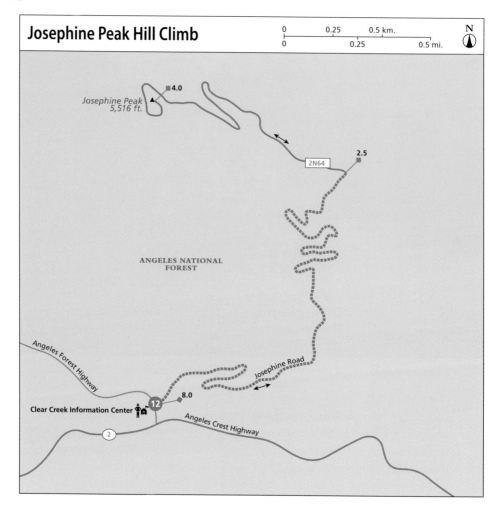

Josephine Peak Hill Climb

0   0.25   0.5 km.

0   0.25   0.5 mi.

N

Josephine Peak
5,516 ft.

■ 4.0

■ 2.5

2N64

ANGELES NATIONAL
FOREST

Angeles Forest Highway

Josephine Road

8.0

Clear Creek Information Center

12

Angeles Crest Highway

2

After 2.5 miles Josephine Peak Road forms a T junction with FR 2N64, a forest service fire road. Turn left at the junction to continue the climb; it is 1.5 miles from here to the crest. The surface becomes somewhat rockier. Whereas Josephine Peak Road is not shaded, FR 2N64 passes through a more lush environment. While there are few big trees, vegetation is plentiful. Despite this being Southern California, there can be snow and ice along this segment of the trail during the colder winter months. After a few switchbacks, FR 2N64 leaves the "protection" of Josephine Peak's vegetation and enters an open environment. The trail literally curls around the mountain from here as it nears the crest. After one final stretch, FR 2N64 ends. The actual peak is to your left, not accessible by bicycle. You will see a few infrastructure items up here, including the concrete footings of an old fire lookout (which actually burned down in the 1976 Big Tujunga Fire), a small wooden shed, communications masts, and a wind-speed measuring device. I do not know how often the facilities are visited or used, but you are not likely to see anyone except other cyclists and hikers up here.

Congratulate yourself on reaching the peak! (As for the highest peak in the San Gabriel Mountains, that would be Mount San Antonio, which crests at a staggering 10,064 feet.) Once you have soaked in the fresh air and the views (as noted above, Strawberry Peak is due east of here), start the descent. Keep control of your machine! It is a fast descent, but not technical. Be sure to hang a right onto Josephine Peak Road at the T junction to continue the descent. If you are still in rapid-downhill mode as you near the bottom, be sure to hit the brakes prior to the gate! End the ride where the trail meets the paved highway.

MILES AND DIRECTIONS

0.0 Start from the base of Josephine Peak Road (dirt fire road) at its intersection with Angeles Forest Highway (CR N3); the trailhead is near the junction of CR N3 and SR 2.

2.5 Turn left onto FR 2N64 (dirt fire road) to continue climbing.

4.0 End of trail atop Josephine Peak; turn around here.

5.5 Bear right onto Josephine Peak Road to continue the descent.

8.0 End ride at the trailhead gate at the Angeles Forest Highway (CR N3).

Mission Point: Weldon Canyon

Start: O'Melveny Park, 17300 Sesnon Blvd., Granada Hills, Los Angeles

Length: 11.2 miles (clockwise loop)

Riding time: 1.25 to 3.5 hours (my time: 1H29:15)

Terrain and surface: 60% dirt trails and fire roads; 40% paved roads

Elevation: Low: 1,302 feet at Balboa and Sesnon Boulevards in Granada Hills; high: 2,765 feet at Jones Junction in the Santa Susana Mountains

Traffic and hazards: The heaviest traffic volumes were on Balboa Boulevard (29,200 vehicles per day in 2004), Balboa Road (21,150 daily vehicles in 2007), and San Fernando Road (20,830 daily vehicles near Balboa Road in 2009). In comparison, the daily volume on Sesnon Boulevard was just 1,300 in 2003.

Map: *The Thomas Guide—Street Guide: Los Angeles and Orange Counties* (any recent year), page 481

Getting there: By car—From central Los Angeles, head north on I-5. Exit at Roxford Street and turn left; once beyond the freeway, the road turns right, becoming Sepulveda Boulevard. At the end of Sepulveda, turn left onto San Fernando Road. Just after crossing under Balboa Boulevard, turn left onto Balboa Road. Turn right at the top of the hill onto Balboa Boulevard and head south. Turn right onto Sesnon Boulevard, entering the Granada Hills neighborhood. Look for O'Melveny Park on the right after about 0.5 mile.

By public transit—From central Los Angeles, ride the Metro Red Line (subway) to the end of the line at North Hollywood. Transfer to the Metro Orange Line (bus rapid transit) to Balboa Boulevard. Transfer to Metro bus route 236 and head north on Balboa to Sesnon Boulevard. Exit here and ride to O'Melveny Park by heading west on Sesnon. Bus route 236 runs approximately every hour on weekdays and weekends.

Starting point coordinates: N34.308361° / W118.510461°

THE RIDE

Mission Point: Weldon Canyon is a mountain bike ride that starts and finishes at O'Melveny Park in the far northern corner of Los Angeles, just south of Newhall Canyon (gateway to Santa Clarita) in the Granada Hills neighborhood. The ride does not use the trails in the park, though, as most of these are off-limits to bicycles. The ride title refers to a couple of topographic features the rider visits along the way. The preferred ride direction is clockwise, making all the turns on paved roads right turns. Park in the small lot at the entrance to O'Melveny Park. The park's namesake was John O'Melveny, a lawyer and owner of C.J. Ranch, which was later converted into the park. At 672 acres, this is L.A.'s second-largest park.

Two riders attack Sulphur Springs Fire Road, climbing up to Mission Point in the Santa Susanas.

Exit the park and turn right to head west on Sesnon Boulevard. Sesnon is a residential collector street that is not too busy; but for an even less-busy street, turn right onto Tuscan Drive after 0.15 mile and climb into the neighborhood. Tuscan curves to the left to parallel Sesnon. Turn right at Neon Way and climb to the end of the street. Continue past the walkthrough gate and onto Sulphur Springs Fire Road. At this point, at the trailhead, you are at an elevation of 1,505 feet. Sulphur Springs is a steep but rideable trail that climbs into the Santa Susana Mountains. The mountains are mostly barren through here, with the exception of indigenous weeds. There are, however, some spectacular views of the land below, including the Los Angeles Reservoir to the south. You will climb exactly 1,000 feet over the next 1.7 miles at a challenging average grade of 11.3%.

Upon reaching the first of several open gates, stay to the left to continue climbing. You are now on Sunshine Canyon Motorway, heading up to Mission Point. (Veering to the right at the gate would ultimately take you to the same crest but via a series of steep switchbacks.) The motorway crests at 2,706 feet 3.0 miles into the ride; a spur trail to your left can be used to access Mission

Beale's Cut and Newhall Pass

The Mission Point: Weldon Canyon route uses Newhall Pass, via The Old Road and San Fernando Road, to take the rider from Weldon Canyon back to Granada Hills. This historical pass separating the San Gabriel Mountains from the Santa Susana Mountains was discovered in 1769 by Gaspar de Portolà during his famous expedition. It was named, however, for a businessman. The steep pass was made easier to cross by Beale's Cut, a deep, slot-like notch that was dug into the mountains. It was originally 50-feet deep, later deepened to 90 feet. The pass was used regularly as a transport passage, including by the legendary Butterfield Overland Mail stagecoach, until 1910. By then the Newhall Tunnel was completed, relegating Beale's Cut to secondary usage. The cut was a favorite of Western films from that era, however, appearing in several Buster Keaton (*Seven Chances*, 1925), Tom Mix (*Three Jumps Ahead*, 1923), and John Ford (*Stagecoach*, 1939) flicks.

Beale's Cut is not visible from anywhere along the Mission Point: Weldon Canyon ride. The ride that comes closest to offering a view is Ruta del Placerita Tujunga, which uses the Sierra Highway. However, a partial collapse wiped away about 60 feet of the cut's depth. Fencing has further restricted access, making the cut difficult if not impossible to see from the Sierra Highway.

Point (aka Mission Peak), a local high point at 2,775 feet. Mission Point is on the Sierra Club's Great Lower Peaks list, which includes seventy-five Southern California mountains with an elevation of less than 5,000 feet. Keep straight, remaining on Sunshine Canyon. The motorway, which bears close resemblance to a fire road, passes through several open gates as it undulates along the ridge. The high point of the ride (at 2,765 feet), comes at Jones Junction, at mile 4.3. Bear right here onto Saugus-to-the-Sea Road.

Despite the name, Saugus-to-the-Sea Road is merely an old dirt road for which there were once grand ambitions. During the 1920s the plan was to link Mulholland Drive (see Circuito de Calabasas and Ride Up over Mulholland for more information

Bike Shops

Cycle World, 8627 Reseda Blvd., Northridge; (818) 349-6900; http://cycleworld bikes.com
John's Serious Cycling, 8819 Reseda Blvd., Northridge; (818) 709-8330; www.bicycle johns.com
Kelly's Bicycles, 8700 Woodley Ave., North Hills; (818) 894-8976; www.kellysbicycle .com

on this famous roadway) to the Santa Clarita Valley via this road. The plans were abandoned once the Great Depression of the 1930s hit, however, and were never revived. The road remains a vital link to get you through this ride, however! The unpaved road begins to descend. After 0.4 mile bear right again onto Weldon Canyon Motorway. This is a fun descent on a wide fire road. To your right, occasionally out of view, is the Sunshine Canyon Landfill. As of this writing, the neighboring community had filed a lawsuit against the landfill for foul odors, although some trail conversion plans were in the works. The motorway drops 439 feet over the next 2.2 miles down to 2,146 feet. At the junction, bear sharply to the left to remain on Weldon Canyon. (Going straight takes you toward the landfill.) The motorway drops 345 feet over the next 0.5 mile, for a steep gradient of 13%. As the motorway is made to accommodate trucks, as well as maintenance and construction vehicles, there are intermittent "washouts" (deep sandy pits) designed to ensure traction and limit runaways. These will slow you down too (as will your brakes!).

The motorway empties out onto Coltrane Avenue; watch for motor vehicles coming from your left before turning right onto the road. Coltrane then curves to the left, becoming Weldon Canyon Road and crossing over I-5. After crossing, turn right onto The Old Road. The road is not literally "old," as in worn-out and pothole-ridden, but it does represent a pre–I-5 passage through Newhall Pass. (For more about this passage, see the sidebar.) The Old Road descends rapidly next to I-5, becoming San Fernando Road at the Sierra Highway intersection. Keep flying along; San Fernando veers under I-5. I recall the underpass being a bit dark, so be cautious of fast motor vehicles through here. In fact, this area gets busy during commute periods as drivers seek alternatives to busy I-5. The shoulder is narrow along some segments, so focus on being visible. Turn right at Balboa Road and climb the 6% grade to Balboa Boulevard. You may find yourself riding past a queue of motor vehicles waiting for the traffic signal. Turn right onto Balboa Boulevard. After 0.6 mile, the latter portion of which is a fast downhill, turn right onto Sesnon Boulevard and enter Granada Hills. After a little over 0.5 mile, look for O'Melveny Park, on the right, to conclude the ride.

MILES AND DIRECTIONS

0.0   Start from O'Melveny Park and turn right onto Sesnon Boulevard.

0.15 Turn right onto Tuscan Drive.

0.65 Turn right at the stop sign onto Neon Way.

0.75 Trailhead: Walk through the gate and continue onto Sulphur Springs Fire Road (climb at 11.3% grade).

2.45 Trail junction at open gate; stay to the left onto Sunshine Canyon Motorway.

3.05 Keep straight at spur trail to Mission Point; elevation here is 2,706 feet.

3.25 Leave Los Angeles and enter Los Angeles County (unincorporated area); no marker.

4.3   Jones Junction; bear right onto Saugus-to-the-Sea Road (dirt fire road).

4.75 Bear right onto Weldon Canyon Motorway (dirt road).

6.95 Bear sharply to the left to remain on Weldon Canyon; downhill at 13% grade.

7.45 End of Weldon Canyon Motorway; turn right onto Coltrane Avenue.

7.65 Coltrane curves to the left, becoming Weldon Canyon Road; cross over I-5.

7.7   Stop sign at The Old Road; turn right.

8.75 Enter the city of Los Angeles.

8.85 Traffic signal at Sierra Highway; keep straight, now on San Fernando Road.

9.5   Traffic signal at I-5 off-ramp; bear left to continue on San Fernando Road.

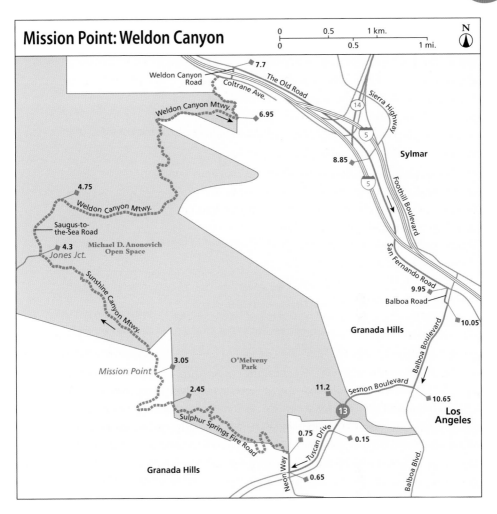

Mission Point: Weldon Canyon

9.95 Traffic signal at Balboa Road; turn right, climbing at 6% grade.

10.05 Traffic signal at Balboa Boulevard; turn right.

10.65 Traffic signal at Sesnon Boulevard; turn right.

11.2 End ride at entrance to O'Melveny Park.

The Oliver Twist

Start: Orcas Park, 11126 Orcas Ave., Lake View Terrace (Los Angeles)

Length: 8.4 miles (5.55 mile clockwise loop, plus 2.85 miles of out-and-back)

Riding time: 45 minutes to 2.5 hours (my time: 1H09:44)

Terrain and surface: 45% paved roads; 50% dirt roads; 5% loose gravel road

Elevation: Low: 1,058 feet at Orcas Park; high: 2,009 feet along Oliver Canyon Road

Traffic and hazards: Foothill Boulevard carried 15,300 vehicles per day near Osborne Street (just east of I-210) in 2009.

Map: *The Thomas Guide—Street Guide: Los Angeles and Orange Counties* (any recent year), page 503

Getting there: By car—From central Los Angeles, head north on I-5. Turn onto SR 118 (Ronald Reagan Freeway) and head east, and then turn onto I-210 and head east. Exit at Foothill Boulevard and turn left. After 0.75 mile turn right onto Orcas Avenue at the traffic signal. Orcas Avenue heads south, entering Orcas Park. Park in the first lot on the left.

By public transit—From central Los Angeles, ride Metro bus route 90 northbound to Orcas Avenue. The bus runs every 20 to 60 minutes on weekdays, every 60 minutes on Saturday, and every 90 minutes on Sunday and holidays. It is a long ride—about 2 hours one way. Ride south on Orcas Avenue to Orcas Park.

Starting point coordinates: N34.271167° / W118.368939°

THE RIDE

The Oliver Twist is a nifty 8.4-mile mountain bike ride that ascends into the San Gabriel Mountains above Lake View Terrace from Orcas Park, rides along Oliver Canyon Road and along a ridge, and then plunges back into Lake View Terrace for the return to Orcas Park. As for the ride title, there really is no "twist";

the featured component of the route is Oliver Canyon Road, from which there are some excellent views of Hansen Dam and Tujunga Wash. The ride does not climb as much or as high as some of the other mountain bike rides in this book, making this an excellent outing for a beginning to intermediate rider. Although, with a steep climb and descent along the way, this ride would suitably challenge even experts. The ride is described as a clockwise loop, with an opening-closing out-and-back. Outstanding climbers might want to try the ride as a counterclockwise loop, but please be aware of the 17% uphill grade (!) on Ebey Canyon Road.

Start from the north edge of the parking lot at Orcas Park, adjacent to the equestrian center. The park is located at the end of Orcas Avenue in Lake View Terrace. Lake View Terrace is a community of Los Angeles located in the northeastern San Fernando Valley with a population of 11,800 in 2009. The

A dramatic rock formation greets riders climbing BP & L Road above Lake View Terrace.

Hansen Dam and Tujunga Wash

Orcas Park abuts Hansen Dam Park in Lake View Terrace. The Los Angeles Flood of 1938 triggered the construction of dams in the Los Angeles region, as the safety of the existing population at the time, as well as future growth, hinged on the taming of floodwaters. In 1939 the US Army Corps of Engineers seized the ranch property of Homer and Marie Hansen and proceeded to build a 2-mile-long, 97-foot-high dam. Today the dam retains a seasonal lake that is suitable for boating, fishing, and swimming. In film, Hansen Dam has been featured in *Easy Rider* (campfire sequence with Peter Fonda and Dennis Hopper), *Charlie's Angels: Full Throttle* (opening ambush sequence with Drew Barrymore, Cameron Diaz, Lucy Liu, and some "bad" guys), and *The Italian Job* (MINI Cooper chase scene with Charlize Theron and Mark Wahlberg), among others.

The Tujunga Wash flows into the dam and then continues southward into heavily populated areas. The potential for flooding along the wash is the reason for the dam's existence. Tujunga Wash is formed in the San Gabriel Mountains, where the Big Tujunga and Little Tujunga Creeks, or washes, converge. (A wash is essentially a creek that runs dry intermittently.) In fact, Tujunga Wash truly flows only during and after heavy rainstorms.

Some distance downstream of Hansen Dam along the Tujunga Wash is the Great Wall of Los Angeles, a 0.5-mile-long mural designed by Judith Baca. The mural depicts the history of California, had numerous collaborators, and is considered to be one of the longest in the world.

community gained notoriety in 1991 as the setting for the beating of Rodney King by Los Angeles Police Department officers; the incident triggered riots that were concentrated toward the south, in south central L.A. Today it is a relatively peaceful and serene, mixed community. The 2008 film *Lakeview Terrace*, starring Samuel L. Jackson, was actually filmed in Walnut.

Turn right onto Foothill Boulevard and head east into the Lake View Terrace community. Although you are still in Los Angeles, it is worlds away from the densely populated hubbub of the rest of the city. In fact, this unique area is still zoned for horse property. At the 1.45-mile mark, turn left onto Esko Avenue and head into the neighborhood. Turn left onto Jimenez Street; the road bends to the right, becoming Dominica Avenue. Climb toward the end of the road—do not go there, though. Just beyond the last residence and its surrounding property, turn left onto the dirt road.

Despite the appearance, the road is public—but take care to avoid straying onto private property.

You are now on BP & L (Burbank Power and Light) Road—history unknown—climbing into the San Gabriel Mountains. The climb is reasonably steep, taking you from 1,275 feet to 1,936 feet at the next junction over a distance of 1.5 miles (8.2% average grade, with some steeper segments). The mountain slopes are effectively barren here, supporting little but noxious weeds. As you near the summit, a dramatic rock formation appears on the right (see photo). At the junction, turn right onto Oliver Canyon Road—a signpost reads FR 2N94, suggesting that this is an old forest road. (Google Maps use the Oliver Canyon designation.) This dirt road travels along the ridge with a few undulations, eventually cresting at the high point of the ride (2,009 feet). To your right there are some excellent views of Hansen Dam as well as of Tujunga Wash (see sidebar). Oliver Canyon, the actual canyon, is also to your right.

After 1.1 miles on Oliver Canyon Road, the trail splits; there is no marker here, but bear right. The trail descends and then climbs around a knoll before descending again rapidly to another junction. While descending, if you look ahead you will see a church on the hilltop—you may think you have reached heaven! You are actually at 1,762 feet elevation here, but the effect is surreal. Upon nearing the church, turn right onto the (paved) Ebey Canyon Road and start to descend.

Bike Shop

Willy's Bikes, 11968 Foothill Blvd., Lakeview Terrace; (818) 896-4249; www.willys bikes.com

And what a descent! The road drops 368 feet over the next 0.4 mile, for an average gradient of 17%. Although the road is paved, it is in poor condition, covered with loose gravel when I rode it. The effect was to reduce the road's traction, making this a wild ride. Also, as you plummet, the road appears to be aiming directly for Tujunga Wash. From this angle the wash looks eroded, hostile, other-worldly, and downright uninviting. Certainly no place for a bicycle! Actually, the road turns to parallel the wash—but the optical illusion is dramatic.

At the base of the descent, turn right onto Conover Street. The downhill continues, but much less steeply. Continue past the gate as you reenter civilization and reach better pavement. (You actually reentered Los Angeles while descending Ebey Canyon.) Conover ends at Foothill Boulevard; turn right at the stop sign, watching for motor vehicle traffic. From here it is a brisk, net downhill 2.0 miles back to Orcas Park, including a left turn from Foothill Boulevard onto Orcas Avenue, to conclude the ride.

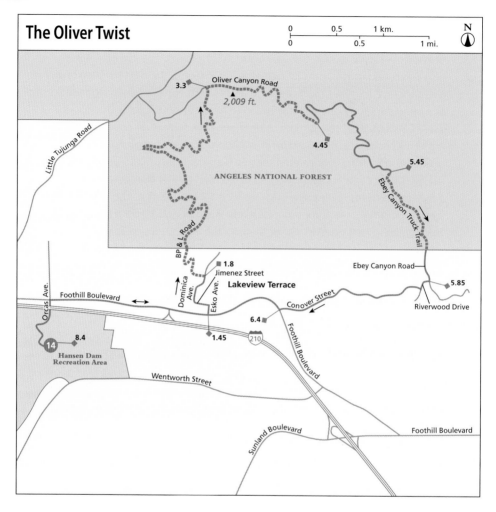

MILES AND DIRECTIONS

0.0 Start at Orcas Park and exit via Orcas Avenue, heading north.

0.25 Traffic signal at Foothill Boulevard; turn right.

1.45 Turn left onto Esko Avenue (residential street).

1.5 Turn left onto Jimenez Street.

1.6 Jimenez bends to the right, becoming Dominica Avenue.

1.8 Turn left onto BP & L Road (dirt road); continue past gate and stay on main dirt road.

3.3 Turn right onto Oliver Canyon Road (dirt road); signpost reads FR 2N94.

4.45 Trail junction; stay to the right, taking unnamed dirt road, and head southeast.

5.45 End of dirt road; turn right onto Ebey Canyon Road (no sign), adjacent to church. Begin descent of 17% grade. (**Caution:** Loose gravel on road may make traction poor.)

5.85 Turn right onto Conover Street; head west.

6.35 Continue past gate, remaining on Conover.

6.4 Stop sign at Foothill Boulevard; turn right.

8.15 Traffic signal at Orcas Avenue; turn left.

8.4 End ride at Orcas Park.

Ride Up over Mulholland

Start: Caballero Canyon trailhead, Reseda Boulevard, Tarzana

Length: 17.3 miles (T-shaped route—3 out-and-backs)

Riding time: 1.5 to 4.5 hours (my time: 1H55:04)

Terrain and surface: 93% on dirt trails and roads; 7% on a paved road

Elevation: Low: 985 feet on the Caballero Canyon Trail, just north of Reseda Boulevard trailhead; high: 1,913 feet on Mulholland Drive at Zelzah Fire Road

Traffic and hazards: 93% of the route is on dirt trails and roads (no motor vehicles). Reseda Boulevard carried 9,570 vehicles per day near Rosita Street, to the north of where the ride ends, in 2007 (traffic volumes along the segment of Reseda used by the ride are lower).

Map: *The Thomas Guide—Street Guide: Los Angeles and Orange Counties* (any recent year), page 560

Getting there: By car—From central Los Angeles, head north on US 101. Exit at Reseda Boulevard; turn left and head toward the Santa Monica Mountains. Look for the Caballero Canyon trailhead on the left, just beyond the El Caballero Country Club. Park on the street.

By public transit—From central Los Angeles, ride the Metro Red Line (subway) to the end of the line at the North Hollywood station. Transfer to the Metro Orange Line (bus rapid transit) and travel to the Reseda Boulevard station. Exit here and head south (by bicycle) on Reseda Boulevard. Follow the above instructions to the Caballero Canyon trailhead.

Starting point coordinates: N34.142731° / W118.540882°

THE RIDE

The Ride Up over Mulholland, the title being a play on the lyrics to a Tom Petty song, features an off-road climb to Mulholland Drive, which snakes through the Santa Monica Mountains; a couple out-and-backs on Mulholland; and

Looking north from "Dirt Mulholland" toward Warner Center and the valley beyond

then a mostly paved descent down Reseda Boulevard. Park as close as you can to the Caballero Canyon trailhead, located on the east side of Reseda Boulevard. The motor vehicles of other trail users will most likely be parked nearby. Start the ride from the trailhead. While not singletrack, the trail is fairly narrow, particularly given the presence of other users. So ride cautiously, holding a predictable line.

Caballero Canyon Trail climbs 566 feet from the trailhead up to Mulholland Drive at an average grade of 6.3%. The gradient is steeper, however, as you near the top. There were a few eroded and rocky segments when I rode it, requiring some bike handling skills. (I walked one of the trickier, steep segments.) Once at Mulholland, you are greeted by a bench and lavatory—you are now at 1,551 feet elevation. Turn right and head west. This segment of Mulholland is often called "Dirt Mulholland," as it is entirely

Bike Shop

Bike Warrior, 19449 Ventura Blvd., Tarzana; (818) 344-0923; http://bikewarrior.com

Mulholland Drive

Not to be confused with the 2001 David Lynch film of the same name, Mulholland Drive is an iconic element of the Los Angeles region's road system. Built in 1924, Mulholland was designed for scenery by developers of the Hollywood Hills. The road is actually in three portions: Mulholland Drive in the east, stretching from Hollywood to west of I-405; central Mulholland, also known as "Dirt Mulholland"; and western Mulholland, which actually splits into two, with Mulholland Drive heading northward into Woodland Hills and Mulholland Highway heading westward into the Santa Monica Mountains and eventually southward to the Pacific Coast Highway. Celebrities known to live just off Mulholland include Paris Hilton, Sylvester Stallone, and Justin Timberlake.

In addition to its breathtaking scenery, Mulholland Drive's twists, turns, and undulations have been known to attract an underground racing scene, including sports cars and motorcycles. In fact, watch out for drivers flexing their muscles on this road. The road also has a bicycling history—for years the Mulholland Road Race was a must-do race on the Southern California calendar (history unknown). The modern-day Tour of California has incorporated portions of Mulholland into its stages. The road continues to be popular among cyclists. Ultra-distance cyclists, in fact, incorporate the road into such events as the Mulholland Double and Mulholland Challenge. For additional riding on Mulholland, see the Circuito de Calabasas, Hollywood Ride of Fame, Topanga to Tuna to Tide, and Zoom Dume Zuma rides in this book.

Finally, no discussion of Mulholland Drive would be complete without a mention of the road's namesake, William Mulholland (1855–1935), considered to have laid the foundations for transforming Los Angeles into a modern-day metropolis. A self-taught civil engineer, Mulholland was responsible for developing and laying the city's water infrastructure. Without his pipelines, dams, aqueducts, reservoirs, and other water facilities, the capacity for Los Angeles would have been severely limited—particularly since Los Angeles' natural water supply is not nearly voluminous enough to sustain a large population. Despite his grand accomplishments and achievements, his career was marred by the 1928 failure of St. Francis Dam, northeast of Los Angeles. He personally inspected the dam, along with other official inspectors, just 12 hours before it failed, leading to a massive flood that took the lives of up to 600 persons. The dam failure is considered to be the worst US civil engineering disaster of the twentieth century—exceeded in California only by the 1906 San Francisco earthquake in terms of lives lost. Mulholland retired after the dam failure, but many positive aspects of his legacy live on.

unpaved. Mulholland is otherwise a through road, stretching from the hills of Hollywood in the east to Malibu in the west (see sidebar). You need not worry about motor vehicles up here except for maintenance trucks, so enjoy the space. To your right as you head west and to your left as you head east (i.e., to the north), there is an expansive vista of the San Fernando Valley. (Looking toward the south, you generally cannot see the ocean, primarily because you are on the "back side" of the Santa Monica Mountains.) The surface of Mulholland is mostly dirt and gravel, with occasional eroded segments that will require your attention as to where to aim your front wheel.

Mulholland climbs gradually (3.6% grade) as you head west. After 0.9 mile take note of the trailhead on your right; you will be returning here later to access Reseda Boulevard. The crest, at least in the westerly direction, comes at the Temescal Canyon Trail junction (1,782 feet elevation), 1.25 miles after you turn onto Mulholland. From here Mulholland descends gradually, passing a few trailheads and turnoffs. You will notice the occasional Santa Monica Mountains National Recreational Area or Conservancy sign, indicating the name of a trail or rules and regulations. Stay on Mulholland through here. After 3.15 miles you come to a gate; continue past the gate and then bear right to continue on Mulholland. The gate marks a barrier to motor vehicles, although you will not see many vehicles even beyond the gate. Mulholland continues to descend toward civilization. (Although gravel was absent along this segment when I rode it, the road was nonetheless quite bumpy.) Street signs suggest a gradual return to civilization. Turn around at Saltillo Street (elevation 1,216 feet here) and begin the trek back. Beyond Saltillo, Mulholland is paved. You are now 4.45 miles west of the Caballero Canyon junction.

It is a long, gradual climb back to the Temescal Canyon trailhead, at 1,782 feet elevation. Beyond this junction, Mulholland Drive descends past the Top of Reseda Trail (to which you will be returning later) and Caballero Canyon Trail. This is a saddle (low point) along Mulholland—the road begins to climb from here at a 5.4% grade. Mulholland reaches the high point of the entire ride (1,913 feet) at the Zelzah Fire Road junction. To the north (your left) you can see the Encino Reservoir. From here Mulholland undulates gradually. The turnaround point is at a gate. Beyond the gate, Mulholland is paved. The elevation here is 1,876 feet, and you are 2.25 miles from Caballero Canyon Trail. Return to Caballero Canyon over a net downhill. Continue past Caballero Canyon to the Top of Reseda Trail. Turn right here. Use caution in navigating the downhill trail (12.6% grade), particularly in the presence of other trail users. Save your speed for paved Reseda Boulevard, which starts just beyond the gate near the bottom of the trail. Reseda descends at a 9.0% grade over 1.2 miles—you will probably hit the highest speeds of the ride here! Conclude the ride at the Caballero Canyon trailhead.

Ride Up over Mulholland

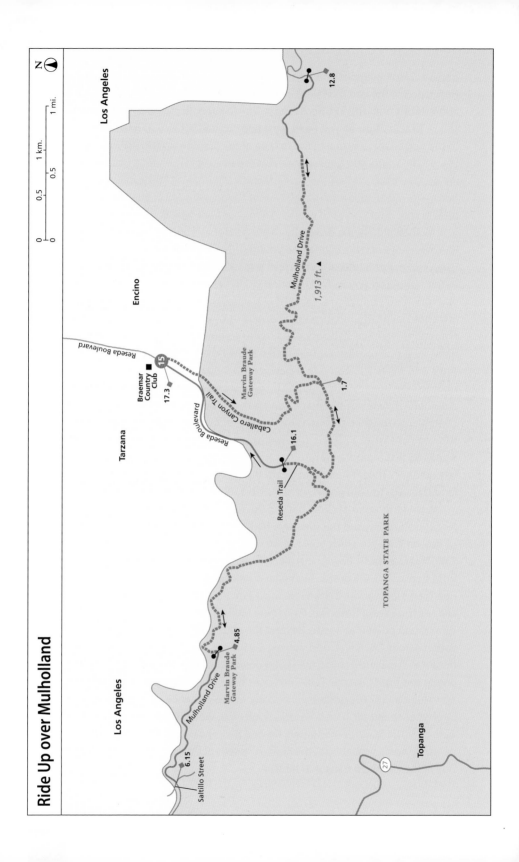

MILES AND DIRECTIONS

0.0 Start from the Caballero Canyon trailhead at Reseda Boulevard in Tarzana. Head south on Caballero Canyon Trail.

1.7 Crest of Caballero Canyon Trail at Mulholland Drive (dirt road); turn right onto Mulholland.

4.85 Gate; continue heading west on Mulholland.

6.15 Turn around at Saltillo Street, near beginning of pavement on Mulholland.

7.45 Continue past gate, heading east on Mulholland.

10.55 Caballero Canyon Trail on the left; continue heading east on Mulholland.

11.75 High point of ride (1,913 feet) at Zelzah Fire Road junction; continue heading east.

12.8 Gate; turn around here—pavement on Mulholland begins just beyond gate.

13.75 Return to high point of ride at Zelzah Fire Road; continue heading west on Mulholland.

15.05 Caballero Canyon Trail on the right; continue heading west on Mulholland.

15.9 Top of Reseda Trail junction; turn right here and begin descent.

16.1 Gate; continue head north (downhill) onto paved Reseda Boulevard.

17.3 End ride at the Caballero Canyon trailhead.

Ruta del Placerita Tujunga

Start: Hansen Dam Park, 11770 Foothill Blvd., Sylmar/ Lake View Terrace (Los Angeles)

Length: 31.95 miles (clockwise loop)

Riding time: 2 to 6 hours (my time: 2H31:16)

Terrain and surface: 100% paved roads

Elevation: Low: 1,074 feet at Hansen Dam Park; high: 2,756 feet on Little Tujunga Canyon Road near Pacoima Road in the Angeles National Forest.

Traffic and hazards: Foothill Boulevard carried 26,230 vehicles per day at Van Nuys Boulevard in 2009.

Map: *The Thomas Guide—Street Guide: Los Angeles and Orange Counties* (any recent year), page 503

Getting there: By car—From central Los Angeles, head north on I-5 to SR 118 (Ronald Reagan Freeway) and head east; at the junction turn onto I-210 and head east. Exit at Foothill Boulevard and turn right. After 0.2 mile look for the entrance to Hansen Dam Park, on the left.

By public transit—From central Los Angeles, ride Metro bus route 90 northbound to Hansen Dam Park. The bus runs every 20 to 60 minutes on weekdays, every 60 minutes on Saturday, and every 90 minutes on Sunday and holidays. It is a long ride—about 2 hours one way.

Starting point coordinates: N34.273639° / W118.383511°

THE RIDE

The Ruta del Placerita Tujunga—or, more linguistically, "La Ruta"—is a challenging loop through the San Gabriel Mountains and Angeles National Forest. The loop includes passages through Placerita Canyon and Little Tujunga Canyon, as well as an urban segment through the northeastern San Fernando Valley. While Little Tujunga Canyon Road is not as long, open, and daunting as Big Tujunga Canyon Road (see Big Tujunga Canyon Epic for comparison), Little Tujunga offers an extra kick by featuring two significant climbs rather than one.

Start the ride at Hansen Dam Park on Foothill Boulevard, just west of I-210 in Lake View Terrace (community of Los Angeles). Hansen Dam Park is a large facility, for which the centerpiece is Hansen Dam (see "Hansen Dam and Tujunga Wash" sidebar), with aquatic, equestrian, fishing, and swimming facilities, athletic fields, a golf course, and hiking trails. There is even a 2-mile-long paved path on top of the dam. While the park itself may entice you to stay there (many of the hiking trails also are suitable for riding), exit the parking lot and turn left onto Foothill Boulevard. You will remain on Foothill for a little over 9 miles as you ride through the northeastern San Fernando Valley. This is the "urban segment" of the ride. While traffic is not too heavy through here (20,000 to 26,000 vehicles per day), there are plenty of traffic signals and cross-streets along the way. The "real" riding starts as you near Newhall Pass, toward the northern end of Foothill, so ride conservatively and safely through the valley.

Once you leave Lake View Terrace, Foothill takes you along the edge of the city of San Fernando and then into Sylmar (community of Los Angeles). Sylmar had a population of 79,614 in 2008, with about 70% of the residents being Hispanic. The area was once rich in olive groves, and the shimmering colors of the olive tree leaves inspired the community's name (loosely

Angeles National Forest

Covering more than 655,000 acres (over 1,000 square miles) of mountainous woodlands, Angeles National Forest is located just to the north of the heavily urbanized Los Angeles region but still within Los Angeles County. Oak, Douglas fir, Coulter pine, California walnut, Jeffrey pine, ponderosa pine, white fir, and lodgepole pine trees are found throughout the forest. There is also a huge array of habitats, ecosystems, and wildlife, as well as opportunities for recreationalists.

The San Gabriel Mountains are the primary topographical feature of the forest, as the mountain range and the forest are nearly contiguous. Nearly 25% of the forest burned during the Station Wildfire of summer 2009. The fire burned for almost one month, destroying ninety-one buildings and resulting in the deaths of two firefighters. The fire's source was determined to be arson. Despite it being a relatively recent event, the fire is considered to be the worst in the Los Angeles region's history.

Entering Angeles National Forest along Sand Canyon Road in the San Gabriel Mountains

translated as "sea of leaves"). Sylmar has seen its share of disasters, including two major earthquakes, a huge underground explosion, a few major fires, and even some gun violence. On any given day, however—hopefully the day you choose to do this ride—Sylmar is a healthy and peaceful L.A. community nestled against the foothills of the San Gabriel Mountains.

After passing under I-210 7.35 miles into the ride, Foothill curves toward the north and leaves the San Fernando Valley. I-5 is immediately to your left as you head toward Newhall Pass (see Mission Point: Weldon Canyon for more info). Once north of Balboa Boulevard, Foothill climbs from 1,359 feet to 1,458 feet at an average grade of 8.5%. The road descends and then gradually climbs from there; turn right onto Sierra Highway, away from the Newhall Pass area, and head northeast. Beale's Cut (also described in the Mission Point ride) is somewhere to your left, hidden by the rugged landscape. Leave Los Angeles as you pass under SR 14 (Antelope Valley Freeway) and enter the city of Santa Clarita. The Sierra Highway is an old passage through here—with SR 14 available as a faster route, traffic volumes on Sierra should be low except during periods when the freeway is congested. Santa Clarita is an amalgamation of several previously separate communities, including Canyon Country (which is where you are now), Newhall, Saugus, and Valencia. The city was incorporated in 1987 and had a population of 209,130 (L.A. County's fourth-largest) as of this writing. You will not see much of Santa Clarita out here; this area remains rugged and lightly developed. Continue along Sierra, parallel to SR 14, as it climbs to 1,729 feet (5% grade), descends, climbs again, and then descends again to Placerita Canyon Road. Turn right onto Placerita Canyon Road and head east.

Placerita Canyon Road takes you out of Santa Clarita and into the Angeles National Forest. The city boundary hovers near the canyon, though, just to the north. This is a two-lane road with a rural feel and light traffic. Just after you enter the canyon and the national forest, just barely visible to the left you may be able to catch sight of a collection of buildings that seem to be from an old Western town. This is the Melody Ranch Motion Picture Studio, traditionally used to film Westerns. Tom Mix and Gene Autry (who also owned the set)

Bike Shop

YG Bicycles, 13751 Foothill Blvd., Sylmar (Los Angeles); (818) 322-7263; http://yg bicycles.com

are among the stars who filmed here. Tours are available, and the studio lot is open once a year for a cowboy poetry festival. Yet another studio, the Walt Disney Golden Oak Ranch, is farther up the canyon. As of this writing there were plans for expansion, and a name change, but still involving Disney. Both studios are considered to be located in the Sierra Pelonas, the mountain range immediately to the north of the San Gabriels separated by Placerita Canyon. The golden oak in the Disney studio name references the "Oak of the Golden Dream," a tree associated with the first recorded finding of gold in California, in 1842. The oak is located in Placerita Canyon State Park, which is to your right as you pedal through the canyon.

Placerita Canyon itself is rich in coast live oak trees, along with cottonwoods, sycamores, and willows. The canyon is uniquely located in a transition zone between mountain (San Gabriel) and desert (Mojave) ecosystems. Ride the 5.0 miles through Placerita Canyon, with its relatively gentle uphills and downhills, to its end at Sand Canyon Road. Turn right and head southeast, reentering Angeles National Forest. Sand Canyon climbs over the next 3.0 miles (average grade 5.5%, with some steeper segments) adjacent to Bear Creek to a crest at Bear Divide (elevation 2,729 feet). There is a ranger station at the pass, to your right as you begin the descent. Sand Canyon Road becomes Little Tujunga Canyon Road as you plunge into Pacoima Creek Canyon. The summit behind you was a false crest—more climbing lies beyond the canyon!

The low elevation through the canyon is 2,074 feet. From here the road twists and winds its way up to Mendenhall Ridge and features some serious hairpin curves. The Pinnacle, one of the taller peaks in this area (3,589 feet), is to your left (and up) as you approach the crest. After crossing the high point of the entire ride (2,759 feet), Little Tujunga Canyon Road begins to descend. This is the long, final descent of the ride. After a steep beginning, which may find you speeding a little out of control, the gradient eases. I found that there was very little traffic along this entire road, seeing no more than ten vehicles the entire way. As you near Lake View Terrace, and civilization, you may hear the sounds of the Angeles Shooting Range, where the L.A. Police Department (and others) get some training and target practice. The USDA Forest Service has a ranger station up a short canyon, off to your right.

After passing some industrial development—there may be some heavy trucks in the vicinity—the road changes its name from Little Tujunga Canyon Road to the less adventurous sounding Osborne Street. Continue to Foothill Boulevard and turn right here. After passing under I-210, it is just another 0.2 mile to Hansen Dam Park, on the left, and the end of the ride.

MILES AND DIRECTIONS

0.0 Start at Hansen Dam Park in Lake View Terrace (Los Angeles). Turn left and head west on Foothill Boulevard.

1.8 Pass under SR 118.

7.35 Pass under I-210.

9.1 Turn right onto Sierra Highway.

9.5 Pass under SR 14 (Antelope Valley).

10.15 Crest of climb along Sierra Highway (1,729 feet).

12.3 Turn right onto Placerita Canyon Road (pass under SR 14).

13.8 Enter Angeles National Forest, adjacent to the entrance to Placerita Canyon State Park.

17.3 Stop sign at Sand Canyon Road; turn right.

20.3 Bear Divide (elevation 2,729 feet); you're now on Little Tujunga Canyon Road.

24.5 Mendenhall Ridge (elevation 2,759 feet—high point of ride); begin descent.

31.1 Enter Lake View Terrace, now on Osborne Street.

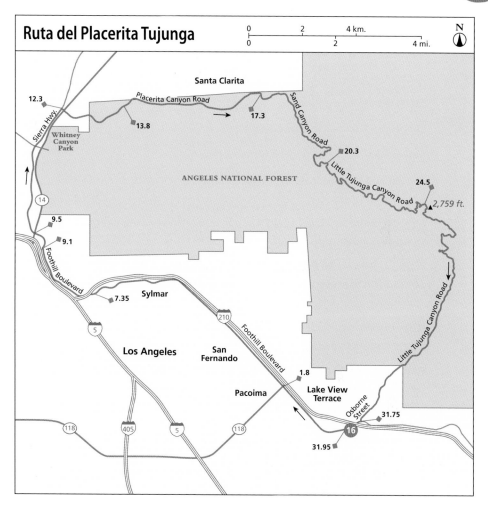

Ruta del Placerita Tujunga

31.6 Traffic signal at Foothill Boulevard; turn right.

31.75 Pass under I-210.

31.95 End ride at Hansen Dam Park (on the left).

Verdugo Mountains Panorama Ride

Start: Brand Library Park, 1601 West Mountain Rd., Glendale

Length: 13.8 miles (clockwise loop)

Riding time: 1.5 to 4.5 hours (my time: 1H50:35)

Terrain and surface: 75% dirt roads; 25% paved roads

Elevation: Low: 792 feet at Brand Park Drive and Mountain Street in Glendale; high: 3,093 feet along Verdugo Mountainway, near Whiting Woods Mountainway junction

Traffic and hazards: Traffic volumes on Sunset Canyon Road in Burbank were known to exceed 2,000 vehicles per day; an exact count was not available.

Map: *The Thomas Guide—Street Guide: Los Angeles and Orange Counties* (any recent year), page 534

Getting there: By car—From central Los Angeles, take I-5 North to Western Avenue in Glendale. Exit and turn right onto Western Avenue. Keep straight, past Mountain Street and into Brand Library Park via Brand Park Drive.

By public transit—From central Los Angeles, ride Metro bus route 92 to Glenoaks Boulevard and Western Avenue in Glendale. Exit the bus and ride uphill on Western Avenue past Mountain Street and into Brand Library Park via Brand Park Drive. Route 92 runs every 20 to 25 minutes on weekdays, every 25 to 30 minutes on Saturday, and every 40 to 45 minutes on Sunday and holidays.

Starting point coordinates: N34.182236° / W118.277814°

THE RIDE

The Verdugo Mountains are an isolated mountain "island," completely detached from other nearby mountain ranges. Millions of years of faulting and uplifting have created the Verdugos. Two Verdugo rides are featured in this book. This one, the "Panorama Ride," penetrates the Verdugos on dirt

Pausing to absorb the commanding view of Burbank and Glendale from the Verdugos

trails, climbing nearly to their 3,126-foot crest. The other, the "Perimeter Ride," completes a full lap around the Verdugos—feasible, given that the range is only 8 miles long by 3.25 miles wide.

The Verdugo Mountains Panorama Ride is an off-road ride, although the opening segment is on paved roads. Be prepared for some steep, relentless climbing, as well as an exhilarating descent. Along the Verdugo Mountainway, the featured segment of the ride along the crest of the Verdugo Mountains, you will be treated to expansive panoramas of the southeastern and northeastern San Fernando Valley, as well as the western San Gabriel Valley. Start the ride at Brand Library Park in Glendale, on the lower slopes of the Verdugos. The park is a worthwhile destination in and of itself, as it features the Brand Library, part of the Glendale Public Library system, with its extensive collection of art and music items. The library is housed, quite literally, in the former Brand mansion, which was occupied by the original owners until 1945. The mansion has a striking East Indian pavilion design. Leave the park by heading downhill on Brand Park Drive to Mountain Street. Turn right here, heading northwest.

Mountain Street climbs gradually from Glendale into Burbank, becoming Sunset Canyon Drive. Burbank had a population of 103,340 in 2010 and was billed as the "Media Capital of the World," being the home of entertainment production facilities for several large companies. These included NBC, Nickelodeon, Walt Disney, Warner Brothers, and Warner Music. The world came to know Burbank during the long-running *The Tonight Show Starring Johnny Carson*, which aired from studios in the city. Numerous well-known films—too many to list here—have been shot in Burbank studios. Continue riding and climbing along Sunset Canyon Drive to Walnut Avenue; turn right here and begin to climb. The elevation at the turn is 961 feet; the gradient is 9.8%. You will continue to climb into the Verdugo Mountains at about a 10% grade, for 1,340 feet of climbing over the next several miles.

Bike Shop

Glendale Cycles, 1250 West Glenoaks Blvd., Glendale; (818) 937-9440; http://glendalecycles.com

Walnut Avenue becomes Stough Canyon Avenue about halfway up the paved portion of the climb. To the left here, Lockheed View Avenue leads to the Starlight Bowl, a well-known outdoor theater. Continue to the end of Stough Canyon Avenue (elevation 1,514 feet) and continue onto Stough Canyon Mountainway, a wide dirt road that continues to climb at the same 10% grade. After 1.2 miles (which might seem longer), bear right onto Verdugo Mountainway (elevation 2,057 feet here). The climb continues at the same gradient. You will notice the occasional sign with a printed elevation to let you know your altitude. Most trail junctions also are marked with a sign. Be sure to stay on Verdugo Mountainway for the next 5.8 miles, although the orientation of some of the signs admittedly makes it difficult to tell which dirt road is Verdugo! (As a general rule, if you start to descend rapidly, you are not on the Verdugo Mountainway.)

Verdugo Mountainway almost imperceptibly enters La Tuna Canyon Park. The La Tuna Canyon Trail junction (elevation 2,300 feet) is just 0.6 mile after you turn onto Verdugo Mountainway. The mountainway leaves the park shortly after the junction. The climbing eases somewhat beyond here, although you still have nearly 800 more feet to gain over the next 3.5 miles. The vistas from either side of Verdugo are spectacular, so enjoy them as you pedal along. A collection of communications towers near Verdugo Peak is a landmark. Many of the dirt roads were built through the Verdugos to provide access for firefighters. As I passed by the communications towers, I observed a large crane, perhaps for some reconstruction or new construction. How did they get such a large piece of equipment up here?

Continue on Verdugo Mountainway, avoiding the side roads. Between the Wildwood Canyon Road and Whiting Woods Mountainway junctions, Verdugo crests at 3,093 feet, immediately adjacent to Verdugo Peak, the high point of the Verdugo Mountains. Beyond the Whiting Woods junction, Verdugo Mountainway descends rapidly to 2,675 feet at the Brand Park Mountainway junction. Bear sharply right here and start the Brand Park descent. The descent is steeper than the climbs you rode earlier, dropping to 1,232 feet in just 2.5 miles (10.9% grade). I observed a woman running up Brand Park Mountainway and was highly impressed, even feeling a bit guilty for taking it in the downhill direction. But controlling your speed will indeed require some effort.

At what seems to be a T junction, turn right to continue on Brand Park Mountainway. For the next segment, the mountainway is very wide and the gradient eases considerably. As the grade begins to increase, the mountainway becomes paved as it enters a series of steep switchbacks. The temptation to blitz through here is great, but watch your speed—there will likely be hikers and other trail users. Upon exiting the switchbacks, stay to the right as the road continues to descend rapidly, at nearly 11%, nearing Brand Park (hence the increased number of trail users). Follow the road as it jogs left and then right, entering the park. Conclude the ride adjacent to the parking area.

MILES AND DIRECTIONS

0.0 Start at Brand Library Park in Glendale. Exit the park and head downhill to Mountain Street.

0.05 Stop sign at Mountain Street; turn right.

0.75 Enter Burbank; Mountain Street becomes Sunset Canyon Drive.

2.05 Stop sign at Walnut Avenue; turn right.

2.5 Walnut Avenue becomes Stough Canyon Avenue at Lockheed View Avenue intersection; keep straight.

3.15 End of Stough Canyon Avenue; keep straight onto Stough Canyon Mountainway.

4.35 Bear right onto Verdugo Mountainway.

4.95 La Tuna Canyon trail junction; remain on Verdugo Mountainway.

8.15 Wildwood Canyon Road (dirt) junction; remain on Verdugo Mountainway.

8.45 High point of ride (3,093 feet) adjacent to Verdugo Peak.

8.85 Whiting Woods Mountainway junction; remain on Verdugo Mountainway.

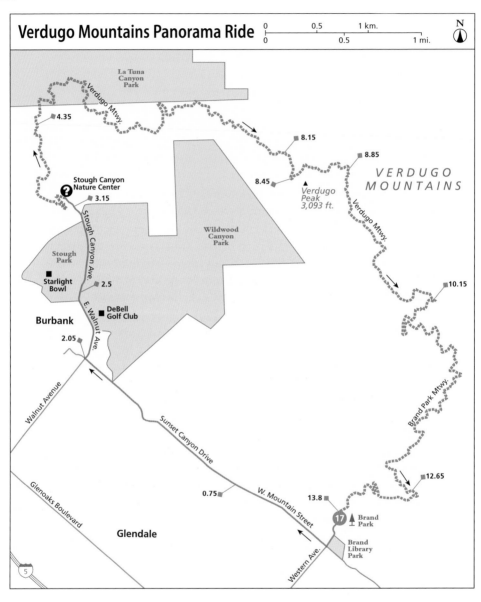

Verdugo Mountains Panorama Ride

10.15 Bear right onto Brand Park Mountainway; begin steep descent.

12.65 Bear right to continue on Brand Park Mountainway.

13.45 Enter Brand Park via Brand Park Drive.

13.8 End ride adjacent to the parking area in Brand Park.

Verdugo Mountains Perimeter Ride

Start: Verdugo Park, 1621 Cañada Blvd., Glendale

Length: 21.7 miles (clockwise loop)

Riding time: 1 to 3.5 hours (my time: 1H29:15)

Terrain and surface: 100% paved roads

Elevation: Low: 606 feet at Mountain Street and Central Avenue in Glendale; high: 1,779 feet along La Tuna Canyon Road, just east of I-210 in Los Angeles

Traffic and hazards: The heaviest traffic volumes were on Sunland Boulevard (26,530 vehicles per day at Penrose Street in 2008) and Glenoaks Boulevard (22,435 vehicles per day at Hollywood Way in 2005).

Map: *The Thomas Guide—Street Guide: Los Angeles and Orange Counties* (any recent year), page 564

Getting there: By car—From central Los Angeles, take I-5 North to SR 2 and head north. Exit at Mountain Street in Glendale and turn left. At the bottom of the steep descent, turn right onto Glendale Road. Bear left onto Cañada Boulevard and continue to Verdugo Park, on the left; enter the park and proceed along the park road to parking.

    By public transit—From central Los Angeles, ride Metro bus route 90 or 91 to Glendale. Exit on Cañada Boulevard at Verdugo Road. The two bus routes, which alternate, run every 15 to 30 minutes on weekdays, every 30 to 35 minutes on Saturday, and every 30 to 45 minutes on Sunday and holidays.

Starting point coordinates: N34.171864° / W118.229019°

THE RIDE

The Verdugo Mountains Perimeter Ride circumnavigates the Verdugo Mountains rather than penetrates them. While there are no 10% climbs and 11% descents, as in the panorama ride, the perimeter ride offers its share of challenges along the undulating roads of the Verdugo foothills. The ride begins at

Verdugo Park in Glendale and then passes through Burbank and Los Angeles before returning to Glendale. Verdugo Park has a place on the local cycling calendar, with its annual Thanksgiving weekend cyclocross races. The park roads, grassy areas, dirt trails, and a sand pit are transformed into a technical cyclocross circuit that competitors must complete several times during a race.

For this ride, exit Verdugo Park, turning right onto Cañada Boulevard. Cañada merges with Verdugo Road just south of the park, adjacent to Glendale Community College. The college boasts among its alumni actress Angie Dickinson, National Football League coach Andy Reid, rapper Schoolboy Q, and three-time Olympic track gold medalist Frank Wykoff. Just past the college, turn right onto Mountain Street, entering an upscale Glendale neighborhood. Glendale had a population of 191,719 in 2010, with about one-third of the residents being of Armenian descent. The rock band System of a Down

A rider speeds along Honolulu Avenue in Verdugo City, with the San Rafael Hills in the distance.

was formed of Armenian-American musicians from Glendale (see sidebar for a further discussion of the city). Follow Mountain Street, with its many traffic-calming interventions (speed humps, stop signs), to its end at Central Avenue. Turn right here; 2 blocks later turn left onto Kenneth Road, a long, two-lane road that passes through residential areas in Glendale and Burbank along with a couple of small commercial districts. You will be on Kenneth for a little over 5.5 miles.

Glendale

The city of Glendale has had a colorful history and seems to be continually redefining itself. The city's proximity to Burbank has been a plus—as entertainment giants have outgrown their Burbank facilities, Glendale has been happy to provide space. The Walt Disney Company, for example, developed several of its animated films at studios in Glendale, particularly from the mid-1980s to the mid-1990s. DreamWorks Animation was established in Glendale in 1994 on land that was formerly used as a helicopter landing pad. When it comes to helicopters, and aviation in general, the city has had a rich past. The former Grand Central Airport, which no longer exists, was the departure point for the first commercial eastbound transcontinental flight, piloted by Charles Lindbergh. Numerous notable personalities hail from Glendale, including actor Robert Englund ("Freddy" in the *Nightmare on Elm Street* films), musician Woody Guthrie, actor Shia LaBeouf, game-show host Pat Sajak, and actor-musician Rick Springfield. Numerous past notables also lived in Glendale, including Indy 500 winner Pat Flaherty, actor-comedian Don Knotts, and legendary actor John Wayne.

Despite the positive energy, a few negatives have set the city back at times. Glendale's proximity to several earthquake faults, including the Sierra Madre, Hollywood, Verdugo, and even the San Andreas, makes it particularly prone to earthquake events. During the 1971 San Fernando earthquake, for example, thirty-one structures in the city were damaged and had to be demolished. During the late 1970s, the bodies of ten murdered women, found in various places throughout the city, led to the arrest of the so-called Hillside Strangler. It was a period of community unease and fright that fortunately has not been experienced since. Today the city exists in relative peace and prosperity, with a diverse population and thriving business community.

At the end of Kenneth, turn left onto Naomi Street for a short trip. Next, turn right onto Glenoaks Boulevard. Enter Los Angeles just beyond the turn, 8.0 miles into the ride. To your right is the campus of Woodbury University. The school was founded in 1884 and is noted for its highly accredited business programs. Roaring to your left along Glenoaks is noisy I-5, a stark reminder that you are indeed doing an urban ride. Glenoaks veers away from I-5 as the road enters the Los Angeles community of Sun Valley. Turn right onto Sunland Boulevard; a couple blocks later, turn right onto La Tuna Canyon Road. This road is the premier segment of the ride. Over the next 5.75 miles, La Tuna Canyon climbs from 872 feet at Sunland Boulevard to 1,779 feet just beyond I-210 before descending to 1,631 feet at Honolulu Avenue. The climbing is mostly gradual.

Bike Shops

Go Green Bicycles, 118 East Alameda Ave., Burbank; (818) 845-6381; www.gogreen bicycles.com

Walteria Bicycles, 310 Fischer St., Glendale; (310) 733-0903

After passing through the La Tuna Canyon community, the road leaves development, traveling adjacent to the Verdugo Mountains and, for just under 2 miles, La Tuna Canyon Park. The riding adjacent the park is challenged by the loss of a shoulder. The "shoulder" is actually a 1.5-mile-long, V-shaped culvert along here, followed by about 0.3 mile of no shoulder, neither of which are comfortable places to ride. Fortunately there are two lanes on the climb, so drivers have plenty of room to pass you if you are in the outside lane. Stay on the road, but to the right, and be alert to passing motorists. In 2009 the traffic volume on La Tuna Canyon Road was 12,270 vehicles per day within the La Tuna Canyon community.

As you pass under I-210, you are nearing the 1,779-foot crest. It is a swift descent to Honolulu Avenue, where you will make a right turn and head back into Glendale. From here, at mile 16.25, it is essentially an all-downhill 5.45 miles to the finish. After passing under I-210 again, and covering another 1.1 miles, turn right onto Pennsylvania Avenue. This road heads south, and then curves to the left, becoming Honolulu Avenue once again. This community of Glendale is Verdugo City, nestled on the northeast side of the mountains. Turn right onto La Crescenta Avenue, passing the Oakmont Country Club, which has hosted qualifying tournaments for the US Open. After merging with Verdugo Road, bear right onto Cañada Boulevard. This is the final segment of the ride. Save for the intermittent traffic signals, this is a speedy stretch. After 1.4 miles, look for the entrance to Verdugo Park, on your right.

Verdugo Mountains Perimeter Ride

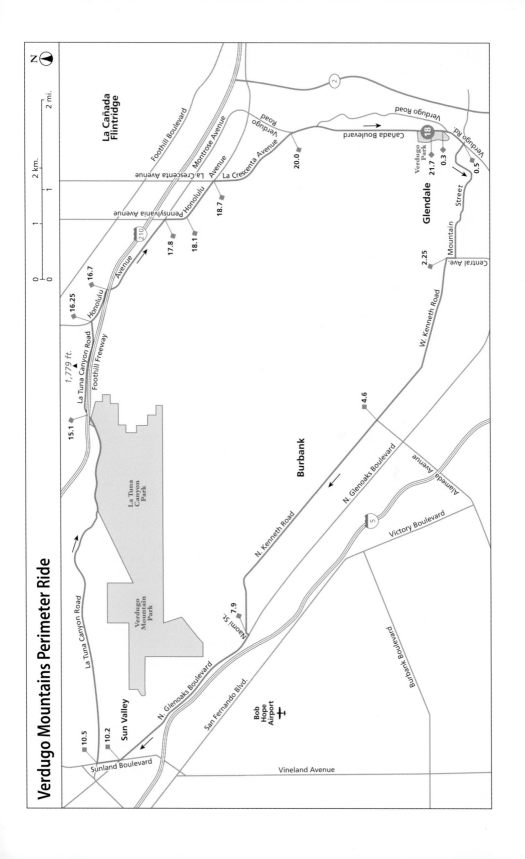

MILES AND DIRECTIONS

0.0 Start at Verdugo Park in Glendale; turn right onto Cañada Boulevard.

0.3 Traffic signal at Verdugo Road merge; bear right.

0.5 Traffic signal at Mountain Street; turn right.

2.1 Stop sign at Central Avenue; turn right.

2.25 Stop sign at Kenneth Road; turn left.

4.6 Leave Glendale and enter Burbank.

7.9 Stop sign at Naomi Street; turn left.

7.95 Stop sign at Glenoaks Boulevard; turn right.

8.0 Leave Burbank and enter Los Angeles.

10.2 Traffic signal at Sunland Boulevard; turn right.

10.5 Traffic signal at La Tuna Canyon Road; turn right.

15.1 Pass under I-210.

15.45 High point of ride (1,779 feet).

16.25 Traffic signal at Honolulu Avenue; turn right.

16.5 Leave Los Angeles and reenter Glendale.

16.7 Pass under I-210.

17.8 Traffic signal at Pennsylvania Avenue; turn right.

18.1 Pennsylvania Avenue curves to the left, becoming Honolulu Avenue.

18.7 Traffic signal at La Crescenta Avenue; turn right.

20.0 Merge with Verdugo Road.

20.3 Bear right onto Cañada Boulevard.

21.7 End ride at entrance to Verdugo Park.

Way of the Wilson and May Canyons

Start: El Cariso Community Regional Park, 13100 Hubbard St., Sylmar (Los Angeles)

Length: 15.2 miles (clockwise loop)

Riding time: 1.5 to 5 hours (my time: 2H14:30)

Terrain and surface: 44% truck trails (wide dirt roads); 24% paved roads; 32% paved truck trail (paved road not accessible to general motor vehicle traffic)

Elevation: Low: 1,428 feet at Hubbard Street and Garrick Avenue (El Cariso Park entrance); high: 3,668 feet at FR 3N17 junction with May Canyon Truck Trail

Traffic and hazards: Traffic volumes averaged 4,000 vehicles per day on Eldridge Street at Astoria Street in 2005; 2,160 vehicles per day on Garrick Avenue at Beaver Street in 2004; 2,280 vehicles per day on Astoria Street at Eldridge Street in 2005; 5,800 vehicles per day on Hubbard Street at Simshaw Avenue in 2007; 4,970 vehicles per day on Olive View Drive at Kennedy Street in 2005.

Map: *The Thomas Guide—Street Guide: Los Angeles and Orange Counties* (any recent year), page 482

Getting there: By car—From central Los Angeles, take I-5 North to SR 118 East, to I-210 North. Exit at Hubbard Street and turn right. Turn right into El Cariso Regional County Park and park.

　　By public transit—From central Los Angeles, ride the Metro Red Line (subway) to the North Hollywood station (end of the line). Transfer to the Metro Orange Line (bus rapid transit) and travel one stop to the Laurel Canyon station. Exit here and transfer to Metro bus route 230. The bus runs every 20 to 35 minutes on weekdays and every 35 to 60 minutes on weekends and holidays. ***Note:*** On weekends and holidays, the bus route terminates at the Sylmar train station on Hubbard Street, about 2 miles southwest of El Cariso Park. Exit the bus here. Transfer to Metro bus route 236 at the station, or simply ride to the park.

Starting point coordinates: N34.318031° / W118.418372°

The Way of the Wilson and May Canyons is a challenging mountain bike loop that begins on pavement in the Los Angeles community of Sylmar, climbs Wilson Canyon, descends the paved May Canyon, and then traverses some Sylmar roads, including an unpaved segment, to return to El Cariso Regional Park. The ride offers several challenges: The first one is to find the Wilson Canyon trailhead, which is somewhat hidden behind the buildings of a medical campus. The second challenge is Wilson Canyon itself, which features deep, loose dirt, making pedaling a challenge. The third challenge, albeit a minor one, is an unrideable segment on the return trip to Sylmar, requiring a dismount and short walk.

Start the ride at El Cariso Community Regional Park in Sylmar. The park is dedicated to the thirteen members of the El Cariso Hotshots firefighting crew who lost their lives battling the Loop Fire in 1966. The fire, which featured 100-foot-tall flames, engulfed the hills into which you will be climbing on this ride. Exit the park and ride straight across Hubbard Street onto Garrick Street. You are now on a gradual climb in a quiet neighborhood of Sylmar. This Los Angeles community had a population of 78,897 in 2010 and occupies the northeasternmost corner of the San Fernando Valley. Continue to the end of Garrick; turn left onto Astoria Street, followed by a right onto Eldridge Street. Turn right onto Polk Street, followed by a left onto Kinbrook Street. At the end of Kinbrook, turn left onto Barner Avenue and head south to Olive View Drive. Turn right here; shortly after the turn the Olive View-UCLA Medical Center will be on your right. This is a large medical facility that serves the immediate region, as well as the Antelope Valley to the north. After riding adjacent to the campus for a stretch—yielding to emergency vehicles of course—turn right onto Cobalt Street. Cobalt enters a quieter section of the campus, heading toward the hills behind the buildings. Keep riding to the end of Cobalt; this is the Wilson Canyon trailhead, despite its off-limits appearance.

Bike Shop

YG Bicycles, 13751 Foothill Blvd., Sylmar (Los Angeles); (818) 322-7263; http://yg bicycles.com

Turn right upon leaving the medical campus onto the wide dirt road. A steep, paved road continues to your left to a dead end. The opening segment of the Wilson Canyon Truck Trail is steep (12.5% grade). The trail eases after about 100 feet of climbing before entering a steady rhythm of nonstop climbing. The trail climbs 1,600 feet over the next 5.0 miles at an average grade of 6.0%. The first 1.7 to 2.0 miles of the climb are especially challenging—much of the road surface is loose dirt. The culprit may be frequent use by equestrians,

A rider chugs up May Canyon Truck Trail. You get to ride down this paved, car-free road!

as well as a general lack of rain. You may have to resort to bike-hiking on some (or most) of the opening section. At 1.2 miles up, be sure to stay to the right at the junction to remain on Wilson Canyon Truck Trail. After about 2.0 miles the loose dirt thins, enabling you to get back on your bike and ride. While the trail is mostly unshaded and barren, especially along its lower reaches, there are a few forested segments as you climb above 2,500 feet.

At the Wilson Canyon Saddle (somewhat large open space at the trail junction—large enough for a truck pit stop!), bear right onto FR 3N17, also known as Santa Clara Truck Trail. The elevation at the junction is 3,116 feet. FR 3N17 climbs another 552 feet over the next 1.65 miles (6.3% grade), until finally reaching the high point of the ride (3,668 feet) at the junction with May Canyon Truck Trail. Although hard-core mountain bikers might scoff at the paved surface of the May Canyon Trail, most riders will be thankful for the easier surface—particularly following the grueling 6.65 miles of dirt-road climbing you have just completed! May Canyon Truck Trail plunges 1,999 feet over the next 4.85 miles at an average grade of 7.8%. The many twists and turns will force some control of your speed, as well as the urge to pull your eyes off the road to enjoy the expansive view. Note that there are a few, short unpaved segments along the way.

About halfway down May Canyon, be sure to check your speed, as you will begin to encounter hikers and other trail users. My sense was that the canyon is a favorite of local residents—I even saw a couple parents pushing strollers up the steep climb! So resist the urge to go kamikaze on the downhill, retaining the truck trail as a pleasant and safe outing for all users. At the bottom of May Canyon, the road somewhat unceremoniously ends at a local residential street, Parkland Circle. Turn left here and continue to descend, followed by another left onto Simshaw Avenue. At the next intersection, turn left to continue on Simshaw, which skirts the edge of Veterans Memorial Park on your left and some residences on your right. The pavement ends at Raven Street; continue onto the dirt road, which effectively ends at the next street. From here, a few large rocks and a drop-off or two make this segment unrideable except for the most skilled mountain bikers. Once across Sayre Street, you're back on pavement. Keep straight on Simshaw to Hubbard Street; turn right here, continuing to descend. When El Cariso Community Regional Park appears on your left, carefully make the left turn into the park, opposite Garrick Street, to conclude the ride.

MILES AND DIRECTIONS

0.0 Start at El Cariso Community Regional Park. Exit the park, cross Hubbard Street, and continue onto Garrick Street.

0.55 Stop sign at Astoria Street; turn left.

0.8 Stop sign at Eldridge Street; turn right.

1.05 Stop sign at Polk Street; turn right.

1.2 Stop sign at Kinbrook Street; turn left.

1.65 Stop sign at Barner Avenue; turn left.

1.7 Stop at Olive View Drive; turn right.

2.5 Turn right onto Cobalt Street; enter Olive View–UCLA Medical Center campus.

2.75 End of Cobalt Street; continue onto trail and bear right, now on Wilson Canyon Truck Trail.

3.95 Bear right at junction to continue on Wilson Canyon Truck Trail.

7.75 Bear right at junction onto FR 3N17 (Santa Clara Truck Trail).

9.4 Turn right onto May Canyon Truck Trail (elevation 3,668 feet).

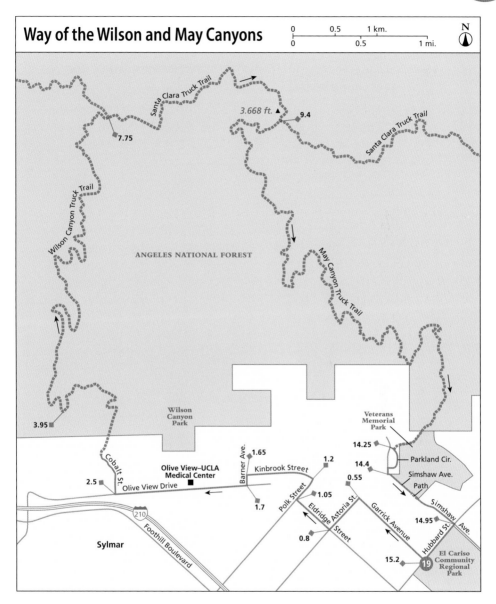

Way of the Wilson and May Canyons

14.25 End of May Canyon Truck Trail; navigate barrier and turn left onto Parkland Circle.

14.4 Turn left onto Simshaw Avenue.

14.45 Stop sign at Astoria Street; turn left to continue on Simshaw Avenue.

14.6 End pavement at Raven Street; keep straight.

14.65 Cross Sayre Street; keep straight on Simshaw Avenue.

14.95 Stop sign at Hubbard Street; turn right.

15.2 End ride at entrance to El Cariso Community Regional Park (at stop sign at Garrick Street).

Best Northeast L.A. Region Rides: San Gabriel Valley and Mountains

The San Gabriel Valley spans east–west to the north and east of Los Angeles, tucked in between the Puente Hills on the south and the massive San Gabriel Mountains on the north. Although the "lower" San Gabriel Valley stretches southward along the San Gabriel River corridor all the way to Long Beach, the true heart of the valley is in the north. The valley—the portion of it covered in this book—had a population of 1.35 million as of 2010, covering an area of 238 square miles. The five largest cities in the subregion include Alhambra, Baldwin Park, El Monte, Pasadena, and West Covina, with Pasadena (population 137,122 in 2010) being the largest. The valley has a rich early history of settlement by the Gabrielino-Tongva peoples, who greeted Spanish explorers during the late eighteenth century. Settlement by Spanish missionaries led to an overhaul of the region's culture and spawned the development of agriculture and, later, oil. A key battle in the Mexican-American War occurred here in 1847.

During the twentieth century, among the most significant events were the establishment of the California Institute of Technology and, later, the Jet Propulsion Laboratory in Pasadena; the building of the nation's first freeway (the Arroyo Seco), also in Pasadena; and the internment of Japanese-Americans at Santa Anita Park during World War II, with up to 17,000 living in horse stables. Yet perhaps the most significant occurrence in the valley has been its settlement by an extremely diverse array of peoples, including Armenians, Chinese, Filipinos, Japanese, Mexicans, Taiwanese, and Vietnamese, among others. In fact, some of the largest Chinese-American communities in the United States are found in several San Gabriel Valley cities. Wealth is evident on the fringes of the valley; the foothills of the San Gabriel Mountains, along with the Puente Hills, feature numerous upscale residences.

The book features five road and six mountain rides in this subregion. The road rides range in length from just 9.4 miles to 39.4 miles; the mountain bike rides range from a quick 3.65 miles to 24.7 miles, the longest (and highest) off-road ride in this book. All the rides feature some climbing, with the lowest elevation change being 617 feet, in the Emerald Necklace Cruise. The Mounts Lowe and Wilson Expedition could have you on your bike for up to 8 hours, making this ride a truly memorable epic.

Ahwingna Pahe Mahar

Start: Orange Grove Park, 14517 Orange Grove Ave., Hacienda Heights

Length: 3.65 miles (counterclockwise loop with short out-and-back segment)

Riding time: 25 to 90 minutes (my time: 37:37)

Terrain and surface: 100% off-road, on dirt and gravel trails

Elevation: Low: 535 feet at the trailhead adjacent Orange Grove Park; high: 1,176 feet at the junction between Seventh Street Loop Trail and Ahwingna Trail

Traffic and hazards: No motor vehicles (100% of the ride is off-road)

Map: *The Thomas Guide—Street Guide: Los Angeles and Orange Counties* (any recent year), page 678

Getting there: By car—From central Los Angeles, head either east on I-10 or south on US 101 to SR 60 eastbound. Exit at Seventh Avenue in Hacienda Heights and turn right. Turn right onto Orange Grove Avenue. Toward the end of the street, turn right to enter Orange Grove Park.

   By public transit—From central Los Angeles, ride the Metro Silver Line (light rail transit)—not the "Silver Streak," which is a commuter rail—to the El Monte Station. Transfer to Foothill Transit bus route 282, traveling toward Hacienda Heights and Puente Hills. The bus runs every 30 to 60 minutes, everyday. Exit at 7th Avenue and Gale Avenue in Hacienda Heights. From here, ride southward on Seventh Avenue. Turn right onto Orange Grove Avenue, as above. Enter Orange Grove Park toward the end of the street.

Starting point coordinates: N34.011422° / W117.998106°

THE RIDE

Ahwingna Pahe Mahar, loosely translated from the Gabrielino-Tongva language, means "Ahwingna Three Five." The title is a reference to the Ahwingna Trail, which in turn is a reference to the ancient Ahwingna village and the length of the ride—"three five," or 3.5 (although the actual length of the ride is 3.65 miles). The ride is a nifty and short but challenging mountain bike ride in the Puente Hills east of Los Angeles. The ride is a great beginner course, while offering enough of a challenge for the expert.

There is archaeological evidence of several Gabrielino-Tongva village sites in the Puente Hills region. One of the villages was named Ahwingna and was located in the vicinity of this ride, although the village of Ajaarvongna may actually have been closer to the route. The staging area for the ride is Orange Grove Park, which was only a few months old as of this writing. The park was too new to be found on maps or even Google Earth! The park and route are located in Hacienda Heights, an unincorporated area sandwiched between the cities of Industry to the north and Whittier and La Habra Heights to the south. The community had a population of 54,038 in 2010. With its stately hillside residences, Hacienda Heights was home to a few notables, including pop superstar Fergie, Olympic gold-medalist swimmer Jill Sterkel, and a number of professional athletes in various sports.

A well-equipped rider stops to check out an ant colony.

Juan Bautista de Anza

The Juan Bautista de Anza National Historic Trail stretches for some 1,210 miles from Nogales, Arizona (at the Mexican border), to San Francisco, California. The trail heads westward from Arizona to Southern California before turning northward toward the Bay Area. De Anza effectively made the trip twice: once in 1774 on an exploratory mission accompanied by 34 padres, servants, and soldiers and 240 cattle, horses, and mules. He then returned to Arizona and between 1775 and 1776 led 240 friars, soldiers, and colonists, with their families, along with 1,080 bulls, cows, horses, and mules. De Anza's efforts led to the settlement of Los Angeles and the establishment of the Presidio and Mission Dolores in present-day San Francisco, as well as a settlement that was the beginning of that great city. De Anza's route was established as the Anza Trail and was used as a regular passage for travel between Mexico, Arizona, and California.

Travelers encountered several hardships along the Anza Trail, including portions of the Sonoran and Mojave Deserts, nearly impassable natural formations such as the Algodones Dunes in southeastern California, and the Colorado River (for which there were few crossings in that day), as well as occasional hostilities from Native American tribes. A few massacres on both sides led to intervention from the Spanish government, which officially "closed" the Anza Trail for a while.

Today's historically commemorative trail was established in 1990. The trail continues to be improved and marked so that modern-day explorers can follow the path. The Ahwingna Pahe Mahar ride covers merely 0.5 mile, or 0.04%, of the 1,210-mile trail, leaving so much more to explore!

The trail's namesake, Juan Bautista de Anza, was born in what is now Mexico (Sonora) in 1736. While it was under Spanish rule, he later became governor of New Mexico. As a captain in the "new Spanish" army, he engaged in hostilities with Native American tribes in Arizona, for which an ancillary outcome was exploration of that region. It was under the approval of Spanish authorities that he began his expeditions; one purpose of these efforts was to facilitate the colonization of "Alta" (upper) California. De Anza passed away in 1788, just one year after completing his term as governor of New Mexico.

Start the ride just beyond the gate at the trailhead at the end of Orange Grove Avenue. The narrow gate intentionally prohibits easy and illicit access and may be a tight squeeze for wide handlebars. Once beyond the gate, turn left and head up the incline on the Seventh Street Loop trail. There is a garden to your right. After 0.25 mile of gradual climbing, bear right as you near the wooded canyon onto Native Oak Trail. There is an information signboard here. The trail quickly narrows and starts to ascend via switchbacks. The average grade along here is 8.5%. Once past the Puma Trail junction, continue to ascend on Native Oak. As suggested by the trail name, coastal live oak trees are plentiful along the hillsides. After climbing at an average grade of 7.3% over the next 1.1 miles, Native Oak Trail crests at the upper junction with Puma Trail. After a short descent, Native Oak Trail merges with Schabarum Trail. This trail—another segment of which is used in the Schabarum Scramble—is part of the Juan Bautista de Anza National Historic Trail (see sidebar).

After riding the false flats of Schabarum Trail along a wide crest (Skyline Fire Road runs parallel to Schabarum, on your right), bear left onto Ahwingna Trail. This is the high point of the ride (1,174 feet). The trail gradually descends from here as it scoots along the ridge. At the junction with Native Oak Trail, bear left. Native Oak descends rapidly from here in a series of switchbacks. When I rode this, the trail was eroded in spots, making this a "technical" descent.

The trail descends just under 300 feet in just over 0.5 mile at an average grade of 10.5%. Once the trail leaves the switchbacks, it curves to the right to race through a wooded canyon. The continuous shade is rare for a trail in this region, so enjoy it! This stretch does not last long, however—just over 0.25 mile—before leaving the canyon and returning to the Seventh Street Loop trail junction. Keep straight here (Native Oak Trail continues to your left; this is where you started to climb earlier). Follow the Seventh Street Loop as it descends to the Orange Grove Avenue trailhead, where the ride ends (although ambitious riders might want to do another lap).

MILES AND DIRECTIONS

0.0 Start at the gate at the end of Orange Grove Avenue, adjacent to Orange Grove Park. Turn left onto the Seventh Street Loop trail (dirt path).

0.25 Bear right onto Native Oak Trail; begin climb on switchbacks.

0.45 Keep straight at junction with Puma Trail (remain on Native Oak).

1.55 Keep straight at upper junction with Puma Trail (remain on Native Oak).

1.6 Junction with Schabarum Trail (Juan Bautista de Anza National Historic Trail); bear left.

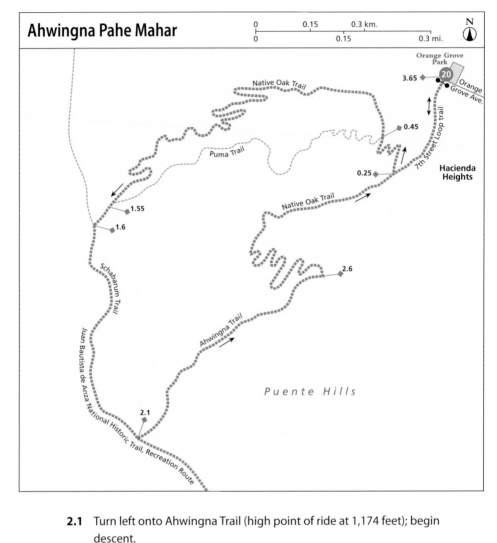

Ahwingna Pahe Mahar

2.1 Turn left onto Ahwingna Trail (high point of ride at 1,174 feet); begin descent.

2.6 Bear left at junction onto Native Oak Trail.

3.4 Exit canyon and keep straight at junction, now on Seventh Street Loop trail (Native Oak Trail turns to the left).

3.65 End ride at Orange Grove Avenue trailhead.

Azusadora 39 Classic

Start: Pioneer Park, 1360 North Dalton Ave., Azusa

Length: 32.7 miles (clockwise loop)

Riding time: 2 to 6 hours (my time: 2H43:34)

Terrain and surface: 100% on paved roads

Elevation: Low: 696 feet at the corner of Sierra Madre Avenue and San Gabriel Canyon Road in Azusa; high: 3,449 feet along Glendora Mountain Road west of Glendora Ridge Road

Traffic and hazards: SR 39 was carrying 2,320 vehicles per day at the San Gabriel River Bridge in northern Azusa in 2013.

Map: *The Thomas Guide—Street Guide: Los Angeles and Orange Counties* (any recent year), page 568

Getting there: By car—From central Los Angeles, take I-10 East to I-605 North and then I-210 East; exit at Azusa Avenue. Turn left and head north to Sierra Madre Avenue. Turn right and go 1 block to Dalton Avenue and turn right; Pioneer Park will be on the left. Park on the street next to the park.

By public transit—From central Los Angeles, ride the Metro Gold Line (light rail transit) to the Downtown Azusa station (Gold Line extension from Pasadena scheduled to be completed in 2016). Head north on Azusa Avenue to Sierra Madre Avenue. Turn right and go 1 block to Dalton Avenue and Pioneer Park.

Starting point coordinates: N34.146742° / W117.905208°

THE RIDE

The Azusadora 39 Classic is an adventurous 32.7-mile road ride that starts and ends in the mountainside suburb of Azusa. The ride travels up San Gabriel Canyon along SR 39, turns to head eastward along the east fork of the river, climbs to Glendora Ridge, and then descends into the city of Glendora before turning to head west for the return trip to Azusa. You are bound to see other cyclists out there; this is a popular route. The title is a play on words, combining

Two cyclists practice a little cat-and-mouse on a climb on Sierra Madre Road in Glendora.

the cities of Azusa and Glendora, through which the route passes, and SR 39, used by just over 30% of the ride.

Start from the intersection of Dalton and Sierra Madre Avenues in Azusa, immediately adjacent to Pioneer Park. Located along a row of cities that hug the San Gabriel Mountains, Azusa had a population of 47,047 in 2012. Contrary to popular belief, Azusa is not short for "everything from A to Z in the USA." Rather, the city's name was derived from the Gabrielino-Tongva place name "Asuksagna." Azusa is home to Azusa Pacific University, a private Christian institution (established in 1899; about 6,500 students). Native "Azusans" have included Rocky Dennis (subject of the film *Mask*, who passed away in his teens from an extremely rare disorder), life coach and author Anthony Robbins, and 1980s women's middle-distance track star Ruth Wysocki.

Carefully make the left turn from Dalton onto Sierra Madre Avenue and head west. Turn right at San Gabriel Canyon Road (SR 39) and start the roughly 10-mile trek up the canyon. At the 1.0-mile mark, where the road is curving to the right, the San Gabriel River Bikeway merges from the left, running parallel to the road. Feel free to cross the road when it is safe and ride on the bikeway.

Best Bike Rides Los Angeles

Alternatively, keep riding in the road (since the bikeway ends after about 0.5 mile). You may have noticed signs near the mouth of the canyon announcing that SR 39 is not a through route to SR 2. (The history behind this disconnected highway is presented in the accompanying sidebar.)

Leave Azusa at the 1.95-mile mark, crossing over the San Gabriel River and entering Angeles National Forest. Over the next 6.0 miles, SR 39 climbs from 839 feet to 1,490 feet at a varying grade that is never particularly steep. The highway passes two bodies of water—first Morris Reservoir and then San Gabriel Reservoir. One reason you do not see water raging in the San Gabriel River is because it is caught in reservoirs such as these and is diverted by other facilities to ensure flood control, hydroelectric power, and water supply.

Turn right onto East Fork Road near the northern end of San Gabriel Reservoir. You are at mile 10.0 of the ride. East Fork literally parallels the east fork of the San Gabriel River. The road climbs gradually through the canyon. Stay right at the fork with Shoemaker Canyon Road, remaining on East Fork Road (at mile 12.5). Shoemaker Canyon continues up the adjacent canyon, passing through a couple of tunnels but leading to nowhere in particular. The road was originally intended to be an evacuation route during nuclear warfare, but the need for it subsided with the end of the Cold War and subsequent treaties.

What Happened to State Highway 39?

North of San Gabriel Reservoir and East Fork Road (where the Azusadora 39 Classic takes a right turn), SR 39 continues north. After 11.3 miles Crystal Lake Road turns off to access the Crystal Lake Recreation Area. SR 39 continues for another 1.8 miles before coming to a locked gate. What happened to the rest of the highway?

The 4.5 miles between the gate and SR 2, the Angeles Crest Highway, have been closed since 1978. A massive rock slide—the Snow Springs slide—damaged the highway and its drainage systems, forcing the highway's closure. Further slides occurred during the winter of 1997–98, although the highway was still closed at that time. Fires and storm damage in the early 2000s led to the closed segment of the highway being declared a state and federal disaster area.

Despite the challenges, the California Department of Transportation has continued to work toward getting the highway reopened. Although the highway has been referred to as "cliff-hanging," as of this writing the plan was for that 4.5-mile segment to reopen in 2015— barring further intervention from Mother Nature. And despite nature's hostilities, the 21.3-mile portion of SR 39 that is open in San Gabriel Canyon is an official State Scenic Highway.

At mile 14.3 East Fork splits, with an access road to Camp Bonita on the left and Glendora Mountain Road to the right. Although Camp Bonita might seem inviting as you peer up at Glendora Mountain Road, turn right and begin the climb. The elevation here is 1,863 feet; the road climbs to 3,316 feet over the next 4.9 miles (average grade of 5.6%). It is a steady grind with no shade, so be prepared to work hard.

The reward comes at the top—well, not quite. At the T intersection with Glendora Ridge Road (which leads to Mount Baldy Village), turn right to remain on Glendora Mountain Road. The crest comes after climbing another 133 feet over the next 0.4 mile (6.3% grade) to the ride's high mark of 3,449 feet. From here it is an exhilarating descent down the mountain. (In Glendora Ridge Stage, you ride up this.) If you have completed that ride, this is payback time! Over the next 9.2 miles, Glendora Mountain Road plummets to 1,007 feet at Sierra Madre Avenue—a 2,442-foot drop at an average grade of 5.0%.

> ## Bike Shops
>
> **Covina Valley Cyclery,** 203 South Citrus Ave., Covina; (626) 332-5200; www.covina valleycyclery.com
> **Irwindale Cycles,** 15708 Arrow Hwy., Irwindale; (626) 814-9437

Turn right onto Sierra Madre Avenue and head west. This moderately busy road travels through residential areas along the "upland" side of the cities of Glendora and Azusa. Sierra Madre undulates, with one short but steep climb; the net elevation change, however, is negative (that is, the road is primarily downhill). Although you may be keeping your eyes on the road, there are some excellent vistas of the San Gabriel Valley to your left. After reentering Azusa, Sierra Madre negotiates a couple of traffic circles. Watch for traffic entering and exiting these circles, while being sure to remain on Sierra Madre. Squeeze the brakes when you see Pioneer Park on your left; turn left onto Dalton Avenue to end the ride.

MILES AND DIRECTIONS

0.0 Start from the intersection of Dalton and Sierra Madre Avenues at Pioneer Park. Turn left from Dalton Avenue onto Sierra Madre Avenue.

0.15 Traffic signal at San Gabriel Canyon Road (SR 39); turn right.

1.2 San Gabriel River Bikeway (paved path) merges from the left to parallel the highway.

Azusadora 39 Classic

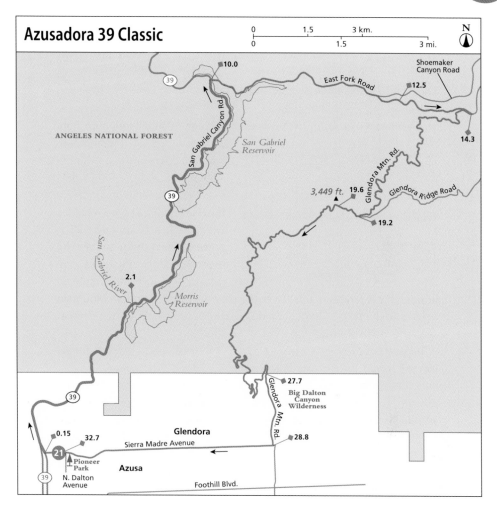

2.1 Cross over San Gabriel River on bridge; leave Azusa and enter Angeles National Forest.

10.0 Turn right onto East Fork Road.

12.5 Stay to the right at Shoemaker Canyon Road; stay on East Fork Road.

14.3 Make a sharp right onto Glendora Mountain Road; begin steep climb.

19.2 Turn right to remain on Glendora Mountain Road (Glendora Ridge Road is to the left).

19.6 High point of ride (3,449 feet); begin descent.

27.7 Leave Angeles National Forest; enter Glendora.

28.8 Traffic signal at Sierra Madre Avenue; turn right.

31.7 Leave Glendora; enter Azusa.

31.8 Traffic circle at MacNeil Drive; continue on Sierra Madre Avenue.

32.55 Traffic circle at Vosburg Drive; continue on Sierra Madre Avenue.

32.7 End ride at Dalton Avenue; turn left to return to Pioneer Park.

Emerald Necklace Cruise

Start: Whittier Narrows Recreation Area (northwest region, off Rosemead Boulevard north of SR 60)

Length: 35.5 miles (figure 8—two connected clockwise and counterclockwise loops)

Riding time: 1.75 to 5 hours (my time: 2H11:10)

Terrain and surface: 70% on paved bicycle paths; 30% on paved roads

Elevation: Low: 210 feet at San Gabriel and Rosemead Boulevards (SR 19); high: 827 feet at end of San Gabriel River Bikeway in Azusa

Traffic and hazards: California Avenue carried 8,595 vehicles per day through Mayflower Village in 2012.

Map: *The Thomas Guide—Street Guide: Los Angeles and Orange Counties* (any recent year), page 636

Getting there: By car—From central Los Angeles, take I-10 East or US 101 South to SR 60 East. Exit at Rosemead Boulevard (SR 19) and turn left. Look for the entrance to Whittier Narrows Recreation Area on the left. Enter the park and find parking.

    By public transit—From central Los Angeles, ride Metro bus route 70 to Rosemead Boulevard in El Monte. Transfer to Metro bus route 266. Exit at Whittier Narrows Recreation Area and enter the park (to your right). Turn right and follow the park road (Cortez Drive) to the "back side" of the park (Loma Avenue), where the ride begins. Route 70 runs every 10 to 20 minutes daily; route 266 runs every 30 to 45 minutes daily.

Starting point coordinates: N34.050664° / W118.068719°

THE RIDE

The ride title, "Emerald Necklace Cruise," may conjure up images of a Frederick Law Olmsted landscape of greenery and bodies of water, all connected by a parkway. This, however, is the L.A. version: There is some greenery, the bodies of water are generally either shallow or dry, and the parkway is actually a series of bicycle paths. An emerald necklace does indeed exist—it's the name given to the path that connects a series of parks that follow the Rio Hondo and San Gabriel Rivers in the San Gabriel Valley. Seventy percent of the ride is on exclusive bicycle paths. Extension of the paths to complete the emerald necklace sometime in the future (unknown date as of this writing) may increase the proportion of the ride that is on paths. In making its way toward the San Gabriel Mountains and then back, this ride visits nine San Gabriel Valley communities: Arcadia, Azusa, Duarte, El Monte, Irwindale, Mayflower Village, Monrovia, Pico Rivera, and South El Monte.

Start the ride on the western, "back," side of Whittier Narrows Recreation Area in South El Monte. This large county recreation park (1,492 acres) spans several major streets and even two cities (South El Monte and Pico Rivera). The park bridges the space between the Rio Hondo and San Gabriel Rivers, both of which are controlled on the south end of the park by the Whittier Narrows Dam (see "Vuelta Tres Rios de Los Angeles"). The ride starts on the side entered from Rosemead Avenue (SR 19) north of SR 60. Ride along Cortez Drive (park road) toward the west side of the park and turn right onto Loma Avenue. At Rush Street, just 1 block up, turn left and ride along the connector path. Turn left at the Rio Hondo Bikeway. You will spend the opening 19.75 miles of the ride on exclusive bicycle paths, save a short segment within the Santa Fe Dam Recreation Area. After just under 1 mile, turn right and follow the bikeway as it swoops under SR 60. After a segment through some surprisingly lush vegetation, the path comes to an end at San Gabriel Boulevard. This is the most awkward part of the route—continue along San Gabriel to Rosemead Boulevard. Your target is the diagonally opposite corner, so you will need to cross both streets.

Once across Rosemead and San Gabriel, the low elevation of the ride (210 feet), continue along the bike path, which is also referred to as Siphon Road. After a straight stretch of 0.7 mile, the San Gabriel River Bikeway enters from the right. By keeping straight, you are now on the San Gabriel River Bikeway. The path makes a sharp left at mile 2.95 and heads north-northeast, running parallel to the San Gabriel River. From here the bikeway climbs in stair-step fashion toward the San Gabriel Mountains. Any climbing is imperceptible between the stair steps, which tend to occur at changes in the river's elevation and at underpasses. The bikeway nimbly passes under I-10 and I-605. Listen to all that traffic as you peacefully cruise past. The bikeway crosses the Arrow Highway at grade in Irwindale at mile 11.2. Irwindale is one of the L.A. region's smaller cities (population 1,412 in 2010), with the majority of the city's land being devoted to quarry operations and sites. Some of the quarries were not in use as of this writing and had been considered for other uses. The Huy Fong Foods sriracha sauce plant

Cyclists—no helmets, guys?—cruise along the Siphon Road connector path in Pico Rivera.

relocated to Irwindale in 2010, agitating local residents with its odors. (Sriracha sauce is made with jalapeño peppers and garlic, which generate the smells.)

After carefully crossing Arrow Highway (use the on-demand signal), the bikeway curves to the left, passes through a gate, and then begins a climb to the crest of Santa Fe Dam. There is one switchback as you make your way up. The path climbs 72 feet in 0.25 mile (5.5% grade). Once atop the dam, the San Gabriel River Bikeway makes a long, sweeping curve to the left, continuing for over 2 miles to the end of the dam and the entrance to the Santa Fe Dam Recreation Area. The dam is actually about 4 miles long and 92 feet high. Completed in 1949, the dam is one of the largest by volume in the United States. Its primary function is flood control. After crossing a recreation area entry road, the bikeway continues for another 0.5 mile. The path ends with an abrupt turn to the left; from here the bike route continues on park roads. Follow the signs as you keep straight for a stretch, then turn right, and then left. After veering left at a fork, the San Gabriel River Bikeway resumes after a turn to the right at mile 14.7. This portion of the path can be referred to as the "Upper" San Gabriel River Bikeway.

US Route 66

In the days prior to the interstate system, US Route 66 was the primary highway between Chicago and Los Angeles. During the Dust Bowl of the 1930s, numerous travelers migrated from the Midwest to the West in search of work and a better life. Route 66 was the main drag at that time, taking migrants through Oklahoma, Texas, New Mexico, and Arizona and across California. The route, which officially ended in Santa Monica, was famously depicted in John Ford's film *The Grapes of Wrath*. A total of 314 of the route's 2,448 miles were in California, where it was known as the National Old Trails Road and then later as the Will Rogers Highway.

After crossing the Mojave Desert in California and descending Cajon Pass, Route 66 entered San Bernardino. The prospect of business along the highway spurred the development of numerous roadside attractions, lodging facilities, and eateries, including the world's very first McDonald's restaurant (in San Bernardino). From there Route 66 headed westward, generally along the base of the San Gabriel Mountains, before entering San Gabriel Valley and Los Angeles and then continuing toward Santa Monica. It was the first US highway to be fully paved, in 1938.

Like many US highways, Route 66 lost its importance with the construction of the interstate system. Although much of the original US highway system remains, Route 66 was actually removed from the system in 1985. Preservation efforts continue to be made to recapture the highway's lore, including route signs, museums, and designations of portions (not all of it) as a National Scenic Byway. The 2.5-mile segment of the Emerald Necklace Cruise along Foothill Boulevard and Huntington Drive in Azusa and Duarte represents just 0.1% of the entire historic route—just long enough to get your kicks on Route 66!

After an interesting segment in which the bikeway undulates and winds its way across the Santa Fe Dam area's landscape, the path returns to the San Gabriel River. The bikeway continues to climb in stair-step fashion, particularly after passing under I-210. The San Gabriel Mountains and San Gabriel Canyon loom ahead. You will see residences of the city of Duarte off to your left and of the city of Azusa off to your right, along with some industrial works closer to the path. At the 18.8-mile mark, the bikeway moves immediately adjacent to SR 39 in San Gabriel Canyon. Stay on the bikeway and continue to its end. (The path literally comes to an abrupt end, to the north of Rock Springs Way.) Turn around here (this is the high point of the ride, at 827 feet) and return along the path as far as Rock Springs. At this point, enter the road and ride along the shoulder. The low-volume highway is generally downhill. At mile 20.25, SR 39 veers away from the bikeway to the left, leaving San Gabriel Canyon and entering a residential area of Azusa (for more information see Azusadora 39 Classic). After a brisk, gradually downhill stretch, turn right onto Sierra Madre Avenue. Turn left onto Todd Avenue as you continue heading south through Azusa.

Turn right onto Foothill Boulevard—this is part of Historic US 66 (see sidebar). At mile 24.0 Foothill crosses over the San Gabriel River and the San Gabriel River Bikeway, where you were just riding awhile ago. Those of you with time travel skills might be able to catch yourself riding below as you cross over above! Just beyond the river (which, as mentioned elsewhere, is generally dry except after storms), Foothill becomes Huntington Drive as you enter the city of Duarte (see White Saddle Challenge for more information). Somehow Huntington sounds more sophisticated than Foothill, in keeping with the somewhat highbrow air of Duarte. Turn left onto Highland Avenue and head south. After passing under I-210 and continuing for a short stretch, turn right onto Duarte Avenue and head west. You may see a Metrolink train racing along immediately to your right. Soon after entering the city of Monrovia, turn left onto California Avenue and head south. California leaves Monrovia and straddles the line between Duarte and the unincorporated community of Mayflower Village. Carefully turn left onto Myrtle Avenue at the end of California and continue heading south.

Once across Live Oak Avenue, Myrtle becomes Peck Road. In swift succession, the road enters and leaves Irwindale, Monrovia, and Arcadia before finally entering the city of El Monte. The city name means "the mountain," although there is no mountain within the city boundaries. Perhaps the reference is to the San Gabriel Mountains in the distance? The city had a population of 113,475 in 2010. The city has had a storied past that belies its relatively passive appearance. During the nineteenth century, El Monte was nicknamed "The End of the Santa Fe Trail," with the settlement serving as a turning point for travelers coming from the east via that trail. It was also a launching point for forty-niners heading for the gold fields of Northern California. In the 1950s El Monte served as the birthplace of TV variety shows, as well as a center of development of rock and roll music. Legendary country musician Cliffie Stone's show *Hometown Jamboree* was broadcast from El Monte. Later, numerous major rock and roll artists performed in El Monte, in part because of a lukewarm reception in Los Angeles to "the devil's music." Ritchie Valens, Johnny Otis, Dick Dale, and host Dick Clark all appeared at the city's Legion Stadium. Think of a rockin' beat as you pedal along the Rio Hondo Bikeway through El Monte.

After riding under the El Monte Busway (bus-only access to I-10) and then I-10 (a long, dark underpass), continue southward into South El Monte. This satellite of El Monte's (population 20,116 in 2010) claim to fame is where you are heading: Whittier Narrows Recreation Area. Look for the connector path to Rush Street and Whittier Narrows; turn left to leave the bikeway here. At Loma Avenue turn right to enter the park. The ride ends at Cortez Drive. ***Note:*** There is a BMX facility just down the road (Loma Avenue) on the right.

MILES AND DIRECTIONS

0.0 Start from Cortez Road and head north on Loma Avenue in Whittier Dam Recreation Area in South El Monte.

0.1 Turn left onto Rush Street (pedestrian-bicycle path).

0.25 Turn left onto Rio Hondo Bikeway.

0.95 Turn right to continue on Rio Hondo.

1.05 Pass under SR 60.

1.95 End of path at San Gabriel Boulevard; continue along San Gabriel.

2.1 Traffic signal at Rosemead Boulevard; cross Rosemead and then San Gabriel; continue along bike path once across both streets.

2.2 Continue through, bearing slightly right to continue on bike path (aka Siphon Road).

2.9 Keep straight at junction, now on San Gabriel River Bikeway.

2.95 Bikeway curves to the left, now heading north-northeast.

4.45 Pass under SR 60.

7.15 Pass under I-10.

10.0 Pass under I-605.

11.2 Cross Arrow Highway at grade; once across, path curves to the left.

11.5 Path curves sharply to the right in climbing Santa Fe Dam.

11.8 Crest of dam climb; you're now on the crest of the dam.

13.7 Path crosses Santa Fe Dam Recreation Area entrance road.

14.2 End of path; keep straight on park road (follow Bicycle Route signs).

14.6 Turn left to continue on bicycle route on park road.

14.65 Bear left at fork to continue on bicycle route on park road.

14.7 Turn right onto San Gabriel River Bikeway (continuation of bike path).

15.7 Pass under I-210.

18.8 San Gabriel River Bikeway is now immediately adjacent to SR 39.

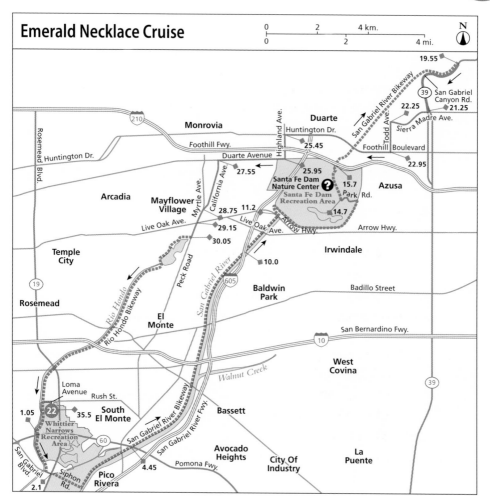

Emerald Necklace Cruise

0   2   4 km.
0   2   4 mi.

N

19.55 End of bikeway; turn around here and return on bike path.

19.75 Leave bike path at Roc Springs Way and enter SR 39 (ride along shoulder).

21.25 Traffic signal at Sierra Madre Avenue; turn right.

22.25 Stop sign at Todd Avenue; turn left.

22.95 Traffic signal at Foothill Boulevard (Historic US 66); turn right.

24.0 Cross over San Gabriel River and San Gabriel River Bikeway.

24.1 Enter Duarte, now on Huntington Drive.

25.45 Traffic signal at Highland Avenue; turn left.

25.7 Pass under I-210.

25.95 Traffic signal at Duarte Avenue; turn right.

27.55 Traffic signal at California Avenue; turn left.

28.75 Stop sign at Myrtle Avenue; turn left.

29.15 Traffic signal at Live Oak Avenue; keep straight, now on Peck Road.

30.05 Turn right to enter Peck Road Park.

30.15 Bear left onto Rio Hondo Bikeway (beginning of bike path).

33.2 Pass under I-10.

35.3 Leave Rio Hondo Bikeway; turn right onto Rush Street path (to Whittier Narrows Recreation Area).

35.45 Turn right onto Loma Avenue.

35.5 End ride at Cortez Drive. Turn left to enter Whittier Narrows Recreation Area and parking.

Glendora Mountain Trails Traverse

Start: Big Dalton Wilderness Park (also known as Glendora Wilderness Park), 2041 Big Dalton Canyon Rd., Glendora (Wren-Meacham/Upper Mystic Canyon trailhead on Big Dalton Canyon Road)

Length: 6.3 miles (clockwise loop)

Riding time: 1 to 3 hours (my time: 1H17:08)

Terrain and surface: 66% dirt trails; 34% paved roads

Elevation: Low: 994 feet at the Palm Drive trailhead at Loraine Avenue; high: 1,918 feet at the junction between Lower Monroe Truck Trail and Upper Mystic Canyon Trail

Traffic and hazards: Glendora Mountain Road was carrying 1,450 vehicles per day north of Sierra Madre Avenue.

Map: *The Thomas Guide—Street Guide: Los Angeles and Orange Counties* (any recent year), page 569

Getting there: By car—From central Los Angeles, take I-10 East to I-605 North to I-210 East. Exit at Lone Hill Avenue and turn left. Head north to Foothill Boulevard and turn left. Head west to Valley Center Avenue and turn right. Valley Center curves to the left, becoming Sierra Madre Avenue. Turn right onto Glendora Mountain Road. Climb to Big Dalton Canyon Road and turn right. Park at the Wren-Meacham/Upper Mystic Canyon trailhead (off-road, unpaved parking area).

By public transit—From central Los Angeles, ride Foothill Transit's Silver Streak (bus line) to the Eastland Center station in West Covina. Transfer to Foothill Transit bus route 851 to Sierra Madre Avenue and Glendora Mountain Road. Head north on Glendora Mountain to the starting point of the ride. **Note:** Bus route 851 runs only during the morning and evening commute periods on weekdays. Transit service should improve with the completion of the extension of the Metro Gold Line (light-rail transit).

Starting point coordinates: N34.158569° / W117.828517°

THE RIDE

The Glendora Mountain Trails Traverse takes advantage of the city of Glendora's short but nifty trails system, making a clockwise loop on a mixture of dirt trails and paved roads. This was the only ride in the book I was unable to complete, because the Colby Trail was closed when I visited during summer 2014. The trail was closed because of the January 2014 Colby Fire, which burned nearly 2,000 acres in the area. The fire, started by three men who lost control of their campfire, destroyed five houses, injured one person, and led to the evacuation of 3,600 residents. The timber and brush had not burned since the 1960s and was ripe for kindling. Regarding the ride, I skipped the Colby Trail and Glendora Mountain Road segments, replacing them with an out-and-back ride on the roads leading to the Colby Trail and an approach to the Lower

An off-road enthusiast looks for a line and shoots the gap on the Lower Monroe Truck Trail.

Monroe Motorway from its east side (rather than its west side). This made my version about 0.3 mile longer than the described route. In any case, this is a good ride for a novice mountain biker, although the downhill may require a dismount (and would thus be suitable for an expert rider). The description presumes that the Colby Trail will have reopened by the time you get out here.

Start the ride at the Wren-Meacham/Upper Mystic Canyon trailhead, located along Big Dalton Canyon Road in Glendora, 0.5 mile east of Glendora Mountain Road. Head west on Big Dalton Canyon Road. This road zips past the lower reaches of Big Dalton Canyon Wilderness Park, on your left and right, as well as the Big Dalton Debris Dam, on the left. Turn left onto Glendora Mountain Road and head downhill. (This road is used in both the Glendora Ridge Stage and Azusadora 39 Classic rides.) After a short descent, turn right onto Palm Drive and head into a typical Glendora neighborhood. Glendora, with a population of 50,073 in 2010, is one of the San Gabriel Valley's many affluent mountainside communities. A diverse set of notables have called Glendora home, including Van Halen bassist Michael Anthony, Olympic decathlon champion Bryan Clay, Motley Crue singer Vince Neil, In-N-Out Burger founders Harry and Esther Snyder, and seminal surf-rock band The Surfaris.

At the end of Palm Drive, keep straight onto the short but useful Palm Drive Trail. After a couple of undulations and a tight squeeze past a residence, the trail ends at Loraine Avenue. Turn right here and climb through the neighborhood. At the end of Loraine, keep straight onto Colby Truck Trail. This trail was closed as of this writing, a result of damage from the Colby Fire. After climbing 537 feet in 0.7 mile (14.7% grade), the trail ends at Glendora Mountain Road. Turn right and head downhill for the next 0.7 mile. Where Glendora Mountain makes a sharp hairpin turn to the right, look to the

Bike Shop

Bicycle Central, 942 South Grand Ave., Glendora; (626) 963-2312; www.thebicyclecentral.com

left for the Lower Monroe Truck Trail. Leave the road here, negotiate the gate, and head north on Lower Monroe. Why this is a truck trail is unknown, as the trail is quite narrow, ranging from double- to singletrack. No room for a truck! Over the first 0.9 mile the trail twists and turns over a frequently rocky surface. Some portions may be technically challenging for beginner riders. The surface changes drastically where Lower Monroe makes a sharp bend to the right. The surface becomes a smoother dirt with few rocks, narrow in places and steeper than the lower segment. The trail climbs 342 feet over the next 1.5 miles at an average grade of 4.3%. The drop-off to the right is quite dramatic in spots—those of you with a fear of heights should keep your eyes on the trail! The vegetation along the trail tends to be thick if not dry, thereby obscuring the

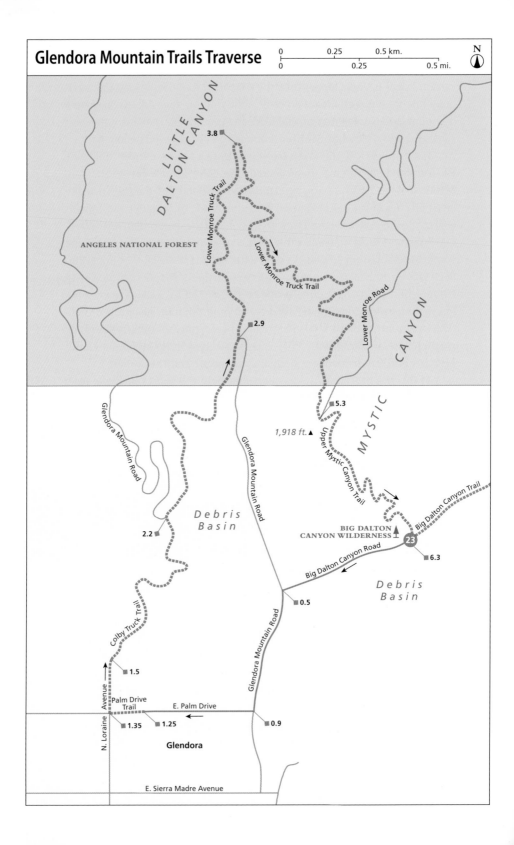

steep slope to your right. There is a variety of plant life, but coastal sage scrub, chaparral, and southern oak are the most abundant.

As Lower Monroe Truck Trail rounds a left-hand bend, look for the marker for Upper Mystic Canyon Trail. Turn right here and then make an immediate left onto Upper Mystic Canyon. (Missing the left puts you on Poop-Out Trail, which is a shortcut back to Big Dalton Canyon but is actually too steep for riding.) Upper Mystic Canyon is a narrow trail, slightly wider than singletrack, which twists and works its way down the canyon. There are several switchbacks, as well as a few rocky segments and even some deep dirt. Skillful riders might use the deep, loose dirt to slow their descending speed. However, many riders may feel more comfortable dismounting. The trail drops from 1,918 feet at the Lower Monroe junction to 1,206 feet at Big Dalton Canyon Road (end of the trail), for an average grade of 13.5% over just 1 mile. Do not be too proud to walk, and be alert to other trail users—these segments are popular. Continue heading downhill at the Big Dalton Canyon Trail junction, which comes just before the end of Upper Mystic Canyon Trail at Big Dalton Canyon Road. The trailhead and parking area where the ride started are right across the street.

MILES AND DIRECTIONS

0.0 Start on Big Dalton Canyon Road and head west from the Wren-Meacham/Upper Mystic Canyon trailhead.

0.5 Stop sign at Glendora Mountain Road; turn left.

0.9 Turn right onto Palm Drive.

1.25 End of Palm Drive; keep straight onto Palm Drive Trail.

1.35 End of Palm Drive Trail; turn right onto Loraine Avenue.

1.5 End of Loraine Avenue; keep straight onto Colby Truck Trail.

2.2 End of Colby Truck Trail; bear right onto Glendora Mountain Road.

2.9 Leave Glendora Mountain Road at hairpin turn; bear left onto Lower Monroe Truck Trail.

3.8 Hairpin turn in Lower Monroe Truck Trail.

5.3 Leave Lower Monroe Truck Trail, turning right onto Upper Mystic Canyon Trail; high point of ride (1,918 feet).

6.2 Junction with Big Dalton Canyon Trail; continue descending on Upper Mystic Canyon Trail.

6.3 End ride at Big Dalton Canyon Road at end of Upper Mystic Canyon Trail.

Start: Carlyle E. Linder Equestrian Park, 1000 Glendora Mountain Rd., Glendora

Length: 39.4 miles (clockwise loop)

Riding time: 2.5 to 6.5 hours (my time: 3H23:00)

Terrain and surface: 100% on paved roads

Elevation: Low: 885 feet at Foothill Boulevard and Valley Center Avenue in Glendora; high: 4,533 feet along Glendora Ridge Road at the crest, 0.9 mile west of Mount Baldy Village

Traffic and hazards: Amelia Avenue in Glendora was carrying 4,865 vehicles per day near Foothill Boulevard; Baseline Road in San Dimas was carrying 2,030 vehicles per day in 2010; Foothill Boulevard in Glendora was carrying 13,705 vehicles per day near Valley Center Avenue. Glendora Mountain Road was carrying 1,450 vehicles per day north of Sierra Madre Avenue; Sierra Madre Avenue in Glendora was carrying 6,495 vehicles per day near Valley Center Avenue; and Valley Center Avenue in Glendora was carrying 6,460 vehicles per day near Sierra Madre Avenue.

Map: *The Thomas Guide—Street Guide: Los Angeles and Orange Counties* (any recent year), page 569

Getting there: By car—From central Los Angeles, take I-10 East to I-605 North to I-210 East. Exit at Lone Hill Avenue and turn left. Head north to Foothill Boulevard and turn left. Head west to Valley Center Avenue and turn right. Valley Center curves to the left, becoming Sierra Madre Avenue. Turn right onto Glendora Mountain Road. Once on Glendora Mountain Road, look for the entrance to Carlyle E. Linder Equestrian Park, on the right.

    By public transit—From central Los Angeles, ride Foothill Transit's Silver Streak (bus line) to the Eastland Center station in West Covina. Transfer to Foothill Transit bus route 851 to Sierra Madre Avenue and Glendora Mountain Road. Head north on Glendora Mountain to the starting point of the ride. ***Note:*** Bus route 851 runs only during the morning and evening commute periods on weekdays. Transit service should improve with the completion of the extension of the Metro Gold Line (light-rail transit).

Starting point coordinates: N34.152408° / W117.837794°

THE RIDE

The Glendora Ridge Stage ride is an epic loop that starts in Glendora; climbs Glendora Mountain to Glendora Ridge; rides along the ridge (which features an additional 1,000 feet of climbing) before dropping into Mount Baldy Village, making a rapid and steep descent of Mount Baldy Road into Claremont and then a casual passage through La Verne and San Dimas before returning to Glendora. With an elevation differential of 3,648 feet, this ride is surpassed only by the Mount Lowe and Wilson Expedition. Also, this ride reaches the third-highest altitude of all of the rides in the book, after the Mount Lowe and Wilson Expedition and the Josephine Peak Hill Climb. Although it is not the longest road ride in terms of distance, it will most likely take you the longest to ride. Nonetheless, at 39.4 miles it is quite doable—even if you need to make a few stops along the way.

Start the ride at Carlyle E. Linder Equestrian Park in Glendora, along Glendora Mountain Road. My research on Mr. Linder revealed little except that he served in the military and lived from 1901 to 1984. Leave the park and immediately begin climbing. The grade here is actually quite steep before easing a bit as you enter Angeles National Forest at mile 0.7. From here Glendora Mountain Road steadily climbs the mountain via a series of curves and the occasional switchback before finally cresting at 3,449 feet at mile 8.4. You can catch some spectacular views of the valley below wherever the road switches back. This road has been ridden as a time trial in the annual San Dimas Stage Race. Tour of Spain champion Chris Horner raced up the climb in under 16 minutes in the mid-2000s, although the route took the racers only part of the way up the mountain. These roads have also been ridden in a stage of the annual Tour of California pro bike race (hence the ride title). A breakaway group charged up the mountain some 2 minutes ahead of the main field before the entire group splintered on the "hors category" climb to the end of Mount Baldy Road.

Once beyond the crest, the road descends to the T intersection between Glendora Mountain and Glendora Ridge Roads (elevation 3,316 feet). Glendora Mountain Road ends here and Glendora Ridge continues on a 12-mile trek to Mount Baldy Village. The road is predominantly uphill, climbing another 1,000

A group of cyclists strategize and share stories on the side of Glendora Mountain Road.

feet before cresting just under 1.0 mile from the village. You will notice cooler temperatures up here, as well as taller trees along the segments of the road that are protected from the sun. The general rule is a 3-degree temperature drop per every 1,000 feet, so it may be 11 to 12 degrees cooler here than in Glendora. Watch out for the occasional spots of road damage and the rare rock in the road. As you are on a ridge, the vistas are both to your left and your right. To the left are Cow, Cattle, and Coldwater Canyons; well beyond to the right is civilization. You may be able to pick out Mount San Antonio to your left (otherwise known as Mount Baldy), which at 10,064 feet is the highest peak in the San Gabriel Mountains. After an arduous 12 miles along the ridge, and reaching the high point of the ride at 4,533 feet, the road finally descends into Mount Baldy Village, at mile 20.8.

Mount Baldy Village is an unincorporated community, actually located in San Bernardino County, which serves as a takeoff point for Mount San Antonio. With an elevation of 4,193 feet, the town experiences weather patterns that are far different from those in the valleys below. Expect cooler temperatures, regular rainfall during the season, and even some snowfall during winter. Tour of California racers turned left here and rode the strenuous climb up Mount Baldy Road. Many of them were probably wishing they could turn right here, like you, and begin the descent. Be sure to take a break in the village, if needed, particularly to replenish water. Mount Baldy Road features a short, steep climb once out of town before descending in earnest. And what a descent it is—8 miles! The average grade is 6.6% over the next 5.0 miles, but there are some steeper segments. High speeds are definitely possible; but with a steady volume of motorists heading to and from Mount Baldy, narrow shoulders, some road damage, and the occasional loose rock, it is best to control your descent. Focus on staying to the right as well as on the road conditions. There are a couple of short tunnels on the way down. Visibility is generally good inside the tunnels (they are short, so plenty of sunlight enters them), but use extra caution when inside.

At the intersection with Mountain Avenue (keep straight on Mount Baldy), the gradient eases to just over 5%. Leave Angeles National Forest and enter the city of Claremont, with the massive San Antonio Dam to your left. With a population of 35,457 in 2012, Claremont is known as the "city of trees and PhDs." The top employer is the Claremont Colleges, and the presence of a highly educated faculty has attracted other doctorates to the city. Hit the brakes at Mills Avenue, which is the end of Mount Baldy Road. Jog to the

Bike Shop

Bicycle Central, 942 South Grand Ave., Glendora; (626) 963-2312; www.thebicyclecentral.com

right and then immediately left to enter Thompson Creek Trail, a paved path. The path parallels Thompson Creek, enabling you to continue the descent without interference from city traffic. Be mindful of other trail users, particularly along the winding segment through Higginbotham Park. After a few at-grade crossings of lightly used roads and some narrow gate openings, the path finally comes to an end after 2.8 miles at Towne Avenue, 31.6 miles into the ride. Turn left here and then right onto Baseline Road.

Baseline Road was formerly part of SR 30, but the numbered route has been gradually removed as the parallel I-210 has been constructed. The freeway roars to your left, although skillful alignment and sound prevention measures have dampened its noise. Enter the city of La Verne at mile 33.1. La Verne, with a population of 31,063 in 2010, has been home to several notables, including pro boxer "Sugar" Shane Mosley, and 1940s-era Heisman Trophy winner Glenn Davis. The city is also home to the University of La Verne, formerly Lordsburg College, so named when the city was known as Lordsburg (which was until 1917). Turn right onto Foothill Boulevard, otherwise known as Historic US Route 66 (see the Emerald Necklace Cruise and its sidebar),

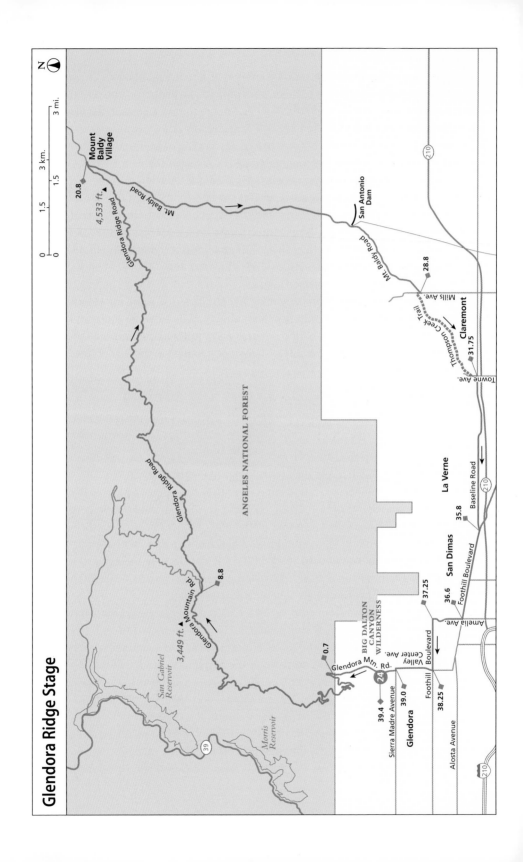

Glendora Ridge Stage

N

0	1.5	3 km.		
0	1.5	3 mi.		

Mount Baldy Village

20.8

4,533 ft. ▲

Glendora Ridge Road

Mt. Baldy Road

San Antonio Dam

Mt. Baldy Road

28.8

Mills Ave.

Thompson Creek Trail

Claremont

31.75

Towne Ave.

ANGELES NATIONAL FOREST

Glendora Ridge Road

La Verne

Baseline Road

35.8

210

San Dimas

8.8

3,449 ft. ▲

Glendora Mountain Rd.

37.25

36.6

Foothill Boulevard

Amelia Ave.

San Gabriel Reservoir

0.7

BIG DALTON CANYON WILDERNESS

Glendora Mtn. Rd.

24

Valley Center Ave.

Foothill Boulevard

39.4

Sierra Madre Avenue

Glendora

39.0

Foothill

38.25

Alosta Avenue

Morris Reservoir

39

210

and continue heading west. Enter the city of San Dimas just past mile 35. San Dimas had a population of 33,371 in 2010, nearly equivalent to that of its next-door neighbor La Verne. While the city does not boast a university, it does lay claim to being the setting for the 1989/1991 "Bill and Ted" films, in which San Dimas is called the "center of the universe." Continue through the city on Foothill. Turn right on Amelia Avenue at mile 36.6, and reenter Glendora.

Only 2.8 miles to go! Amelia passes the Glendora Country Club, an exclusive course that occasionally attracts pro golfers. Turn left onto Foothill Boulevard—this is "upper" Foothill (the "other" Foothill continued from Amelia as Route 66)—and head west, passing more Glendora residences. Turn right at Valley Center Avenue, at 885 feet above sea level, the low point of the course. Glendora High School, on your left just before the turn, counts among its graduates songstress Anna Nalick, pro hoops player Tracy Murray, and motivational speaker and author Anthony Robbins. Head north on Valley Center; the road curves to the left at mile 39, becoming Sierra Madre Avenue. Just after the turn, make a right onto Glendora Mountain Road and start the short climb back to Carlyle Linder Equestrian Park, where the ride ends.

MILES AND DIRECTIONS

0.0 Start at Carlyle Linder Equestrian Park; turn right and head north on Glendora Mountain Road.

0.7 Enter Angeles National Forest.

8.8 Keep straight at T intersection onto Glendora Ridge Road.

20.8 Stop sign at Mount Baldy Road in Mount Baldy Village; turn right.

28.8 Stop sign at Mills Avenue; keep straight across, jogging slightly to the right onto Thompson Creek Trail (paved path).

31.6 End of Thompson Creek Trail; turn left onto Towne Avenue.

31.75 Traffic signal at Baseline Road; turn right.

34.8 Traffic signal at Foothill Boulevard (Historic US Route 66); turn right.

36.6 Traffic signal at Amelia Avenue; turn right.

37.25 Stop sign at Foothill Boulevard; turn left.

38.25 Traffic signal at Valley Center Avenue; turn right.

39.0 Stop sign at Sierra Madre Avenue; turn left.

39.05 Traffic signal at Glendora Mountain Road; turn right.

39.4 Traffic signal at Boulder Spring Road and entrance to Carlyle Linder Equestrian Park; turn right and end the ride.

Hahamongna Watershed Shred

Start: Loma Alta County Park, 3330 Lincoln Ave., Altadena

Length: 8.7 miles (clockwise loop)

Riding time: 45 minutes to 2.5 hours (my time: 1H12:50)

Terrain and surface: 58% dirt fire roads; 42% paved roads

Elevation: Low: 1,157 feet in Arroyo Seco basin; high: 2,397 feet at Brown Mountain Saddle (junction of Lower Brown Mountain Fire Road and Fern Truck Trail)

Traffic and hazards: Altadena Drive carried 5,310 vehicles per weekday near Casitas Avenue in 2007; Loma Alta Drive carried 2,750 vehicles per weekday at Lincoln Avenue in 2008.

Map: *The Thomas Guide—Street Guide: Los Angeles and Orange Counties* (any recent year), page 535

Getting there: By car—From central Los Angeles, head north on SR 110. Continue to the end of the freeway in Pasadena and turn left onto Colorado Boulevard. Turn right onto Fair Oaks Avenue and head north. Turn left onto Orange Grove Avenue and then right onto Lincoln Avenue. Head north on Lincoln Avenue into Altadena. Once past Loma Alta Drive, look for the entrance to Loma Alta County Park, on the right.
   By public transit—From central Los Angeles, ride the Metro Gold Line to Memorial Park station in Pasadena. Transfer to Metro bus route 267 northbound. Exit at Lincoln Avenue and Altadena Drive. Head north on Lincoln Avenue to Loma Alta County Park. Bus route 267 runs every 30 minutes on weekdays and every hour on weekends and holidays.

Starting point coordinates: N34.201864° / W118.159150°

THE RIDE

The Hahamongna Watershed Shred is a nifty 8.7-mile clockwise loop up and down the slopes of the lower San Gabriel Mountains in and above Altadena. The course is excellent for a beginner mountain biker who is eager to test his or her

Cyclists gather to practice their trick-riding skills on North Arroyo Road in the Arroyo Seco basin.

fitness and skills on a real mountain ride. Yet the route features enough climbing and descending to challenge the fittest. The off-road portions of the ride are primarily on fire roads, making the surfaces not too technical. Start the ride at Loma Alta County Park in Altadena, an unincorporated community with a population of 42,777 in 2010. The community is located immediately to the northwest of Pasadena. In fact, loosely translated the name simply means "higher than Pasadena." Altadena was home to a number of notable residents, including physicist Richard Feynman (Nobel Prize, 1965), Olympic swimming gold medalist Shannon Stouder (1964), and author Alice Walker (*The Color Purple*).

Head south on Lincoln Avenue and then right onto Altadena Drive. Follow Altadena to its end, overlooking the Arroyo Seco basin. Keep straight onto the connector trail, which can be rocky, and drop down into the basin (10.0% grade). Enter Hahamongna Watershed Park, a 1,400-acre wetlands habitat that serves as a debris basin, ecosystem, and recreational facility. Hahamongna was the name of an ancient Gabrielino-Tongva village that once occupied this site. Once at the bottom, turn right onto the paved North Arroyo Road. Almost directly across the basin from you is NASA's Jet Propulsion Laboratory (JPL). This is the United

States' premier space exploration institute, where the nation's space missions are spawned. Needless to say, the brainpower is very high there. After perhaps catching a little spark of inspiration from your proximity to JPL, turn right onto North Arroyo and head into the canyon. This is the low point of the ride (1,157 feet). To the south of here is Devil's Gate Reservoir (mostly dry) and Dam. Legend has it that rock formations near the dam are a portal to another world. Surprisingly, a cofounder and former director of JPL was involved in the occult in his spare time and purposefully sited the lab near "The Gate" to tap into its energy field.

About 0.6 mile up the canyon, bear right onto Lower Brown Mountain Fire Road. The fire road begins to climb at an 8.4% grade. The road leaves the wooded canyon behind, making a sharp left turn. This is the end of the pavement. From here it is a steady 2.5-mile climb to the high point of the ride at Brown Mountain Saddle (2,397 feet). The fire road makes a seamless exit from Hahamongna Watershed Park partway up the climb, immediately entering Angeles National Forest. The fire road is quite rideable, with only a few short rocky, eroded, and/or sandy segments. Once at the saddle, keep straight to remain on the fire road. Begin to descend in earnest, rapidly passing the trademark coastal sage scrub and chaparral that is common throughout the region. After a hairpin turn in a wooded canyon, the fire road bottoms out (1,984 feet) at mile 5.1. A 6.2% gradient climb is next, taking you back up to 2,112 feet before starting another descent. Watch out for the sign that directs you to turn left at mile 6.0 (keeping straight leads to a dead end). The fire road descends into a wooded (oak trees) canyon—the rustic structures and parking area here are part of Millard Campground.

Bike Shop

BlackSwift Bicycles, 6635 N. Baltimore Ave., Altadena; (626) 806-2649; http://black swiftbicycles.com.

Continue past the campground and onto the paved road. Ready for one last climb? This one is steep, at 9.8%, but paved. You are now on Chaney Trail (paved road). After a 0.5-mile climb, the road bends sharply to the right, cresting once again (2,083 feet). From here the road plummets at a 12.2% grade, with some spectacular views of the valley below. Watch your speed, especially as the road nears a gate that is occasionally closed. The gate marks the Angeles National Forest boundary; on the other side is Altadena. Navigate the gate and continue to descend, now having returned to an Altadena residential area. Turn right onto Loma Alta Drive (mile 7.8) and continue to descend. Although traffic volumes are light (2,750 vehicles per weekday), be mindful of slowing and turning motorists. Your speed is likely to be high here. The ride ends at Lincoln Avenue, at the end of Loma Alta Drive. Turn right onto Lincoln to return to Loma Alta County Park.

Hahamongna Watershed Shred

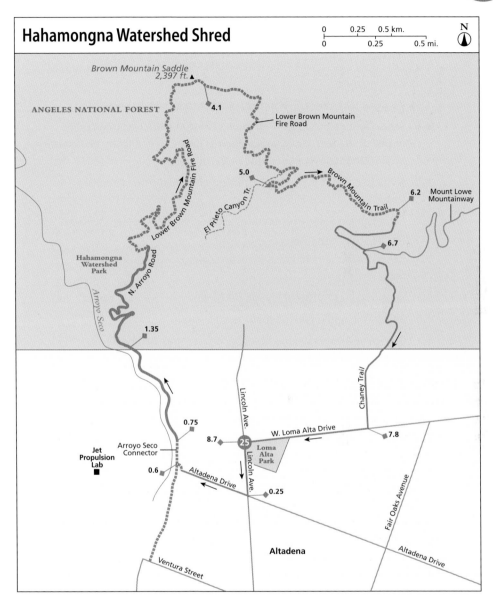

0	0.25	0.5 km.
0	0.25	0.5 mi.

N

Brown Mountain Saddle
2,397 ft.

ANGELES NATIONAL FOREST

4.1

Lower Brown Mountain
Fire Road

Lower Brown Mountain Fire Road

5.0

Brown Mountain Trail

6.2

Mount Lowe
Mountainway

El Prieto Canyon Tr.

6.7

Hahamongna
Watershed
Park

N. Arroyo Road

Arroyo Seco

1.35

Chaney Trail

Lincoln Ave.

0.75

Jet
Propulsion
Lab

Arroyo Seco
Connector

8.7

25

W. Loma Alta Drive

7.8

Loma
Alta
Park

Lincoln Ave.

0.6

Altadena Drive

0.25

Fair Oaks Avenue

Altadena

Altadena Drive

Ventura Street

MILES AND DIRECTIONS

0.0 Start at the intersection of Loma Alta Drive and Lincoln Avenue in Altadena, adjacent to Loma Alta County Park. Head south on Lincoln.

0.25 Traffic signal at Altadena Drive; turn right.

0.6 End of road; continue straight onto Arroyo Seco connector trail. The trail curves to the right and heads downhill (10.0% grade).

0.75 Turn right at bottom of hill onto North Arroyo Road.

1.35 Bear right onto Lower Brown Mountain Fire Road; begin climbing at 8.4% gradient.

1.55 Road switches back, becoming a dirt fire road; continue climbing.

4.1 Brown Mountain Saddle—junction with Fern Truck Trail (high point of ride: 2,397 feet). Keep straight across junction, remaining on Lower Brown Mountain Fire Road, and begin descent.

5.0 El Prieto Canyon Trail junction; remain on Lower Brown Mountain Fire Road.

5.1 Enter canyon area—hairpin turn followed by short descent followed by climb (6.2% grade).

5.25 Keep straight at junction; remain on Lower Brown Mountain Fire Road.

5.5 Second crest (2,112 feet); begin descent.

6.0 Bear left to remain on fire road.

6.2 Base of descent in wooded canyon; begin climb on paved road (Chaney Trail) at 9.8% grade.

6.7 Sharp right to remain on Chaney Trail; third crest (2,083 feet) just beyond turn. Begin descent at 12.2% grade.

7.4 Gate—may be closed, requiring a dismount.

7.8 Stop sign at Loma Alta Drive; turn right.

8.7 End ride at stop sign at Lincoln Avenue. Turn right to return to Loma Alta County Park.

Little Old Ride through Pasadena

Start: Brookside Park, 360 N. Arroyo Blvd. (Central Arroyo Seco), Pasadena

Length: 17.5 miles (clockwise loop)

Riding time: 50 minutes to 3 hours (my time: 1H17:08)

Terrain and surface: 100% paved roads

Elevation: Low: 569 feet at Colorado and Eagle Rock Boulevards; high: 1,356 feet at Chevy Chase Drive and Figueroa Street

Traffic and hazards: The heaviest traffic volumes were in Eagle Rock, with 34,055 vehicles per weekday on Colorado Boulevard (at Eagle Rock Boulevard) in 2009 and 24,820 vehicles per weekday on Broadway north of Colorado in 2003. Daily traffic volumes on Pasadena streets (2010–2014) were lighter, including 4,800 on North Arroyo Boulevard near Brookside Park, 2,900 on South Arroyo Boulevard, 4,200 on La Loma Road, 9,100 on Linda Vista Avenue south of Lida Street, and 13,500 on Seco Street near Linda Vista.

Map: *The Thomas Guide—Street Guide: Los Angeles and Orange Counties* (any recent year), page 565

Getting there: By car—From central Los Angeles, take I-5 North to SR 2 North to SR 134 East. Exit at San Rafael Avenue; turn right and then left onto Colorado Boulevard. Turn left onto Linda Vista Avenue, passing under the freeway. Turn left onto Seco Street, which is part of the ride route, and descend into the Arroyo Seco basin. Turn right onto North Arroyo Boulevard; enter the Brookside Park parking area on your left.

    By public transit—From central Los Angeles, ride the Metro Gold Line (light-rail) to Memorial Park station in Pasadena. Exit the station and head west (by bicycle) on Walnut Street. Turn right onto Orange Grove Boulevard and then left onto Rosemont Avenue. At Seco Street turn left; Brookside Park is on the left.

Starting point coordinates: N34.155728° / W118.167281°

THE RIDE

According to a legendary 1960s Jan and Dean song, Colorado Boulevard attracts speeding drivers who are "terrors" of the road. This ride uses Colorado Boulevard—albeit in Eagle Rock (L.A. community), not Pasadena—which has become much more bicycle-friendly since the days of that song. So fear not the old lady! The Little Old Ride through Pasadena is a 17.5-mile loop through Pasadena, Eagle Rock, and Glendale. The route features plenty of curves and turns along wooded roads in and near the Arroyo Seco corridor. This ride is not without some climbing: Chevy Chase Drive in Glendale ascends nearly 600 feet to the ride's high point. This is one of four rides in the book that are entirely on urban roads. All the other road rides incorporate either bicycle paths or mountainous roads that leave city limits.

Start from Brookside Park, located just south of the Rose Bowl (see sidebar) in Pasadena. Pasadena had a population of 137,122 in 2010. The city has evolved over the years from being considered L.A.'s "twin" to being a resort destination for wealthy easterners, to being an arts and sciences center, to unfortunately becoming a center for gang violence. The violence has subsided since the mid-1990s, the arts and sciences have been retained, and the population has transformed into a diverse mixture of ethnic groups and income levels. Today Pasadena is well known as the home of the Jet Propulsion Laboratory, California Institute of Technology, Norton Simon Museum, Art Center College of Design, Rose Bowl, and of course the Tournament of Roses Parade. The ride officially begins by heading south on North Arroyo Boulevard from Seco Street. The opening 2.5 miles are along Arroyo, which parallels the Arroyo Seco parkway adjacent to parklands and park-side residences.

After passing under Holly Street, SR 134, and Colorado Boulevard, look for the Home Laundry building (432 S. Arroyo Blvd.) and the Batchelder House (626 S. Arroyo Blvd.). Both buildings are on the National Register of Historic Places (NRHP), and in the Lower Arroyo Seco Historic District, which stretches as far south as La Loma Road. At the Grand Avenue intersection, keep right to

Bike Shops

Performance Bike, 323 South Arroyo Pkwy., Pasadena; (626) 395-9796; www.performancebike.com

Incycle Bicycles, 175 South Fair Oaks Ave.; (626) 577-0440; http://incycle.com

Empire Bike Shop, 546 North Fair Oaks Ave.; (626) 578-9350

Pasadena Cyclery, 1670 East Walnut St., Pasadena; (626) 795-2866; http://pasadenacyclery.com

A rider hike-a-bikes under the freeway along North Arroyo Boulevard.

continue on South Arroyo. Turn right onto San Rafael Avenue and cross over the Arroyo Seco. Although San Rafael turns to the right after crossing the bridge, keep straight onto Laguna Road through a shady residential neighborhood. Turn left at La Loma Road and continue heading west. The Poppy Peak Historic District is just past Avenue 64 and the adjacent residential area to your left.

La Loma Road enters Los Angeles and the Eagle Rock community just before Figueroa Street. Eagle Rock had an estimated population in 2014 of about 34,000. The community was a separate city from 1911 until 1923, when because of the lack of an adequate water supply, it elected to become part of Los Angeles. The community is home to Occidental College, where during the late 1990s, a young Ben Affleck was a student sharing a residence with his roommate, Matt Damon. During their residency, the two developed the screenplay for the film *Good Will Hunting*, which would go on to win two Academy Awards—one for the screenplay and one for best supporting actor, Robin Williams. Turn left from La Loma onto Colorado Boulevard and head west.

Colorado Boulevard is perhaps the nerve center of Eagle Rock. This ride covers 2.0 miles of the road. Despite the lyrical suggestion of Jan and Dean,

The Rose Bowl and Rose Parade

The Rose Bowl is the name of a venerable stadium as well as a major end-of-season championship-caliber collegiate football game. The game is actually older than the stadium, which was built in 1922. With a seating capacity in excess of 90,000, which exceeded 100,000 before some renovations, it is one of the largest stadiums in the United States. The stadium's primary use is for football—it is the home stadium for the University of California, Los Angeles (UCLA), as well as the site of the annual Rose Bowl, which is always held on January 1 (unless that date falls on a Sunday).

The Rose Bowl has been held annually since 1916, although the first official game was in 1902. One of the most exciting games was perhaps in 2006, the Rose Bowl's last as college football's Bowl Championship Series (BCS) title game, in which the University of Texas—guided by masterful quarterback Vince Young—defeated the University of Southern California 41 to 38. The Rose Bowl was used again for the BCS Championship in 2010 and 2014, but the Rose Bowl games, pitting the top Pacific 12 Conference team against the top Big 12 Conference team, were separate matches held on the traditional January 1 date. The Rose Bowl also has an exciting history as the venue for championship-level soccer matches, including the 1984 Olympic Games final (France over Brazil 2–0), the 1994 FIFA (Men's) World Cup (Brazil over Italy on penalty kicks), and the 1999 Women's World Cup (United States over China on penalty kicks). The stadium is also a concert venue and has been the site of the NFL's Super Bowl.

Older than the Rose Bowl (game and stadium) is the Rose Parade ("Rose Parade presented by Honda," as of this writing), which dates back to the 1890s. The parade showcases natural materials, particularly flowers (not just roses) on the many floats that move along the parade route. Some of the floats under construction can be viewed in an area on the north side of Brookside Park along Seco Street, which is along the ride route. During the parade, in between the floats are a number of marching bands and equestrian teams and of course a Rose Parade queen.

The Little Old Ride through Pasadena does not cover any of the parade route, which focuses on Colorado Boulevard through central Pasadena. The parade route's overall length is 5.5 miles, suggesting that those marching band members must be in decent physical condition for their "moving" performances!

mentioned earlier, two vehicle lanes had been removed on Colorado to make way for bicycle lanes. The street is still busy, as noted above, but frequent crosswalks and pedestrian signals keep motor vehicle speeds down—and a bicyclist's morale up. The intersection with Eagle Rock Boulevard is the ride's low point, 569 feet above sea level. You may recognize some of the scenes along the way from films (e.g., 1981's *The Incredible Shrinking Woman*), television shows (*Beverly Hills 90210* and *Glee*), and music videos (e.g., for Avril Lavigne's "Complicated"). The Eagle Rock Branch Library (2224 Colorado Blvd.) is on the NRHP. Eagle Rock's original city hall is at 2035 Colorado Blvd. Colorado and Broadway split at the western edge of the community; stay right to continue on Broadway. Turn right at Harvey Street (mile 6.75) and enter the city of Glendale. At the end of Harvey, turn right onto Chevy Chase Drive.

The turn onto Chevy Chase Drive begins a long climb into the San Rafael Hills. The climb starts gradually and then gets steeper, with an average grade of 5.6% toward the crest (1,356 feet) at Figueroa Street. Along the way, enjoy the road's curves while staying safely to the right. Also, glance at the attractive residences along the way. The James Daniel Derby House, at 2535 Chevy Chase, is on the NRHP. You'll reach Figueroa Street at mile 10.35 after climbing just under 600 feet in just over 2.0 miles. Enter the city of La Cañada-Flintridge just before Figueroa. Continue past Figueroa as Chevy Chase starts to descend. Turn right onto Highland Drive; this pretty residential street follows a bench in the San Rafael Hills, curving to the east and then to the south, effectively returning you to Pasadena. After riding next to the Foothill Freeway (I-210) for a stretch and passing an overpass to your left, you are now on Linda Vista Avenue. Linda Vista continues southward, generally downhill, through another pleasant, wooded residential area that runs parallel to the Arroyo Seco. Hang a sharp left at Seco Street, heading downhill into the Arroyo Seco basin. Although Brookside Park is just to your right, the ride is not over—it is time to do a 3.0-mile loop on roads that circle the Rose Bowl.

At the T intersection at the base of the descent, keep straight onto West Street. The Rose Bowl is to your right; also to your right is the Brookside Golf Course. Keep straight on West Street. You may wonder why you are working so hard to sustain your speed; this is actually a false flat, climbing from 795 to 907 feet in the 1.3 miles along the west side of the Rose Bowl. Turn right onto West Washington Boulevard and then right onto Rosemont Avenue. You will notice other road users all along the loop. Cyclists regularly congregate here for some fast laps. The roads are also popular for running races and the occasional triathlon. Follow Rosemont, which is mostly downhill, as it passes the Rose Bowl on its east side. Turn right onto Seco Street; the loop and the ride end at North Arroyo Boulevard. Brookside Park is to your left.

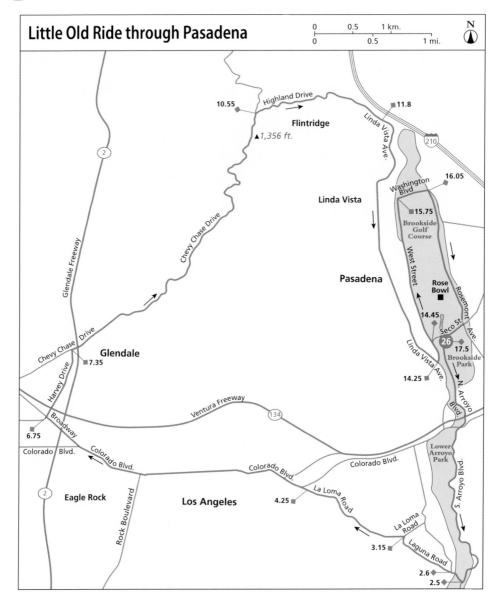

Little Old Ride through Pasadena

0   0.5   1 km.
0   0.5   1 mi.

N

10.55

Highland Drive

11.8

Flintridge

▲ 1,356 ft.

Linda Vista Ave.

210

Washington Blvd

16.05

15.75

Linda Vista

Brookside Golf Course

Glendale Freeway

Chevy Chase Drive

Pasadena

West Street

Rose Bowl

Rosemont Ave.

2

14.45

Chevy Chase Drive

Glendale

7.35

Linda Vista Ave.

Seco St.

26

17.5

Brookside Park

Harvey Drive

14.25

N. Arroyo Blvd

Ventura Freeway

134

Broadway

6.75

Lower Arroyo Park

Colorado Blvd.

Colorado Blvd.

Colorado Blvd.

Colorado Blvd.

S. Arroyo Blvd.

2

Eagle Rock

Los Angeles

Rock Boulevard

4.25

La Loma Road

La Loma Road

3.15

Laguna Road

2.6

2.5

MILES AND DIRECTIONS

0.0 Start from North Arroyo Boulevard and Seco Street, adjacent to Brookside Park in Pasadena; head south on North Arroyo.

0.5 Holly Street underpass.

0.7 SR 134 underpass.

0.9 Colorado Boulevard underpass; now on South Arroyo Boulevard.

2.3 Bear right at Grand Avenue to remain on South Arroyo Boulevard.

2.5 Stop sign at San Rafael Avenue; turn right.

2.6 Continue straight onto Laguna Road (San Rafael Avenue turns right).

3.15 Stop sign at La Loma Road; turn left.

3.95 Leave Pasadena and enter Los Angeles (Eagle Rock community).

4.25 Traffic signal at Colorado Boulevard; turn left.

6.35 Traffic signal at Broadway; keep straight, now on Broadway (Colorado bears left).

6.5 SR 2 underpass.

6.75 Traffic signal at Harvey Drive; turn right. Leave Los Angeles and enter Glendale.

7.35 End of Harvey Drive at Chevy Chase Drive; turn right.

8.35 Begin steady 2.0-mile climb at 5.6% grade.

10.3 Leave Glendale and reenter Pasadena.

10.35 High point of ride (1,356 feet) at Figueroa Street; begin descent.

10.55 Stop sign at Highland Drive; turn right.

11.8 Stop sign at Linda Vista Avenue (freeway overpass); keep straight, now on Linda Vista.

14.25 Turn right onto Seco Street.

14.45 Keep straight, now on West Street; begin Rose Bowl loop.

15.75 Turn right onto West Washington Boulevard.

16.05 Turn right onto Rosemont Avenue.

17.25 Turn right onto Seco Street.

17.5 End ride (and Rose Bowl loop) at North Arroyo Boulevard.

Mounts Lowe and Wilson Expedition

Start: General Charles S. Farnsworth County Park, 568 Mount Curve Ave., Altadena

Length: 24.7 miles (clockwise loop)

Riding time: 3 to 8.5 hours (my time: 4H39:50)

Terrain and surface: 60% on dirt fire roads; 29% on paved roads; 11% on a paved mountain road not open to general traffic

Elevation: Low: 1,239 feet on Mount Wilson Toll Road across Eaton Wash Dam; high: 5,683 feet at Mount Wilson Red Box Road and Mount Wilson Circle, high atop Mount Wilson

Traffic and hazards: 4,020 vehicles per day on Lake Avenue north of Concha Avenue in 2014; 1,950 vehicles per day on Loma Alta Drive at Loma View Drive in 2010

Map: *The Thomas Guide—Street Guide: Los Angeles and Orange Counties* (any recent year), page 536

Getting there: By car—From central Los Angeles, head north on SR 110. Continue to the freeway's end in Pasadena. Turn right onto Colorado Boulevard and then left onto Lake Avenue. Continue on Lake into Altadena. Along the 8% uphill grade, look for General Charles S. Farnsworth Park on the left; turn left onto Concha Street, followed by a right turn into the park's parking lot.

 By public transit—From central Los Angeles, ride Metro's Gold Line (light-rail) to the Lake Avenue station in Pasadena. Transfer to Metro bus route 180 or 485. Travel to Altadena Avenue in Altadena; exit here and ride up Lake Avenue (~8% grade) to Farnsworth County Park. Route 180 runs every 35 minutes seven days a week; route 485 runs every 40 to 50 minutes Monday through Friday.

Starting point coordinates: N34.199222° / W118.131214°

THE RIDE

The Mounts Lowe and Wilson Expedition is a 24.7-mile mountainous affair, opening with 13.3 miles of continuous climbing at grades of 9% to 11%, followed by 8.5 miles of downhill at grades of 9% to 10%, and then closing with 2.5 miles of moderate climbing to complete the ride. The net elevation change is 4,444 feet, making this the "mother" of all mountain bike rides in this book. To give the reader an idea of the challenge, many riders bypass the climb and get shuttled to the top for the exciting downhill! We of course are hardier than that, with the descent being our reward after the climb. Most of the climbing is on Mount Lowe Road, followed by the descent on Mount Wilson Toll Road. Mount Lowe Road summits within 300 feet of the crest of Mount Lowe, which peaks at 5,606 feet. The two mountains are adjacent to each other. The transition between the two involves about 2.5 miles of riding, some of it additional climbing, to a second summit that is within 24 feet of Mount Wilson's peak (5,710 feet).

Although the highest peaks in the San Gabriel Mountains are to the east, with Mount San Antonio reaching 10,064 feet, the comparatively "short" Mounts Lowe and Wilson may be the most well known. After two decades of experimentation with telescopes, Mount Wilson Observatory, featuring the Hooker Telescope, was finally opened in 1917. It was the world's largest telescope for the next thirty years. During the 1920s, Edwin Hubble worked at the observatory, making several significant astronomical discoveries. Radio and television antennas and equipment dominate the landscape atop Mount Wilson in addition to the observatory. A total of twenty-five L.A.-area TV stations were relaying their broadcasts through equipment on the mountain as of this writing. While Mount Lowe has not seen any mountaintop development, the mountain has its own legacy (see sidebar).

Give yourself plenty of time for this ride. A morning start is recommended to avoid running out of daylight. Also bring plenty of liquids with you—the Mount Wilson Observatory is open to the public only on weekends.

Bike Shops

Steve's Bike Shop, 859 East Mariposa St., Altadena; (626) 798-8703; http://stevesbikeshop.wordpress.com
Performance Bike, 323 South Arroyo Pkwy., Pasadena; (626) 395-9796; www.performancebike.com
Incycle Bicycles, 175 South Fair Oaks Ave.; (626) 577-0440; http://incycle.com
Empire Bike Shop, 546 North Fair Oaks Ave.; (626) 578-9350
Pasadena Cyclery, 1670 East Walnut St., Pasadena; (626) 795-2866; http://pasadenacyclery.com

(The water fountain in the Henninger Flats picnic area had been capped off when I did this ride, and the restrooms were closed.) Check the weather as well—expect cooler temperatures at higher elevations, and avoid doing this ride when there is rain or snow in the mountains.

Start from the corner of Lake Avenue and Concha Street in Altadena, adjacent to General Charles S. Farnsworth County Park. General Farnsworth (1862–1955)

Mount Lowe Railway

Mount Lowe Road, also known as Mount Lowe Mountainway and Mount Lowe Railway Trail, follows the alignment of the Mount Lowe Railway. The railway was an extremely ambitious project undertaken by Thaddeus S. C. Lowe in 1891. Using the millions that he had made from patents on hydrogen gas manufacturing and ice-making machines, Mr. Lowe funded the effort in conjunction with the designs of David J. McPherson, a civil engineer. The project was quickly completed, and by 1896 a three-tiered rail system to Crystal Springs, adjacent to Mount Lowe, had been built.

The first tier was a narrow-gauge trolley that climbed from central Altadena to the foot of Echo Mountain in Rubio Canyon. The second tier was an incline, or "funicular," that climbed at up to a 62% grade to Echo Mountain. The third tier, the Alpine Division, was another narrow-gauge rail line that negotiated 127 curves and 18 trestles over 3.5 miles to the terminal at the springs. Alpine Tavern, a twelve-room Swiss chalet, was built adjacent to the terminal. Mount Lowe Road from Echo Mountain Trail to Inspiration Point Trail (Muir Peak Road) follows the exact alignment of the Alpine Division.

The Mount Lowe Railway thrived for just a few years before it began to suffer financially. In those days, getting a large number of people to come to Altadena was nearly as challenging as getting up the mountain. Mother Nature also took its toll: Two of the four hotels along the line burned down in the early 1900s. An electrical storm and high winds in 1909 and 1928, respectively, caused further destruction. In 1936 Alpine Tavern, which by then had been renamed Mt. Lowe Tavern, caught fire and burned down. Finally, a three-day rainstorm in 1938 effectively washed away the railway. It has been abandoned ever since, but revival efforts began in the 1990s with its placement on the National Register of Historic Places.

It is estimated that about 3 million people rode the railway during its lifetime. Thaddeus Lowe had long since passed (d. 1913) before nature's dismantling of the railway. Yet he had the distinction of Oak Mountain being renamed Mount Lowe in his honor during his lifetime.

was honored for distinguished service during World War I and was Chief of Infantry with the US Army. Later in life, having retired to Altadena, he helped establish Altadena Park, which was named in his honor in 1939. After climbing Lake Avenue's 8.7% grade, turn left onto Loma Alta Drive for a 6.25% descent.

Watch for the flashing overhead light up ahead; turn here onto Chaney Trail, which is a paved road (and is ridden in the opposite direction in the Hahamongna Watershed Shred ride). At 11.3%, the Chaney Trail climb into the Angeles National Forest is the steepest of the entire ride. At Chaney Trail's crest (2,085 feet of elevation), turn right and head onto Mount Lowe Road, going around the gate. Mount Lowe Road is also known as Mount Lowe Mountainway and Mount Lowe Railway Trail. The opening 2.6 miles are paved. Hard-core mountain bikers will scoff at the "sissy" pavement but may end up being thankful for the traction—the climb is at a steady 9.2% grade. Keep straight past the (also paved) side road to the Camp Sierra site. The trailhead for the Echo Mountain Trail is on the right at mile 2.6. Keep straight here onto the unpaved portion of Mount Lowe Road. You are now at 3,483 feet of elevation. The next 6.3 miles are dirt, with the surface becoming quite rocky in places for the final 5.4 miles or so. Signs along the road offer photos and information on the Mount Lowe Railway, with a few challenging you to compare a historical shot with the current scene.

Although fatigue may be setting in, keep climbing. Note that the gradient of the climb eases once the road hits dirt, dropping to an average of 5.3%. The easier grade is offset, though, by the reduced traction and frequent rocks. You will see quite a bit of granite along the road, particularly at the higher elevations. One of the Mount Lowe Railway signs describes how some granite outcroppings had to be blasted to make way for the train track. At mile 8.7 bear left at the T junction to remain on Mount Lowe Road. The sign at the junction is hard to read, but the trail to the right leads to Inspiration Point on Muir Peak. The junction is at 4,490 feet. After another 2.2 miles along "open" trail (i.e., little to no shade), Mount Lowe Road finally crests at 5,292 feet. To your right is a trail to the summit of Mount Lowe. By now you will have noticed that, despite being at an elevation of over 5,000 feet, there has been minimal tree growth anywhere along the route. Part of this is the result of the 2009 Station Fire, which burned more than 160,000 acres during a nearly two-month period. Keep straight onto the descent. After 0.2 mile Mount Lowe Road enters Mueller Tunnel, built in 1942. There is no lighting in the tunnel, so brace yourself for a short, dark passage.

After exiting the tunnel, Mount Lowe Road continues for another 0.3 mile to its end at Mount Wilson Red Box Road. The canyon to your right as you approach the road is deep and spectacular. At mile 11.4 go around the gate and turn right onto the paved road (elevation 5,119 feet). This two-lane road provides access to Mount Wilson and its many facilities. After 1.9 miles and another 564 feet of climbing, you finally reach the high point of the entire ride—5,683 feet, where the road turns right, becoming the one-way Mount Wilson Circle. The next 0.3 mile is the flattest part of the entire ride. Just prior to the Mount Wilson Observatory entrance, turn right and leave the road, heading onto Mount Wilson Toll Road. The signage here is somewhat misleading, but the road is indeed open to the public. The toll road immediately begins to descend at a 10.4% grade. After 1.0 mile bear left at the split in the fire road to continue on the toll road—heading straight takes you to a (usually) locked, gated fence, and a dead end.

Mount Wilson Toll Road was built in 1891 to facilitate travel to and from the mountain from Altadena and Pasadena, mainly to transport observatory equipment. A mountaintop hotel was later built to accommodate sightseers. The road started off as a narrow (less than 6 feet wide) trail, charging 25 cents for hikers and 50 cents for riders on horseback. By 1917 the road had been widened to 12 feet to accommodate two-way motor vehicle travel and to transport pieces of the Hooker Telescope. After the construction of better roads to Mount Wilson, including the Angeles Crest Highway and Mount Wilson Red Box Canyon Road, the toll road was turned over to the USDA Forest Service in 1936. Today the road is open to nonmotorized users, such as yourself, along with maintenance and emergency vehicles. And the road sure

Getting up the nerve to enter Mueller Tunnel along Mount Lowe Road (elevation 5,200 feet)

is rocky along its upper reaches! Keep control of that bicycle, and choose your lines carefully as you pick your way down the mountain. Be sure that your brake pads are intact—and that your handlebar grips are cushioned.

After 19.4 miles in the saddle, and some 5.5 miles down the mountain, enter Henninger Flats. This oasis at 2,550- to 2,600-feet elevation is a campground, picnic area, and nursery—a welcome respite from the bone-jarring descent of the Toll Road and mostly shade-free riding up until now. The Flats were settled in 1880 by William K. Henninger, a gold prospector who built a house and water cistern and planted a nursery here. By the 1890s the property had been sold to the Mount Wilson Toll Road Company, which later turned it over to the forest service. An experimental nursery was established here in 1928—the variety of vegetation and trees here are a result of diligence. During my third passage through here, in autumn 2014, the water fountain in the picnic area had been capped off and the restrooms closed. Previously this had been a great place to refresh, given that there is no water anywhere along the route.

Continue the descent at a 9% grade as you move beyond Henninger Flats. You can now see Altadena and Pasadena more clearly down below, as well as the Toll Road snaking its way down the side of the mountain. This segment of the road is popular, so be mindful of other users. After plummeting down the final, steep portion of the descent, the road levels out to cross a bridge over Eaton Wash. Be careful in making the slight, left-hand turn onto the bridge to avoid the protruding abutments as well as the lip between the dirt road and the paved bridge surface. At 1,239 feet above sea level, this is the low point of the entire ride. After crossing the bridge, it is a short, 0.2-mile paved climb at a 10.4% grade to the Pinecrest gate.

You now have 2.4 miles to go. Given that the gate is at 1,338 feet and Farnsworth County Park is at 1,651 feet, there is still some climbing to do. Turn right onto Pinecrest Drive and begin the climb into a wooded Altadena neighborhood. Keep straight onto East Loma Alta Drive where Pinecrest turns to the left. The road makes a sweeping right-hand bend, with more climbing, to cross over Rubio Wash. Once across the bridge, you are on Rubio Canyon Road. The road descends now, curving to the right at Via Madera. Turn right onto Maiden Lane and resume climbing, followed by a right onto Mount Curve Avenue and more climbing. Mount Curve eventually levels as it curves to the left. Once at Lake Avenue, turn left, watching for both uphill and downhill traffic. Farnsworth County Park is on your right. End the ride at the Concha Street intersection.

MILES AND DIRECTIONS

0.0 Start at Farnsworth County Park and head north on Lake Avenue from Concha Street (8.7% uphill grade).

0.35 Turn left onto East Loma Alta Drive; head downhill (6.25% grade).

1.35 Flashing overhead signal at Chaney Trail (paved road); turn right and begin climb (now at 1,468 feet).

1.8 Gate (typically closed 8 p.m. to 6 a.m.); enter Angeles National Forest. Climb continues at 11.3% grade.

2.5 Turn right onto Mount Lowe Road (go around gate), also known as Mount Lowe Mountainway and Mount Lowe Railway Trail. Now at 2,085 feet, continue climb at 9.2% grade.

4.25 Keep straight at junction with road to Camp Sherpa site (elevation 2,927 feet).

5.1 Echo Mountain Trail on the right; keep straight—end of pavement. Elevation is 3,483 feet; average gradient is 5.3% from here.

6.4 Trail to Dawn Mine on the left; Mount Lowe Road becomes rockier.

8.7 Junction with trail to Inspiration Point (also called Muir Peak Road); turn left to remain on Mount Lowe Road. Elevation is 4,490 feet.

10.9 Summit (5,292 feet) and junction with trail to Mount Lowe. Keep straight on Mount Lowe Road and begin descent.

11.1 Enter Mueller Tunnel (short but dark).

11.4 End of Mount Lowe Road at Mount Wilson Red Box Road (gate). Turn right and head toward Mount Wilson on paved road (elevation 5,119 feet); grade of climb is 5.7%.

13.3 Turn right onto one-way Mount Wilson Circle. High point of ride (5,683 feet).

13.65 Leave road and bear right onto Mount Wilson Toll Road (no real signage). Begin descent (9.6% grade).

14.65 Bear left at split in fire road to remain on Mount Wilson Toll Road (elevation 5,148 feet). Continue to descend at 10.4% grade.

19.4 Enter Henninger Flats (elevation 2,551 feet; campground, picnic tables, nursery). Follow signs; bear left to continue past tables on Mount Wilson Toll Road. Continue to descend at 9.0% grade.

22.15 Base of Mount Wilson Toll Road; cross dam and then ride short climb (10.4% grade) to Pinecrest gate.

22.35 Continue through gate; turn right onto Pinecrest Drive.

22.65 Stop sign at East Loma Alta Drive; keep straight, now on East Loma Alta (Pinecrest turns to the left).

23.7 Cross Rubio Wash; now on Rubio Canyon Road.

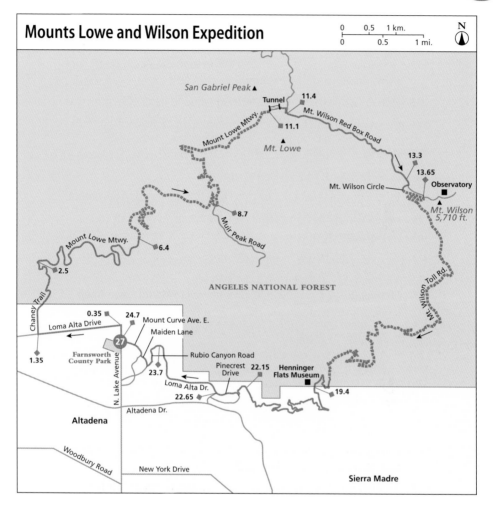

Mounts Lowe and Wilson Expedition

24.0 Rubio Canyon Road curves to the right at Via Madera; stay on Rubio Canyon.

24.1 Stop sign at Maiden Lane; turn right.

24.3 Stop sign at Mount Curve Avenue; turn right.

24.55 Stop sign at Lake Avenue; turn left—short downhill.

24.7 Turn right onto Concha Street, adjacent Farnsworth County Park, to conclude the ride.

Santa Anita Canyon Call

Start: Sierra Vista Park, 611 E. Sierra Madre Blvd., Sierra Madre

Length: 9.4 miles (out-and-back, with a small loop at the end)

Riding time: 40 minutes to 2.5 hours (my time: 56:15)

Terrain and surface: 100% paved roads

Elevation: Low: 657 feet at Santa Anita Avenue and Sierra Madre Avenue in Arcadia; high: 2,186 feet at Chantry Flats, at the high end of the parking area.

Traffic and hazards: Traffic volumes on Santa Anita Canyon Road are light but steady on weekends and holidays, when the parking area at Chantry Flats fills up.

Map: *The Thomas Guide—Street Guide: Los Angeles and Orange Counties* (any recent year), page 567

Getting there: By car—From central Los Angeles, take I-5 North to SR 2 North to SR 134 East; continue onto I-210 East. Exit at Santa Anita Avenue in Arcadia and turn left. Turn left onto Sierra Madre Avenue; Sierra Vista Park is on the right, just after you leave Arcadia and enter Sierra Madre.

By public transit—From central Los Angeles, ride the Metro Silver Line (bus rapid transit) to the El Monte station. Transfer to Metro bus route 487 and head north. Exit the bus at Sierra Vista Park in Sierra Madre. Bus route 487 runs every 10 to 40 minutes on weekdays, every 55 minutes on Saturday, and every 50 minutes on Sunday and holidays.

Starting point coordinates: N34.162050° / W118.039294°

THE RIDE

The Santa Anita Canyon Call is a challenging out-and-back hill climb and descent in Santa Anita Canyon. The canyon straddles the line between the cities of Sierra Madre and Arcadia, which are located in the San Gabriel Valley, although the upper reaches of the canyon are in the Angeles National Forest in the San Gabriel Mountains. Santa Anita Canyon Road is the feature of the

A cyclist grazes the shoulder of Santa Anita Canyon Road while climbing toward Chantry Flats.

ride—the road is popular with hikers, cyclists, a few runners, and motorists heading for Chantry Flats Recreation Area. The Chantry Flats parking area fills up on weekends and holidays and even the occasional weekday, and you may find vehicles parked along the side of the road in pullout areas. (Trails continue from Chantry Flats, leading farther up into the San Gabriel Mountains.) After an opening gradual downhill on Sierra Madre Avenue, the 9.4-mile ride is actually at its steepest along Santa Anita Avenue within the city of Arcadia and then Sierra Madre (9.1% gradient). The grade eases (8.0%) slightly past the gate that marks the starting point of Santa Anita Canyon Road, also known as Chantry Flats Road. The grade eases even more (6.4%) after you enter Angeles National Forest, 2.55 miles into the ride.

Once arriving at Chantry Flats Recreation Area, continue along the parking road to the end. The road curves to the left and then dead-ends. There are a couple of water fountains here, as well as lavatories. Aliens landed at Chantry Flats in the original *War of the Worlds* film (1953). The turnaround point is at mile 4.4. The downhill ride is slightly longer (5.0 miles) because I have you riding to the north of Sierra Vista Park on Grandview Avenue before turning onto Canon Avenue and then onto Sierra Madre Avenue to return to the park. This makes the ride more interesting and avoids having you build up too much speed on Santa Anita Avenue before having to turn off it.

The ride starts in Sierra Madre, which had a population of 10,917 in 2010. Nestled against the San Gabriel Mountain foothills, the city was the home of Alan Wood (1922–2013), the soldier who brought the US flag to Iwo Jima during World War II. The ride also travels through Arcadia, which had a population of 56,364 in 2010. The city is best known for the Santa Anita horse racing track and the Los Angeles County Arboretum and Botanical Gardens. The latter was famously used in the opening segment of the *Fantasy Island* TV series, in which the character "Tattoo" points and shouts at a plane. Of particular note, at the end of the route and back in Sierra Madre is the Pioneer Cemetery, located immediately adjacent to Sierra Vista Park. This may be one of the scariest cemeteries around, having been used in the films *Invasion of the Body Snatchers* (1956, with Kevin McCarthy), *A Family Plot* (Alfred Hitchcock, 1976), *Hallowe'en* (one scene, 1978), and *Twin Peaks* (David Lynch, 1990).

Bike Shops

Helen's Cycles, 142 Huntington Dr., Arcadia; (626) 447-3181; http://helenscycles.com
Open Road Bicycle Shop, 60 N. Sierra Madre Blvd.; (626) 683-9986; www.sidemountpedal.com

MILES AND DIRECTIONS

0.0 Start at Sierra Vista Park and turn left onto Sierra Madre Avenue.

0.05 Leave Sierra Madre and enter Arcadia.

0.45 Stop sign at Santa Anita Avenue; turn left and begin climbing at a 9.1% gradient (low point of ride: 657 feet).

0.8 Leave Arcadia at Grandview Avenue and reenter Sierra Madre.

1.1 Gate (closed 8 p.m. to 6 a.m.); continue climbing 8.0% gradient, now on Santa Anita Canyon Road (also called Chantry Flats Road).

2.55 Enter Angeles National Forest (elevation 1,579 feet), now officially on FR 2N40 but informally still on Santa Anita Canyon Road. Continue climbing (6.4% gradient).

4.25 Enter Chantry Flats Recreation Area (elevation 2,154 feet); continue riding through parking area to the end of the road.

4.4 End of road (elevation 2,186 feet); turn around here and begin descent.

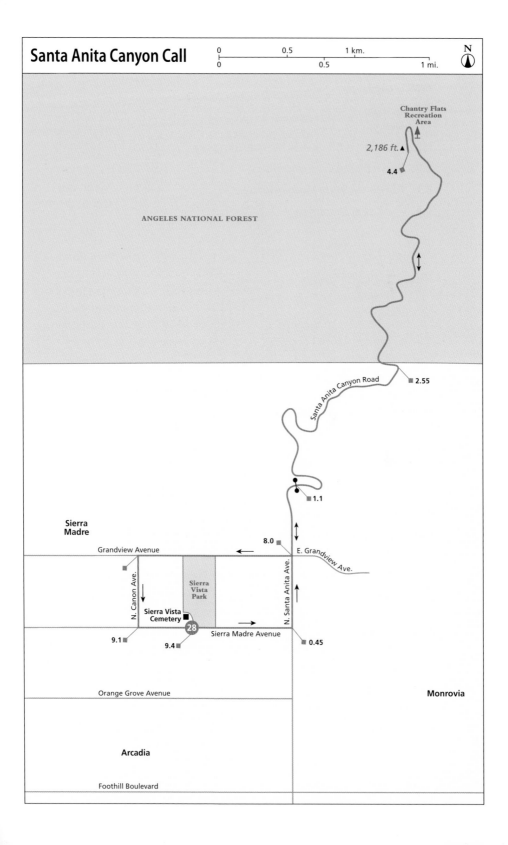

Santa Anita Canyon Call

0   0.5   1 km.
0   0.5   1 mi.

N

Chantry Flats
Recreation
Area

2,186 ft. ▲

4.4

ANGELES NATIONAL FOREST

Santa Anita Canyon Road

2.55

1.1

Sierra
Madre

Grandview Avenue

8.0

E. Grandview Ave.

N. Canon Ave.

Sierra
Vista
Park

N. Santa Anita Ave.

Sierra Vista
Cemetery

28

9.1

9.4

Sierra Madre Avenue

0.45

Orange Grove Avenue

Monrovia

Arcadia

Foothill Boulevard

4.55 Leave Chantry Flats Recreation Area.

6.25 Leave Angeles National Forest.

7.7 Gate; leave Santa Anita Canyon and return to residential area (Sierra Madre).

8.0 Stop sign at Grandview Avenue; turn right.

8.75 Turn left onto Canon Avenue.

9.1 Turn left at Sierra Madre Avenue.

9.4 End ride at Sierra Vista Park, on the left.

Schabarum Scramble

Start: Peter F. Schabarum Regional Park, 17250 East Colima Rd., Rowland Heights (motor vehicle entrance fee)

Length: 9.5 miles (clockwise loop)

Riding time: 1 to 3 hours (my time: 1H19:57)

Terrain and surface: 97.5% on dirt trails; 2.5% on paved park roads

Elevation: Low: 465 feet on the north side of Schabarum Regional Park on Adams Road; high: 1,330 feet at the junction between the Purple Sage and Buena Vista Trails

Traffic and hazards: 100% of the ride is within Schabarum Regional Park, with only 2.5% on paved roads shared with motor vehicles accessing the park.

Map: *The Thomas Guide—Street Guide: Los Angeles and Orange Counties* (any recent year), page 678

Getting there: By car—From central Los Angeles, head east on SR 60. Exit at Azusa Avenue in Industry and turn right, entering Rowland Heights. Turn left onto Colima Road and then turn right to enter Peter F. Schabarum Regional Park. Pay the entrance fee and head toward the left side of the park to find parking.

    By public transit—From central Los Angeles, ride Foothill Transit express bus route 493 to Colima Road and the Puente Hills Mall, which is immediately adjacent to Schabarum Regional Park. The bus leaves Los Angeles on weekday afternoons every 5 to 20 minutes between 2:30 and 6:30 p.m. For all-day and weekend service, ride the Metro Silver Line to El Monte station and then transfer to Foothill Transit bus route 178 or 282. Both routes travel to Puente Hills Mall.

Starting point coordinates: N33.989106° / W117.927519°

THE RIDE

The Schabarum Scramble is a reasonably challenging mountain bike ride in Schabarum Regional Park, located in Rowland Heights. The route uses dirt trails within the 575-acre park (some sources say 640 acres), which is located on the north side of the Puente Hills. (See Ahwingna Pahe Mahar and Whittier–Workman Hill Workout for other Puente Hills mountain bike rides.) For mountain bikers, the Puente Hills are hallowed ground—the original training grounds of legendary off-road cyclist David "Tinker" Juarez. His rise as an off-road cycling star occurred during the 1980s, when the sport was in its fledgling stages and all equipment—as well as training techniques—was subject to "tinkering." As of this writing, far from being retired, Juarez was still racing, collecting his share of Masters national and world titles (and still living and training in the

An off-road specialist tames a climb on the Schabarum Trail in Schabarum Regional Park.

Puente Hills). Despite the Juarez legend, the namesake of the park is Peter F. Schabarum. Mr. Schabarum played professional football for the San Francisco 49ers during the early 1950s, taking a break to serve in the Korean War. Later he served in the California State Assembly, with a stint on the Los Angeles County Board of Supervisors between 1967 and the early 1990s.

The ride begins in Rowland Heights, an unincorporated community of 48,993 persons (as of 2010), sandwiched between the cities of Industry to the north and La Habra Heights to the south. The population of Rowland Heights was 60% Asian in heritage as of the last US census, with a heavy concentration of Taiwanese—so heavy, in fact, that China Airlines was operating a special bus from the community to Los Angeles Airport specifically to feed flights to China. Enter the park and bear left, following the main park access road (the Powder Canyon Mountainway).

Find a parking spot.

The ride officially begins at the trailhead, located where Powder Canyon Mountainway intersects an unnamed road that heads toward the east side of the park to Albatross Road. I found that most—but not all—the trail junctions along this ride were

> ## Bike Shops
>
> **Beach Cruiser Bikes/ Fixie Fixed Gear Bikes,** 17531 Railroad St., Rowland Heights; (626) 626-7311; www.bikebuyers.com
> **GreenLine Bicycles,** 1314 John Reed Ct., Industry; (626) 810-3500; www.greenline bicycles.com

marked. It is a brisk start to the ride, as the trail immediately begins to climb up into the Puente Hills. This trail, which is Schabarum Trail, is part of a loop around the main part of the park. The "main part" is where the park's recreational facilities and picnic areas are located and where most of the park's users congregate. You, however, are headed for the remote upper reaches of the park in the Puente Hills. Thus, although this part of the ride has some stiff climbing, it is actually just a warm-up for the main course. Follow the trail as it climbs and then descends sharply toward the south side of the park. After passing a stable and equestrian facility (Ray's Equestrian Center), bear left to enter Powder Canyon via Powder Canyon Trail.

Just 0.2 mile up the canyon, look for the Schabarum Trail Extension on the left. Bear left here and begin an ascent on switchbacks, along which there are some spectacular views. The elevation at the mouth of Powder Canyon is 600 feet, while that at the crest of the Schabarum Extension is 1,040 feet. The extension is part of the Juan Bautista de Anza National Historic Trail. The trail approximates a segment of the route of de Anza's famous late-eighteenth-century overland expedition. From the crest it is an exhilarating view to the north and east of cities in the San Gabriel Valley. Along the descent, the trail crosses a paved water tank access road—I recall having to dismount here to clear curbs. An aerial view of one of Rowland Heights' neighborhoods, to your left, is a feature of this stretch of the trail. As the trail continues to descend to Fullerton Road, look for an unnamed connector trail on the right. Take the connector to the wide fire road and turn left. The fire road, which serves as an access for an easement, descends steeply. Watch out for sandy areas and debris.

At the bottom of the descent, adjacent to some industrial activity and near a parking area off Fullerton Road, turn right onto Black Walnut Trail. There is a wooden marker; the elevation here is 640 feet. The trail climbs steeply before descending into Powder Canyon. At the end of Black Walnut, turn right onto Powder Canyon Trail. The trail crests at 860 feet at a junction between several trails. Turn left to take Purple Sage Trail (the wider trail on the left). It is yet another ascent—this one will take you to the highest point of the ride, eventually cresting at 1,330 feet at the junction with Buena Vista Trail. Stay on Purple Sage here, as well as at a previous junction with a trail on the left. Beyond Buena Vista turn right and continue on Schabarum Trail, also known as Bixby Road.

Just 0.1 mile downstream, Bixby keeps straight while Schabarum turns right. Take Schabarum and follow it as it starts to descend sharply into the main part of Schabarum Regional Park. As you approach the "busier" areas of the park, bear left at the junction to continue on Schabarum. You are now on the west side of the park, with a view of activities in its central area. At the next trail junction, stay to the left. To your left there will be a parking area that is unrelated to the park. The trail empties out into an open space. Keep riding, aiming for the road up ahead. At the road negotiate the curb and turn right to continue. You are now on Adams Road, which is completely within Schabarum Regional Park. The road crosses a bridge, coming to an end at Powder Canyon Mountainway, the main park road. Turn right here and return to the trailhead where you started.

MILES AND DIRECTIONS

- **0.0** Start at the trailhead, located adjacent to the intersection between Powder Canyon Mountainway (the main park access road) and an unnamed road that heads to Albatross Road on the east side of the park. Head south (and up) via Schabarum Trail.
- **0.9** Pass by stables and equestrian facilities plus a small parking area.
- **1.0** Bear left at junction to continue southward on Schabarum Trail.
- **1.2** Bear left onto Schabarum Trail Extension; begin climb.
- **3.3** Cross over paved access road to water tank; keep straight on trail.

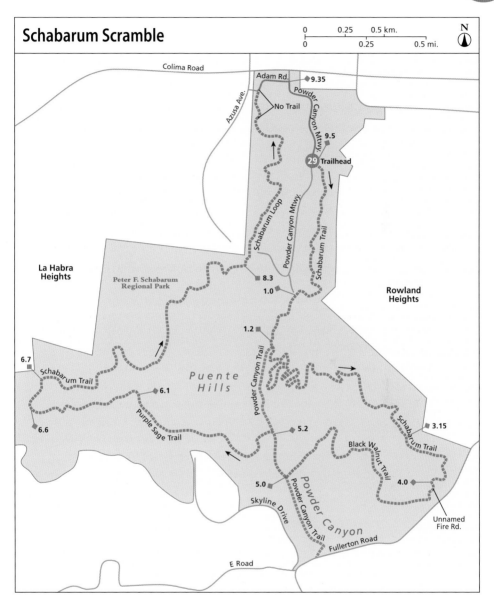

Schabarum Scramble

0   0.25   0.5 km.

0   0.25   0.5 mi.

N

Colima Road

Adam Rd. ◆ 9.35

Powder Canyon Mtwy.

Azusa Ave.

No Trail

■ 9.5

29 Trailhead

Schabarum Loop

Powder Canyon Mtwy.

Schabarum Trail

La Habra
Heights

Peter F. Schabarum
Regional Park

■ 8.3

■ 1.0

Rowland
Heights

■ 1.2

6.7
■

Schabarum Trail

Puente
Hills

Powder Canyon Trail

Schabarum Trail ■ 3.15

◆ 6.1

◆ 5.2

6.6 ◆

Purple Sage Trail

Black Walnut Trail

◆ 4.0

◆ 5.0

Powder Canyon Trail

Skyline Drive

Powder Canyon

Unnamed
Fire Rd.

Fullerton Road

E Road

3.65 Turn right onto unnamed connector trail (Schabarum Extension continues from here to road).

3.7 End of connector; turn left onto wide unnamed fire road. Begin descent.

4.0 Bear right onto Black Walnut Trail, adjacent to Fullerton Road access; begin climb.

5.0 End of Black Walnut Trail; turn right onto Powder Canyon Trail.

5.2 Turn left at multi-trail junction at crest of climb onto Purple Sage Trail (also called Skyline Drive); begin climb.

5.65 Trail junction; stay to the right.

6.1 Junction with Buena Vista Trail; keep left to stay on Purple Sage Trail.

6.6 Turn right onto Schabarum Trail (also called Bixby Road).

6.7 Bear right to continue on Schabarum Trail; begin descent.

8.3 Reenter main part of park; stay to the left at junction to continue Schabarum Trail loop.

9.1 Bear left at Y junction; trees and a large parking lot not associated with the park are to your left.

9.15 Trail ends; continue across open space to park road, which is up ahead.

9.2 Enter Adam Road, which is inside the park; turn right.

9.35 End of Adam Road; turn right onto main park road (Powder Canyon Mountainway).

9.5 End ride adjacent to the trailhead where the route started.

White Saddle Challenge

Start: Royal Oaks Park, 2627 Royal Oaks Dr., Duarte

Length: 17.0 miles (clockwise loop)

Riding time: 1.75 to 5.5 hours (my time: 2H32:58)

Terrain and surface: 57% on dirt fire roads; 34% on paved roads; 9% on a paved bike path

Elevation: Low: 548 feet at Duarte Bike Trail (also known as Royal Oaks Walking Trail) and Buena Vista Street in Duarte; high: 3,618 feet on Van Tassel Mountainway, about 1.3 miles beyond White Saddle

Traffic and hazards: The busiest segment is along Foothill Boulevard in Monrovia (traffic volume data unavailable).

Map: *The Thomas Guide—Street Guide: Los Angeles and Orange Counties* (any recent year), page 568

Getting there: By car—From central Los Angeles, head east on I-10 to I-605 north; continue to the end of the freeway in Duarte. Continue straight onto Mount Olive Drive. Turn right onto Royal Oaks Drive and continue to Royal Oaks Park, on the left, just past Vineyard Avenue.

    By public transit—From central Los Angeles, ride the Metro Silver Line (bus rapid transit) to the El Monte station. Transfer to Foothill Transit bus route 494 and travel to Duarte. Exit at Huntington Drive and Las Lomas Road. Ride northward on Las Lomas to Royal Oaks Drive. Turn left onto Royal Oaks; Royal Oaks Park will be on your right. Service on bus route 494 is limited to just three trips per day, during rush hour on weekdays.

Starting point coordinates: N34.143575° / W117.949031°

THE RIDE

The White Saddle Challenge is a challenging off-road ride that begins tamely on paths and roads in Duarte and Monrovia. After entering Monrovia Canyon, the ride leaves civilization and climbs earnestly into the San Gabriel Mountains, with a junction at White Saddle (3,229 feet). From there, after more

Long before the arduous climb to White Saddle, a rider cruises along the Duarte Bike Trail.

climbing to the high point of 3,618 feet, the route plummets dramatically into San Gabriel Canyon. This portion of the ride is not for the squeamish—those with a fear of heights might be alarmed by the experience. The descent is otherwise exhilarating, eventually returning the rider to the quiet residential environment of Duarte.

Start the White Saddle Challenge in Duarte at Royal Oaks Park. Duarte is named for Mexican corporal Andrés Duarte, who at one time owned all the land in Duarte and the surrounding area. The city (population of 21,321 in 2010) is perhaps best known as the crucible of the City of Hope National Medical Center, one of the leaders in the fight against cancer. Leave Royal Oaks Park via the Duarte Bike Trail, a paved bike path that runs parallel to Royal Oaks Drive. There are a number of at-grade street crossings along the path, so be sure to stop and look both ways. Although the bike path remains in Duarte until its end, immediately to your right is the city of Bradbury. This small city (population 1,048 in 2010) was formerly listed by *Forbes* as being the most expensive zip code in the United States. No, you cannot afford it. The bike path ends at Buena Vista Street, 1.6 miles into the ride (low point of the ride: 548 feet). Turn right here and then make an immediate left onto Orange Avenue.

Enter the city of Monrovia immediately after turning onto Orange. Monrovia (population 36,590 in 2010) is the fourth-oldest city in Los Angeles County. The city is perhaps best-known as the birthplace of McDonald's restaurants. The first "McDonald's" was called "The Airdrome" (1937); in 1940 it was relocated to San Bernardino, renamed, and the rest is history. The city was also the residence of Mary Ford, one-time partner of Les Paul, both of whom were pioneers in the development of the electric guitar and multi-track recording. At the end of Orange Avenue, turn right onto Bradbury Avenue and head north. The road curves to the left, becoming Wildrose Avenue. Turn right onto Mountain Avenue and then left onto Foothill Boulevard. After a short ride on the busiest street of the entire ride, turn right onto North Canyon Boulevard. The climbing begins here, at mile 3.25.

The opening climb on North Canyon is at a 6.1% grade as the road passes by some of Monrovia's interesting and appealing houses. Turn right at East Scenic Drive to remain on North Canyon. The grade steepens to 7.8% for this segment. At Oakglade Drive bear right to remain on North Canyon (elevation: 954 feet). The grade eases a bit here, to 4.9%, as you leave the city and enter Monrovia Canyon. Enter Monrovia Canyon Park at mile 4.85 (elevation: 1,103 feet). Look for the road leading to Camp Trask (Trask Boy Scout Reservation) at mile 5.0; turn right here. You are still on North Canyon—this is the steepest climb of the entire ride! The road ascends from 1,149 feet at the turn to 1,572 feet past the dam at the Monrovia Canyon Truck Trail (fire road) trailhead. The average grade along here is 11.4%, although there are steeper segments, especially in the middle of the switchbacks. Watch for motorists traveling to and from the camp, as the road is narrow.

Leave the paved road to the right at mile 5.95 and head onto Monrovia Canyon Truck Trail, a wide fire road with a good surface. The trail climbs at a steady 8.3% grade over the next 3.8 miles, so settle into a rhythm. As you are climbing, generally above Monrovia Canyon, you may be envious of the sound of rushing water and rustling trees coming from below. Camp Trask stretches into the canyon and contains a busy ecosystem that includes bigleaf maple, white alder, and coast live oak trees. In comparison, Monrovia Canyon Truck Trail offers little shade, and there is no water. There is a lavatory, however, on your

Bike Shops

Empire Bikes, 625 South Myrtle Ave., Monrovia; (626) 930-1983; http://empirebikes.us
Stan's Monrovia Bicycles, 880 South Myrtle Ave., Monrovia; (626) 357-0020; www.facebook.com/pages/Stans-Bike-Shop/506565879356087

left at about 2,600 feet elevation. Intermittent guide signs along the way indicate the elevation and provide a brief note on connecting trails leading down into the canyon. These are worth exploring. Some of the signs also indicate how far it is to points of interest, such as White Saddle. Speaking of which, you finally reach White Saddle (elevation: 3,229 feet) at mile 9.75. The feature is so named because the truck trail meets Silver Fish Truck Trail here, and their wide juncture has the appearance (perhaps from above) of a brightly colored saddle.

Turn right onto Silver Fish and—keep climbing! No, you have not yet reached the crest. Silver Fish climbs in stages rather than steadily to a junction with Van Tassel Mountainway. Stay to the right here to continue on Van Tassel. After another mile of climbing, the crest of the entire ride is finally reached at 3,618 feet. While on Van Tassel, you may catch a few glimpses of the valley below and may be surprised (perhaps even shocked) at how far up you are. Those of you with a hint of acrophobia may feel uneasy at the thought of descending into the valley below. But what goes up must come down, and the Van Tassel descent is a doozy. The average grade is 13.3%, although there are steeper segments. You may marvel at the parked construction and earth-moving equipment on the way down, wondering how those big rigs ever made it up here. Deep, loose dirt sections occur intermittently on the way down. These are there to slow the heavy vehicles during descent, and perhaps provide traction. A skillful mountain biker might similarly use these to slow his or her descent. Or, if you are like me, your hands will be feeling the strain from squeezing the brake levers. Soft, cushioned handlebar grips are highly recommended.

Avoid looking away from the trail, and control your speed on the way down. Then again, take a short glance every now and then to check how much progress you are making during the downhill. The valley rapidly comes into view, getting closer and closer. Near the bottom, Van Tassel makes sharp left and then right turns. After the last turn, at mile 15, the fire road enters a small community of ranch properties. Ride on through; the steep descent is now over. Turn right onto Fish Canyon Road and return to pavement. Watch out for trucks accessing nearby quarry operations. Soon after the turn, the road enters Duarte, becoming Encanto Parkway. Watch the street signs for easy-to-miss Royal Oaks Drive; turn right here. From here it is a pleasant 0.8 mile through Duarte to Vineyard Avenue (Royal Oaks Park is to your right) and the end of the ride.

MILES AND DIRECTIONS

0.0 Start from Vineyard Avenue, adjacent to Royal Oaks Park, and head west on the Duarte Bike Path.

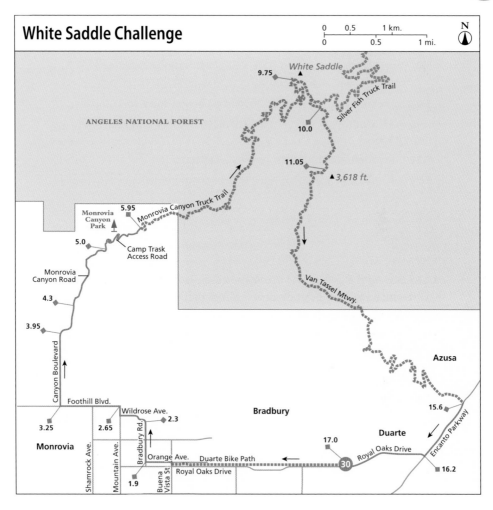

30

White Saddle Challenge

| | 0 | 0.5 | 1 km. |
| | 0 | 0.5 | 1 mi. |

1.6 Stop at Buena Vista Street; turn right.

1.65 Stop at Orange Avenue; turn left.

1.9 Stop at Bradbury Road; turn left.

2.3 Road curves to the left; now on Wildrose Avenue.

2.55 Stop at Mountain Avenue; turn left.

2.65 Stop at Foothill Boulevard; turn left.

3.25 Traffic signal at North Canyon Boulevard; turn right.

3.95 North Canyon turns to the right at East Scenic Drive; remain on North Canyon.

4.3 Road curves to the right at Oakglade Drive; now on Monrovia Canyon Road.

4.85 Enter Monrovia Canyon Park.

5.0 Turn right at entrance to Trask Scout Reservation (Camp Trask), still on Monrovia Canyon Road.

5.95 End of road; veer right onto Monrovia Canyon Truck Trail (unpaved fire road—elevation: 1,571 feet). Begin climb at an average 8.3% grade.

6.25 Gate; continue around on Monrovia Canyon.

9.75 Junction with Silver Fish Truck Trail; bear right onto Silver Fish (elevation: 3,229 feet).

10.0 Junction with Van Tassel Mountainway; keep right, now on Van Tassel.

11.05 High point of ride (3,618 feet).

11.15 Stay right at fork in trail to remain on Van Tassel Mountainway (elevation: 3,568 feet). Start descent (average grade: 13.3%).

15.05 Van Tassel Mountainway makes a sharp right-hand curve, entering mountainside community (elevation: 828 feet).

15.6 Stop sign at Fish Canyon Road; turn right (elevation: 677 feet).

15.7 Now on Encanto Parkway.

16.2 Turn right onto Royal Oaks Drive.

17.0 End ride at stop sign at Vineyard Avenue, adjacent to Royal Oaks Park.

Best West and Southwest L.A. Region Rides

Destination: beaches and the ocean! What Los Angeles–area guidebook would be complete without a discussion of the region's coastline? While the inland areas of L.A. certainly have a pounding vibe and may be the region's heart, the true soul of the region may be along the coast. The subregion is effectively that of area codes 310 and 424, reaching from Malibu in the west to Beverly Hills in the east and then to the Palos Verdes Peninsula and San Pedro in the south. The subregion's population was 1.29 million as of 2010. The largest cities included Los Angeles (west-central and southern portions of the city, with a total population of 350,000, representing less than 10% of the city's total), Torrance, Inglewood, Santa Monica, and Hawthorne. Between Malibu and Redondo Beach, the county boasts 44 miles of coastline, nearly all of it accessible beaches and oceanfront (with more than half in Malibu). The only real interruptions are at Marina del Rey and Redondo Beach's harbor. Farther to the south, Long Beach features another 3 miles of beachfront. Living along, within walking distance, or in view of the ocean is expensive; hence the L.A. region's richest communities tend to be in this subregion. Even though you (and I) may not be able afford any of the residences you can see during the ride, you get to experience firsthand the SoCal surfside lifestyle.

Rather than doing one long out-and-back coastal ride, this book breaks the coastline into several segments, heading inland as needed to explore the Santa Monica Mountains and a few communities. Going inland allows the rider to temporarily escape the busy coast and explore surprisingly quiet (and hilly) country and residential roads. There are seven road and five mountain bike rides in this section. The road rides range in length from 3.9 to 38.2 miles; the mountain bike rides range from just 3.35 to 16.75 miles. Net elevation changes range widely as well—from just 53 feet (Rondo Redondo Beach) to 2,192 feet (Rambla Piuma Pacifico). Outside of the scenic beauty and accessibility, the climate is the main draw. Described as Mediterranean, beach and ocean weather is literally year-round. Eighteenth-century Spanish missionary Juan Crespi and nineteenth-century author Richard Henry Dana—although they never met—fully agreed that Los Angeles was ripe for settlement. They both foresaw the transformation of the region from a dry coastal basin into a thriving metropolis.

The greater proportion of the L.A. region's coastline is Santa Monica Bay, which features a seemingly endless string of beaches and includes Santa Monica Pier. The rocky Palos Verdes Peninsula, complete with tide pools and a rugged shoreline, separates Santa Monica Bay from San Pedro Bay. The latter features two major ports: the Port of Los Angeles and the Port of Long Beach. Combined, the two ports are among the ten busiest container ports in the world. Venice, one of the first major oceanside developments, was built in 1892 and modeled after Italy's Venice. The community featured canals, gondolas, and a true resort environment that was actually an independent city until 1926. The city was then annexed by L.A. The canals are still there, but the rest has been transformed into a residential rather than resort community. Yet Venice Beach remains a center of waterfront performance, with artists, fortune-tellers, musicians, fitness fanatics, and countless onlookers. The waterfront is so busy, in fact, that bicycling through here is nearly impossible. Therefore the rides in this book skip Venice—not to say that the oceanfront walk is not worth a visit!

Best Bike Rides Los Angeles

Baldwin Hills Hahn-wind

Start: Norman O. Houston Park

Length: 3.35 miles (counterclockwise loop)

Riding time: 20 minutes to 1 hour (my time: 26:15)

Terrain and surface: 71% on dirt trails; 29% on a paved path; 10% on a paved park maintenance road

Elevation: Low: 260 feet at the end of La Brea Loop Trail, at intersection with park maintenance road; high: 487 feet at the beginning of Boy Scout Trail

Traffic and hazards: None of the route is shared with motor vehicles. To get to the starting point from Norman O. Houston Park, the rider must cross La Brea Avenue.

Map: *The Thomas Guide—Street Guide: Los Angeles and Orange Counties* (any recent year), page 673

Getting there: By car—From central Los Angeles, head west on I-10. Exit at La Brea Avenue and head south. Turn left onto Don Lorenzo Drive, followed by a right turn onto Stocker Street and then a right turn onto La Brea Avenue (now heading north). Norman O. Houston Park is on the right.

    By public transit—From central Los Angeles, ride the Metro Expo Line (light-rail) to the Expo/La Brea station. Transfer to Metro bus route 212 or 312 and head south on La Brea Avenue. Exit at Don Lorenzo Drive; Kenneth Hahn State Recreation Area is on your right. Route 212, occasionally alternating with route 312, runs every 5 to 12 minutes on weekdays, every 15 minutes on Saturday, and every 20 minutes on Sunday and holidays.

Starting point coordinates: N34.041667° / W118.359328°

THE RIDE

The Baldwin Hills Hahn-wind is a 3.35-mile jaunt through Kenneth Hahn State Recreation Area in the Los Angeles community of Baldwin Hills. Although the

Moguls and picturesque scenery along Boy Scout Trail in Kenneth Hahn State Recreation Area

ride is short, it offers a little bit of everything: fast descents, steep climbs, dirt trails—rough and smooth, paved paths, and even a few moguls. It is a choice ride for a beginning mountain biker who wants a few, but not too many, technical tests. It is also a great ride for someone who is pressed for time (as I was once, on my way to Los Angeles International Airport to catch a flight). Although the title implies that you will "Hahn-wind" in this ride, prepare for a few bumps!

Norman O. Houston Park in Baldwin Hills is the staging area for this ride. The ride officially begins on the other side of La Brea Avenue, however, in Kenneth Hahn State Recreation Area (opposite Don Lorenzo Drive). This side of Hahn Park is easier to access than its official entrance point, which is off Baldwin Hills Avenue. Norman O. Houston (1893–1981) was a businessman and president of Golden State Mutual Life Insurance Company, at one time the largest African American–owned business west of the Mississippi.

To get to Kenneth Hahn Park, ride along La Brea Avenue to Don Lorenzo Drive. Cross the street here, and then climb the stairs to enter the park. There is a large sign posted here. Kenneth Hahn was a forty-year member of the Los

1932 Summer Olympic Games

A little over half a century before the 1984 Summer Olympic Games, Los Angeles held the 1932 Summer Olympics—the Games of the 10th Olympiad. The community of View Park, located less than a mile east-southeast of Kenneth Hahn Park, was the site of the Olympic Village. All 1,206 male athletes stayed in the village, while the 126 female athletes stayed in a hotel on Wilshire Boulevard! The Olympic Village was demolished long ago, but Olympiad Drive still snakes through the neighborhood as a commemoration. Athletes from thirty-seven nations were represented at the Games, despite Los Angeles being somewhat remote at the time. There were no freeways back then, and the major airports were in Burbank and Glendale—Los Angeles International was still in the early phases of development. Participation, in fact, was down by about 50% compared to the 1928 Games in Amsterdam. Yet, unlike today's intense competition and bidding process among potential host cities, L.A. was the only city that offered to stage the Games. The United States had the largest team by a factor of nearly four, and its 103 medals (41 gold) easily outpaced Italy's 36 medals (12 gold). Among the standout athletes were Mildred "Babe" Didrikson, triple gold medalist and double world-record setter in track and field; Eddie Tolan, double gold medalist in the sprints; and Kusuo Kitamura, still the youngest-ever (age 14) male gold medalist in an individual event: swimming.

Four track cycling events were held on a velodrome constructed inside the Rose Bowl in Pasadena. There were two road biking events: a 100-kilometer (km) individual time trial, and a 100 km team time trial, in which the results were determined by adding the times of a team's top three men in the individual race. The distance was originally set at 100 miles but was shortened to ensure that the entire course was safe and closed to traffic. The point-to-point route took the riders from Moorpark in Ventura County, northwest of L.A., along Los Angeles Avenue (which still exists but is now also designated as SR 118) to Oxnard. Once in Oxnard, the route turned southward onto Vineyard Avenue and then onto the Roosevelt Highway, which later was incorporated into the Pacific Coast Highway (SR 1). From there the route continued along the coast to Santa Monica, where the race ended. Attilio Pavesi of Italy won the time trial in 2 hours, 28 minutes, 5.6 seconds—a 25.2-mile-per-hour average on a vintage 1930s-era road bike! (Granted, there was a net elevation loss of about 500 feet.) By taking first, second, and fourth in the individual race, the Italian men easily won the team event.

Angeles County Board of Supervisors and an ardent supporter of civil rights. His namesake recreation area covers 401 acres in the middle of Baldwin Hills and features a wide variety of recreational opportunities, wildlife, and plant life. The park has been used as a filming location, including Dr. Dre and Snoop Dogg's music video for "Nothin' But a G Thang." Hahn Park occupies the former site of the Baldwin Hills Dam and Reservoir. In December 1963 a breach was discovered in the dam and the authorities ordered local residents to evacuate. Within three hours, the dam burst, flooding the surrounding region with 250 million gallons of water. The evacuations limited the loss of life to just three deaths. The dam was never rebuilt, and Kenneth Hahn State Recreation Area was opened in 1984.

Head north on La Brea Loop Trail—and hang on! It is a wild start to the ride as the trail undulates and twists its way downhill, parallel to La Brea Avenue. You might envision yourself keeping up with traffic on the adjacent road as the trail drops from 440 to 260 feet, the ride's low point. After a rapid descent to get your heart pumping, the trail comes to an abrupt end at a park maintenance road. Turn left here and climb up to "The Bowl," also known as "Janice's Green Valley," one of the park's feature sites. The climb is steep, with an average grade of 14.1%. At the top of the hill, perhaps gasping for breath, turn right onto the Community Loop Trail (also known as Bowl Loop). The paved trail is popular, so be courteous to other trail users. The trail features a few undulations. The loop is actually discontinuous—bear left onto the short dirt connector at mile 1.2, and then pick up the paved path on the other side. Continue around the loop, heading nearly back to where you entered the loop.

Bike Shops

Penuel Bicycles, 1329 N. La Brea Ave., Inglewood; (310) 412-5836
Primo's Bike Shop, 1645 W. Vernon Ave., Los Angeles; (323) 294-7640

At mile 1.7 turn right, off of the loop, and ride along the edge of the parking area. Head toward the canyon and look for the trailhead to Boy Scout Trail. There are a couple of steps (downhill) to negotiate—you may either ride or walk these. A bit wider than singletrack, Boy Scout Trail featured a few moguls when I rode it. The trail heads downhill, into the canyon. Just over 2.0 miles into the ride, Boy Scout makes a sharp hairpin turn to the right. You are now heading south on Ron's Trail. This trail, like Boy Scout, is a bit wider than singletrack and is gradual uphill. Portions of the trail are rough. There are a few tight turns that may test your bike-handling skills. Keep straight where Ron's Trail merges with another trail. At the trail split at mile 2.9, keep right. You are now on Five Points Trail; follow this to the south side of this section of Kenneth Hahn Park. The trail merges with the La Brea Loop Trail (portions of which have been converted

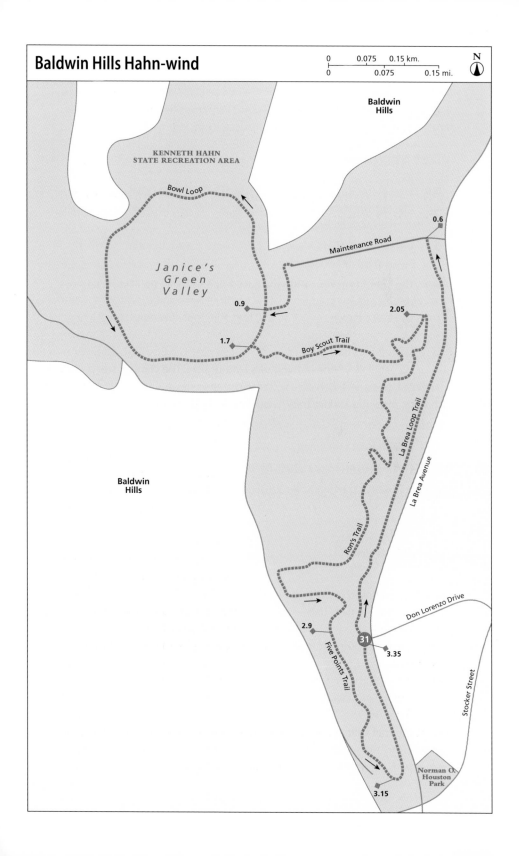

Baldwin Hills Hahn-wind

0   0.075   0.15 km.

0   0.075   0.15 mi.

N

Baldwin
Hills

KENNETH HAHN
STATE RECREATION AREA

Bowl Loop

0.6

Maintenance Road

Janice's
Green
Valley

0.9

2.05

1.7

Boy Scout Trail

La Brea Loop Trail

La Brea Avenue

Baldwin
Hills

Ron's Trail

Don Lorenzo Drive

2.9

31

3.35

Five Points Trail

Stocker Street

Norman O.
Houston
Park

3.15

into a fitness walking trail). After curving to the left, you are now heading north on La Brea Loop. You are now within 0.2 mile of completing the ride—a couple of steep downhill drops await you, so you can finish with an exclamation point!

MILES AND DIRECTIONS

0.0 Start at the top of the stairs opposite Don Lorenzo Drive, adjacent to the large information sign and La Brea Avenue in Kenneth Hahn State Recreation Area. Head north on La Brea Loop Trail.

0.6 Turn left at end of La Brea Loop Trail onto paved maintenance road; begin climb (14.1% grade).

0.9 Top of hill; turn right onto the paved Community Loop Trail (also known as Bowl Loop).

1.2 Bear left onto short unpaved connector trail.

1.3 Turn left to continue on paved Bowl Loop (Community Loop Trail).

1.7 Turn right, off loop, and ride adjacent to parking area.

1.75 Cut across junction of footpaths and down short (rideable) staircase to access Boy Scout Trail (head toward canyon).

2.05 Boy Scout Trail makes hairpin turn; now on Ron's Trail.

2.9 Bear right at trail junction; now on Five Points Trail.

3.15 Curve left; return to La Brea Loop Trail.

3.35 End ride at starting point, adjacent to large sign.

Beverly Hills Brevet

Start: Will Rogers Memorial Park, 9650 Sunset Blvd., Beverly Hills

Length: 11.3 miles (clockwise loop)

Riding time: 35 minutes to 2 hours (my time: 46:32)

Terrain and surface: 100% on paved roads

Elevation: Low: 354 feet at Beverly and Cañon Drives, adjacent to Will Rogers Memorial Park; high: 1,314 feet on Mulholland Drive east of Sumatra Drive

Traffic and hazards: 18,605 vehicles per day on Benedict Canyon Drive at Hillgrove Drive in 2006; 6,230 vehicles per day on Mulholland Drive west of Coldwater Canyon Drive in 2006; 25,050 vehicles per day on Coldwater Canyon Drive at Heather Road in 2005

Map: *The Thomas Guide—Street Guide: Los Angeles and Orange Counties* (any recent year), page 592

Getting there: By car—From central Los Angeles, head west on Cesar Chavez Avenue, which becomes Sunset Boulevard just west of downtown. Continue on Sunset Boulevard to Beverly Drive in Beverly Hills. Turn left and then turn right onto Cañon Drive. Park adjacent to Will Rogers Memorial Park (no off-street parking available).

By public transit—From central Los Angeles, hop on Metro bus route 2 to head west on Sunset Boulevard. Exit at Beverly Drive in Beverly Hills adjacent to Will Rogers Memorial Park and cross the street to get to the park. Route 2 alternates with Route 302 during weekday commute periods. The bus runs every 10 minutes on weekdays, every 13 minutes on Saturday, and every 15 to 18 minutes on Sunday and holidays.

Starting point coordinates: N34.080153° / W118.413822°

THE RIDE

The Beverly Hills Brevet is a pleasant 11.3-mile loop up and back down the hills above Beverly Hills. A brevet is typically a long-distance cycling event, but this route is short and sweet—although, with about 1,000 feet of climbing along the way, the rider is destined for a good workout. The entire ride takes place within the 90210 zip code, which, through the TV series *Beverly Hills 90210* and a consistent *Forbes* magazine ranking as one of the most expensive in the United States, has become iconic (see sidebar). While riding along, you may happen to observe the many fine houses along the way, but you will probably be watching the road as well. Start the ride at the intersection of Sunset Boulevard and Cañon Drive, adjacent to Will Rogers Memorial Park. The park was established in 1915 as Sunset Park but was renamed in 1952. Will Rogers (1879–1935) was a popular actor, humorist, social commentator, and vaudeville performer. Although the man got around (born in Oklahoma, died in Alaska), he served as the honorary mayor of Beverly Hills from 1926 to 1928.

A cyclist enjoys serenity along one of the most famous roads to ride in Los Angeles, Mulholland Drive.

Beverly Hills 90210

Beverly Hills 90210 is an actual place. The 90210 zip code, in fact, encompasses much of the Beverly Glen community of Los Angeles in addition to "northern" Beverly Hills. The zip code is consistently ranked among the top ten most-expensive places to live in the United States by *Forbes*, based on the value of real estate. Beverly Hills had a population of 34,590 in 2010. The city was incorporated in 1914 and resisted annexation by Los Angeles during the 1920s (in part because the city had its own water resources). Because of its proximity to Hollywood, actors and actresses such as Douglas Fairbanks, Mary Pickford, Rudolph Valentino, and others established residences in the city and built opulent mansions. During the 1900s, housing restrictions had been established to ensure that the city remained an all-white, non-Jewish community. Nonetheless, African-American actors and actresses began to move in during the 1940s, opposing the covenants, which were eventually overturned by the US Supreme Court in 1948.

Modern-day Beverly Hills is still predominantly white, but about one-fourth of the residents identify themselves as Persian Jews, the largest such community in the United States. Numerous actors and actresses—too many to list here—have made and continue to make Beverly Hills their home. Guided tours of the "stars' homes" are offered by various organizations for those eager to get a glimpse of the lifestyles of the rich and famous. The wealth in the city is real, and TV shows and films—*The Beverly Hillbillies, Beverly Hills Cop (I, II & III), Beverly Hills Chihuahua, The Real Housewives of Beverly Hills*, and the aforementioned *90210*—have cemented the city's high-brow reputation. In the Weezer song "Beverly Hills" (music video not filmed in the city), Rivers Cuomo yearns for the celebrity lifestyle the city offers. Well, at least you get to take an exciting ride into the hills above the revered city!

In 1998 singer-songwriter George Michael was arrested in the park's restroom for performing a "lewd act."

Head northwest, away from the park, on Cañon Drive, crossing busy Sunset Boulevard. Once across, you are on Benedict Canyon Drive (also spelled Benedict Cañon Drive). The road begins a gradual climb into the canyon. After leaving Beverly Hills and entering Los Angeles at mile 1.1, the canyon closes in and the road narrows. Although the average grade is a doable 3.7%, the climb gradually gets steeper. Shortly after entering L.A., Benedict Canyon passes

Cielo Drive, which is where Sharon Tate and four others were murdered by members of the Charles Manson "family" in 1969. The residence where the incident occurred has since been razed and another home built.

After you negotiate a couple of hairpin turns that afford some excellent vistas, Benedict Canyon closes in on Mulholland Drive (see the Circuito de Calabasas ride for more on Mulholland). Turn right here (5.05-mile mark; elevation: 1,261 feet) and head east. Mulholland snakes and twists its way along the crest. The high point of the entire ride (1,314 feet) comes 1.0 mile after the turn onto Mulholland.

Continue heading east along Mulholland, enjoying the vistas to the left and to the right. Coldwater Canyon Drive merges from the left at an awkward intersection at mile 7.2. Keep straight on Mulholland. Look for the "lower part" of Coldwater Canyon to be on the right, at mile 7.5. Turn right here and begin the descent. This is a fun descent that starts out steep and then gradually eases. In this canyon, as in Benedict Canyon, you will observe a wide variety of vegetation, including oak, sycamore, cypress, pine, and eucalyptus trees, along with chaparral, ferns, lupine, and vines.

Bike Shop

Beverly Hills Bike Shop (not actually in Beverly Hills), 10546 W. Pico Blvd., Los Angeles; (310) 275-2453; www.bhbikeshop.com

Reenter Beverly Hills at mile 9.45. Coldwater Canyon Drive becomes Beverly Drive just south of Coldwater Canyon Park. At the stop sign at Rexford Drive, turn right to continue on Beverly Drive. Continue heading southward on Beverly and cross Sunset Boulevard, with Will Rogers Memorial Park on your left. To complete the ride, continue to Cañon Drive and turn right. Head up Cañon back to Sunset to finish the loop.

MILES AND DIRECTIONS

0.0 Start from Will Rogers Memorial Drive and head northwest on Cañon Drive. Cross Sunset Boulevard; the street becomes Benedict Canyon Drive.

1.1 Leave Beverly Hills and enter Los Angeles (Beverly Glen community).

5.05 Traffic signal at Mulholland Drive; turn right.

6.05 High point of ride (1,314 feet), east of Sumatra Drive.

7.2 Coldwater Canyon Drive merges from the left; keep straight on Mulholland.

7.5 Traffic signal at Coldwater Canyon Drive; turn right and begin descent.

Best Bike Rides Los Angeles

218

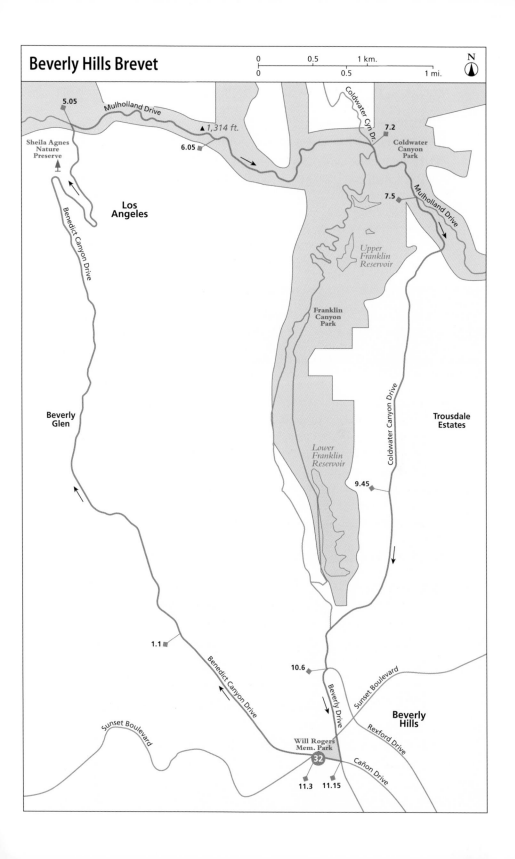

Beverly Hills Brevet

0   0.5   1 km.
0   0.5   1 mi.

N

5.05
Mulholland Drive
▲ 1,314 ft.
6.05
Coldwater Cyn Dr.
7.2
Coldwater
Canyon
Park

Sheila Agnes
Nature
Preserve

Los
Angeles

7.5
Mulholland Drive

Benedict Canyon Drive

Upper
Franklin
Reservoir

Franklin
Canyon
Park

Beverly
Glen

Coldwater Canyon Drive

Trousdale
Estates

Lower
Franklin
Reservoir

9.45

1.1
Benedict Canyon Drive

10.6
Beverly Drive
Sunset Boulevard

Sunset Boulevard

Will Rogers
Mem. Park
32
Cañon Drive

Rexford Drive

Beverly
Hills

11.3   11.15

9.45 Enter Beverly Hills.

10.35 Traffic signal at Beverly Drive; keep straight, now on Beverly Drive.

10.6 Stop sign at Rexford Drive; turn right to remain on Beverly Drive.

11.0 Traffic signal at Sunset Boulevard; keep straight.

11.15 Stop sign at Cañon Drive; turn right.

11.3 End ride at Sunset Boulevard, adjacent to Will Rogers Memorial Park.

Crankin' Franklin Canyon

Start: Franklin Canyon Park, 2600 Franklin Canyon Dr., Beverly Hills

Length: 6.05 miles (two connected clockwise loops, plus an out-and-back on a trail)

Riding time: 20 to 60 minutes (my time: 30:32)

Terrain and surface: 69% on dirt trails; 31% on paved roads

Elevation: Low: 657 feet at Discovery Trail trailhead along Lake Franklin Drive; high: 1,195 feet at the Hastain Trail crest.

Traffic and hazards: Franklin Canyon Drive was carrying 305 vehicles per day on the north side of Franklin Canyon Park in 2007.

Map: *The Thomas Guide—Street Guide: Los Angeles and Orange Counties* (any recent year), page 592

Getting there: By car—From central Los Angeles, head west on Cesar Chavez Avenue; the road becomes Sunset Boulevard just west of downtown. Continue all the way to Beverly Hills. Turn right onto Rexford Drive, followed by a right onto Beverly Drive. At the traffic signal adjacent to Coldwater Canyon Park, turn left to remain on Beverly Drive. Follow Beverly as it narrows and winds through the neighborhood. Just past the gate, the steep and narrow road becomes Franklin Canyon Drive. Continue along Franklin Canyon to its intersection with Lake Franklin Drive. Pull off the road and park here.

By public transit—From central Los Angeles, hop on Metro bus route 2 to head west on Sunset Boulevard. Exit at Beverly Drive in Beverly Hills and ride north on Beverly Drive to Coldwater Canyon Park. Turn left and follow the "by car" instructions. Route 2 alternates with Route 302 during weekday commute periods. The bus runs every 10 minutes on weekdays, every 13 minutes on Saturday, and every 15 to 18 minutes on Sunday and holidays.

Starting point coordinates: N34.115842° / W118.413972°

THE RIDE

Urban mountain bike routes are not easy to find, especially in a dense, heavily developed city such as Los Angeles. Trails are often restricted to foot traffic only, as is the case in some of L.A.'s parks (such as Griffith Park). Franklin Canyon Park is an exception—a bit of an oasis affording a pleasant and popular respite amid Los Angeles' urbanization. Franklin Canyon Park is located in the lower, south-side slopes of the Santa Monica Mountains, making it easily accessible from Beverly Hills, Hollywood, and central L.A. Its accessibility to Hollywood is evident in the staggering number of TV shows and films that have been shot here. One of the most notable is the opening scene in the 1960s' *Andy Griffith Show*, in which Andy and Opie (a young Ron Howard) are walking to Myers Lake to do some fishin'. The scene was shot in Franklin Canyon Park; the lake is Franklin Lake. (And all the while I thought that they were in Mayberry, North Carolina!) Also filmed in the park was the hitchhiking scene from *It Happened One Night* (1934), in which Claudette Colbert pulls her dress up to expose a shapely leg to attract a ride for herself and Clark Gable. In *The Creature from the Black Lagoon* (1954), the creature emerges from Franklin Lake.

With plenty of TV and movie nostalgia in the air, start the ride from the intersection of Franklin Canyon and Lake Franklin Drives, in the middle of the park. Head north on Franklin Canyon. You will notice that the park is heavily wooded with oak, sycamore, walnut, and even redwood trees (although these are not native to Southern California). A variety of wildflowers grows in the park as well. Just up the road, bear left onto the unnamed dirt trail. The trail runs essentially parallel to the road but offers a more interesting segment. At the end of the trail, turn right and head south on Franklin Canyon. At the next intersection turn left, 1.1 miles into the ride, to circumnavigate Upper Franklin Canyon Reservoir. The reservoir is partially obscured by the dense vegetation. The road curves its way around the lake, eventually merging with Franklin Canyon Drive, near where you started. At Lake Franklin Drive, where you actually did start, turn left and head down the hill.

Bike Shop

Beverly Hills Bike Shop (not actually in Beverly Hills), 10546 West Pico Blvd., Los Angeles; (310) 275-2453; www.bhbikeshop.com

Look for the Hastain Trail trailhead on the left at mile 2.05, 0.3 mile after making the turn. Enter the trail through the narrow gate—a dismount is necessary, and wide handlebars just barely fit through the opening. Hastain Trail climbs at 6.4%, with some nice views of the canyon, to a hairpin turn. Beyond the hairpin, the trail's gradient increases to a whopping 12.0%, leaving you to

This is Los Angeles? On the Hastain Trail in Franklin Canyon, in the hills above Beverly Hills.

move about as fast as the hikers. In 0.3 mile—which may seem longer—Hastain Trail peaks at 1,195 feet above sea level. Continue past the junction at the crest and begin the gradual descent. The trail comes to an abrupt end at a gate; turn around here and return the way you came. While navigating the descent, enjoy the views of the canyon, L.A., and Beverly Hills. This trail is quite popular, so always be mindful of other users. After navigating the narrow gate at the base of the trail, turn left onto Lake Franklin Drive.

After a short distance, look for the Discovery Trail trailhead on the right. I do not recall seeing a sign posted. This trail climbs up the side of the canyon, opposite that of the Hastain Trail, at a grade of 8.5%. This trail is narrower than Hastain, slightly wider than singletrack. At the top turn right onto the paved Hillcrest Drive. At the end of Hillcrest, turn right onto Franklin Canyon Drive. This is the way you entered the park. The road gently twists and winds its way down into the canyon—watch out for oncoming motor vehicle traffic. The ride ends at the Lake Franklin Drive intersection.

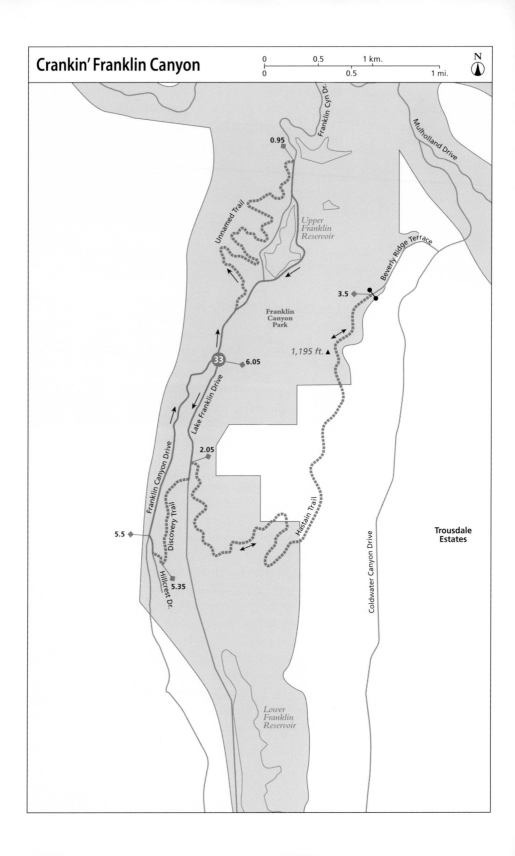

Crankin' Franklin Canyon

Franklin Cyn Dr.

Mulholland Drive

0.95

Unnamed Trail

Upper
Franklin
Reservoir

Beverly Ridge Terrace

3.5

Franklin
Canyon
Park

1,195 ft. ▲

33   6.05

Lake Franklin Drive

Franklin Canyon Drive

2.05

Hastain Trail

Discovery Trail

5.5

Coldwater Canyon Drive

Trousdale
Estates

Hillcrest Dr.

5.35

Lower
Franklin
Reservoir

N

0   0.5   1 km.
0   0.5   1 mi.

MILES AND DIRECTIONS

0.0   Start at the corner of Franklin Canyon and Lake Franklin Drives in Franklin Canyon Park. Head north on Franklin Canyon.

0.15 Veer left off the road onto the unnamed dirt trail.

0.95 End of trail; turn right onto Franklin Canyon Drive.

1.1   Turn left to circumnavigate Upper Franklin Canyon Reservoir.

1.4   End of loop around reservoir; merge with Franklin Canyon Drive and head south.

1.75 Turn left onto Lake Franklin Drive.

2.05 Bear left onto Hastain Trail (narrow entryway); begin climb (6.4% grade).

2.95 Hastain Trail executes hairpin turn to the left (elevation: 980 feet); climb gets steeper (12.0% grade).

3.3   Crest of Hastain Trail (elevation: 1,195 feet); keep straight onto short downhill segment.

3.5   End of trail at gate; turn around and return.

3.65 Back at Hastain Trail crest; begin descent.

4.0   Hairpin curve to the right.

4.9   End of Hastain Trail; proceed through gate and then turn left onto Lake Franklin Drive.

4.95 Turn right onto Discovery Trail (low point of ride: 657 feet); begin climb (8.5% grade).

5.35 End of Discovery Trail; turn right onto Hillcrest Drive.

5.45 Stop sign at Franklin Canyon Drive; turn right.

6.05 End ride at Lake Franklin Drive intersection.

Malibulldog MASH 4077 Tour

Start: Malibu Creek State Park, 1925 Las Virgenes Rd., Calabasas

Length: 16.65 miles (clockwise loop)

Riding time: 2 to 6 hours (my time: 2H50:12)

Terrain and surface: 89% on dirt fire roads and trails; 11% on paved roads

Elevation: Low: 472 feet on Malibu Canyon Road, crossing Malibu Creek; high: 2,419 feet at Castro Peak Motorway and Bulldog Mountainway

Traffic and hazards: 98% of the ride is on unpaved and paved park roads; 2% is on Malibu Canyon Road (CR N1), which carried 19,325 vehicles per day across Malibu Creek in 2012.

Map: *The Thomas Guide—Street Guide: Los Angeles and Orange Counties* (any recent year), page 588

Getting there: By car—From central Los Angeles, take I-10 West. At the end of the freeway in Santa Monica, continue onto SR 1 (Pacific Coast Highway). Once in central Malibu, turn right onto Malibu Canyon Road (CR N1) and head north. The road name changes to Las Virgenes Road north of Piuma Road. Look for the entrance to Malibu Creek State Park on the left, before the intersection with Mulholland Highway. Enter the park (day-use fee).

    By public transit—There is no transit service to Malibu Creek State Park.

Starting point coordinates: N34.099192° / W118.714256°

THE RIDE

The Malibulldog MASH 4077 Tour is a popular loop ride that travels from Malibu Creek up into the mountains above the canyon, then plunges into the canyon for a special ride through the old *M*A*S*H* TV show set, and then finishes with an undulating ride along Malibu Creek's canyon. Most of the ride takes place within Malibu Creek State Park except for a short, 0.4-mile segment along Malibu Creek Canyon Road. The ride starts in Malibu Creek State Park, from the first parking lot inside its Las Virgenes Road entrance. From here, follow the park entrance road toward the park's interior. Veer off the road onto an unnamed dirt road that leads to a campground after 0.4 mile. As you make your way up this road, look for the (dirt) parking area to your left. Turn in here and ride toward the opposite side of the lot. Look to the right for the Tapia Spur Trail trailhead. Yes, it is a little hard to find.

The Tapia Spur Trail opens the ride with a moderately challenging, twisting, doubletrack trail that climbs and then descends into Tapia County Park. Stay to the right as the trail enters the park. The trail will end at Dorothy Drive, which is actually a park road. Turn left here to head through the park toward the exit. Turn right onto Las Virgenes Road, which becomes Malibu Canyon Road just south of here, to continue the ride. This is the only segment of the ride along which traffic volumes are significant. After crossing Malibu Creek, leave the road and enter the trailhead for Backbone Trail. Backbone Trail is primarily an east–west ridge trail that runs nearly continuously from Will Rogers

M*A*S*H 4077th Set

Although it was entirely fictional, the M*A*S*H TV series made the trials and triumphs of a medical team during the Korean War seem quite real. The show, which ran from 1972 until 1983, lasted much longer than the actual war, which was over in three years (1950–1953). Based on the 1970 film of the same title, the show offered a successful blend of comedy, tragedy, and commentary on war that resonated with its viewers. Although a lot of production was filmed in a studio, all the outdoor scenes were shot here at the park. Most of the set burned down in a 1982 brush fire, close to the end of the TV show's long run. (The fire was later written into the script as an enemy action.) After the final episode, which was the most-watched show in TV history at the time, the set was abandoned, with little to no intervention.

A quarter century later, in 2008, several of the stars from the series—Mike Farrell (B. J. Hunicutt), Loretta Swit (Margaret Houlihan), and William Christopher (Father John Mulcahy), along with director Charles S. Dubin and two of the producers—reunited at the site to celebrate a partial restoration of the set. Today a few signs, including a large one that is posted on weekends, a rusty old jeep, and an equally rusty old ambulance occupy the site. The set and site have not gone entirely unused: Several TV commercials have been shot here. The original M*A*S*H film was shot here, as well as How Green Was My Valley (1941) and the Planet of the Apes TV show (1974).

Riders examine a rusty old Army jeep on the set of *M*A*S*H*, adjacent to the Goat Buttes.

State Park in L.A. in the east to Point Mugu State Park in the west. Only portions of the trail, such as this portion, are accessible to bicycles. Follow Backbone as it climbs the hillside. After just under 1.0 mile, Backbone Trail merges with Mesa Peak Fire Road, also known as Mesa Peak Mountainway. From here (mile 3.9 of the ride) the fire road climbs at an average 8.5% grade.

The 3.0-mile climb is relentless, with the gradient easing for only short episodes along the way. The views to the right and left are spectacular, and there are some very scenic rock formations along the trail itself. Backbone and Mesa Peak crest at 2,237 feet (mile 6.95). The two trails finally diverge at the 8.0-mile mark. Backbone veers to the right through some unrideable terrain, while Mesa Peak veers left toward its end at the paved Corral Canyon Road. Turn right here onto this lightly traveled road and head toward its end. The pavement ends at the Castro Peak Motorway trailhead. Keep straight onto this unpaved fire road. Castro Peak climbs at a 10.1% grade to the high point of the ride—continue past all turnoffs until you reach the crest (elevation: 2,419 feet). At 2,824 feet, Castro Peak is the tallest mountain in the area. Turn right at the crest onto Bulldog Road, also known as Bulldog Mountainway.

Bulldog is a thrilling descent, at an average grade of 9.7%, into the Malibu Creek canyon. The fire road twists and winds while plummeting, demanding good bike control. After 1.1 miles look for the right turn onto Bulldog Lateral Road, which is also an unpaved fire road. Bulldog Road continues to the left at the junction. Bulldog Lateral continues the descent at a 7.7% grade into the canyon. Bulldog Lateral ends at mile 13.1 at Crags Road (unpaved); turn right here (elevation: 692 feet). You are now riding in the canyon, generally parallel to Malibu Creek. At mile 13.3 Crags Road enters a clearing that contains—surprise!—old props and signing from the former set of *M*A*S*H*, a popular TV show that aired from 1972 until 1983 (see sidebar). Take a few moments to check out the set, which is surprisingly accessible (no barriers, very little fanfare). After you have finished practicing a "Hawkeye" quip or humming the "Suicide Is Painless" theme song, continue the ride as Crags Road curves to the left, passing amid the impressive Goat Buttes.

Bike Shops

Santa Monica Mountains Cyclery, 21526 Ventura Blvd., Woodland Hills; (818) 456-4105; www.smmcyclery.com
Wheel World Cyclery, 22718 Ventura Blvd., Woodland Hills; (818) 224-2044; http://wheelworld.com

Upon entering the passage, there's another surprise: The trail surface becomes very rocky and technical. Although the terrain is flat, the tricky surface may force you to put a foot—or both—down. Also, always be alert for other trail users (the hike to the *M*A*S*H* set is popular). Crags Road leaves the rocky segment at mile 13.9, curving to the right to once again head east. Stay to the left at the fork at mile 14.35 to remain on Crags. The next 2.0 miles of the ride are on Crags Road, which is generally wide and nontechnical from here. There are a number of trail crossings; follow the signing and stay on Crags Road. At the split at mile 16.1, turn right to remain on Crags. Crags finally arrives at the park entrance road at mile 16.4. Turn left here to conclude the ride in the parking lot where you started.

MILES AND DIRECTIONS

0.0   Start from the first parking lot inside the Malibu Creek State Park entrance; head into the park on the park entrance road.

0.4   Veer off the road onto an unnamed dirt road that leads to a campground.

0.55 Bear left into parking area; continue to opposite side and look for trailhead.

Malibulldog MASH 4077 Tour

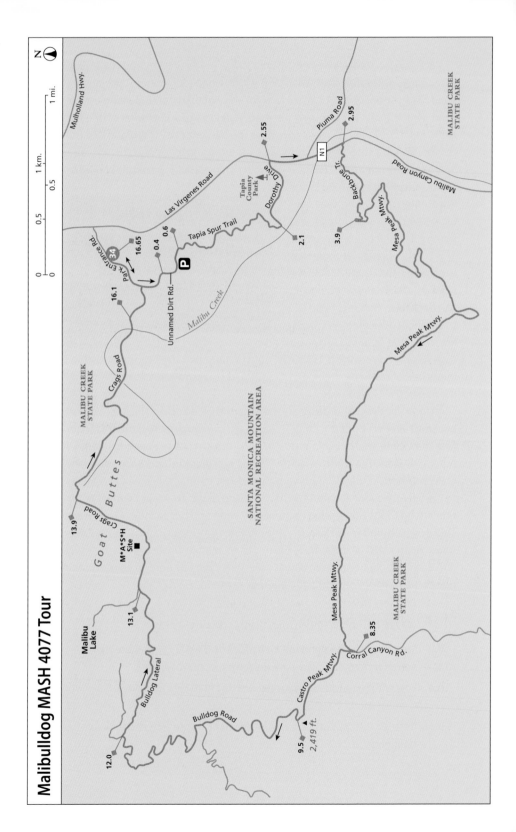

0.6   Continue onto Tapia Spur Trail.

2.1   End of Tapia Spur Trail; turn left onto Dorothy Drive (paved park road) and enter Tapia County Park.

2.55 Leave Tapia County Park; turn right onto Malibu Canyon Road (CR N1).

2.85 Bridge over Malibu Creek.

2.95 Leave the road, turning right into trailhead parking area; continue onto Backbone Trail.

3.9   Merge with Mesa Peak Mountainway (also known as Mesa Peak Fire Road and as a continuation of Backbone Trail). Climb 8.5% grade.

4.45 Keep straight at junction with Coral Canyon Trail (elevation: 791 feet).

6.95 Crest of Mesa Peak Mountainway (Backbone Trail) at 2,237 feet.

8.0   Mesa Peak Mountainway and Backbone Trail split; stay left on Mesa Peak.

8.35 End of Mesa Peak Mountainway; turn right onto Corral Canyon Road (paved).

8.7   End of paved road; continue onto unpaved Castro Peak Mountainway (elevation: 1,994 feet). Begin climb (10.1% grade).

9.5   Junction with Bulldog Mountainway (also known as Bulldog Road); high point of ride (elevation: 2,419 feet). Begin descent (9.7% grade).

12.0 Junction with Bulldog Lateral (also known as a continuation of Bulldog Road); turn right (elevation: 1,142 feet). Continue descent (7.7% grade).

13.1 End of Bulldog Lateral at junction with Crags Road (unpaved); turn right (now at 692 feet of elevation).

13.3 Enter old *M*A*S*H* TV show set site, adjacent to Goat Buttes.

13.5 Leave *M*A*S*H* site; enter canyon and rocky, technical trail.

13.9 Exit canyon; Crags Road curves to the right.

14.35 Stay left at fork to remain on Crags Road.

16.0 Stay left at split in trail to remain on Crags Road.

16.1 Turn right at junction to remain on Crags Road.

16.4 Turn left onto park entrance road.

16.65 End ride at entrance to parking lot.

Passeio de Palos Verdes

Start: Deane Dana Friendship Park, 1805 West 9th Street, San Pedro

Length: 26.8 miles (counterclockwise loop plus an out-and-back of just under 3 miles each way)

Riding time: 80 minutes to 4 hours (my time: 1H42:07)

Terrain and surface: 100% paved roads

Elevation: Low: 159 feet along Palos Verdes Drive South adjacent to Abalone Cove Shoreline Park in Rancho Palos Verdes; high: 941 feet at Palos Verdes Drive East and Crest Road in Rancho Palos Verdes

Traffic and hazards: Western Avenue (SR 213) was carrying 27,000 vehicles per day through San Pedro in 2013; Palos Verdes Drive East carried 14,520 vehicles per day near Miraleste Drive in Rancho Palos Verdes in 2010; Palos Verdes Drive South carried 15,780 vehicles per day near Palos Verdes Drive East in 2010; Palos Verdes Drive West carried 14,700 vehicles per day near Hawthorne Boulevard in 2010.

Map: *The Thomas Guide—Street Guide: Los Angeles and Orange Counties* (any recent year), page 824

Getting there: By car—From central Los Angeles, head south on I-110 (Harbor Freeway). Continue to San Pedro and exit at Gaffey Street. Turn left and head south of Gaffey. Turn right onto West 9th Street and head west. At Friendship Park Drive, turn left and head up the hill to enter Friendship Park. Park here.

   By public transit—From central Los Angeles, ride Metro bus route 450 to San Pedro. The bus runs every 16 to 19 minutes during weekday morning and evening commute periods. Exit at Pacific Avenue and 9th Street and head west on 9th Street to Friendship Park Drive. Turn left here and climb the hill into the park. Alternatively, Metro bus route 550 runs to San Pedro from Exposition Park, which is located just south of central L.A. This bus runs every 30 to 60 minutes all day on weekdays. Exit at Gaffey Street and 9th Street and head west as above.

Starting point coordinates: N33.732075° / W118.318250°

THE RIDE

The Passeio de Palos Verdes is a comprehensive tour of the Palos Verdes Peninsula. The ride begins and ends with an out-and-back segment through San Pedro, in Los Angeles' southernmost community. The main course is a counterclockwise loop around the Palos Verdes Peninsula on the aptly named Palos Verdes Drives: East, North, West, and South. There are superb vistas of the Pacific Ocean on the west and south sides of the ride. In between, the ride visits some of the L.A. region's most exclusive cities, including Palos Verdes Estates, Rancho Palos Verdes, Rolling Hills, and Rolling Hills Estates.

Start the ride at Deane Dana Friendship Park in San Pedro. Deane Dana (1926–2005) was a member of the Los Angeles County Board of Supervisors for sixteen years, although his primary vocation was engineering. San Pedro,

A great day for riding! Cyclists cruise along Palos Verdes Drive West in Palos Verdes Estates.

formerly a separate city but annexed to L.A. in 1909, had a population of about 80,000 as of this writing. The community is a gateway to the Port of Los Angeles, which in combination with the Port of Long Beach is the largest container port in the United States. San Pedro has been the home to numerous notable natives and residents, including Michael Lookinland (Bobby Brady on TV's *The Brady Bunch*), Eugene L. Daub (sculptor of the Rosa Parks statue at the US Capitol), rock group Ambrosia, R&B-soul singer Miguel, and jazz saxophonist Art Pepper. Outside of its famous citizenry, San Pedro is known as a working-class community, with large ethnic populations of Croatians, Italians, and Norwegians. Descend Friendship Park Drive (8.4% grade) to leave the park—you may catch some air on the intermittent speed bumps.

Turn right at the bottom of the hill onto West 9th Street, followed by another right onto Western Avenue. This is the busiest street of the ride. After a little over 1.0 mile, turn right at the signal onto West 25th Street. Leave L.A. after another mile and enter the city of Rancho Palos Verdes (RPV). The Palos Verdes Peninsula features four cities that hug the coastline and climb the Palos Verdes Hills, and this is the first of the *passeio*. RPV had a population of 41,643 in 2010 and a median annual household income of about $120,000. Just under 3.0 miles into the ride, make a sharp right onto Palos Verdes Drive East and begin to climb. This is the main climb of the ride, at an average 5.2% grade, taking you up to the highest point of the route—941 feet at Crest Road. As the road switches back, enjoy the expansive views of the ocean. Beyond Crest, after a transitional segment, the road descends. Be careful as the road twists and winds its way to the north side of the peninsula. Stay to the right, and be alert to motor vehicles approaching from behind. That said, these roads are popular with cyclists, so sharing the road *should* be the norm among the local drivers.

Leave RPV and enter Rolling Hills at mile 8.9 on the way down Palos Verdes Drive East. This small city (population of just 1,860 in 2010) is entirely gated except for the main through roads. As of 2010, the city's per capita income was ranked fourth in the United States among cities of 1,000 persons or more. At Palos Verdes Drive North (mile 9.3) turn left. This is the main drag on the north side of the peninsula. The road climbs gradually, leaving Rolling Hills and entering Rolling Hills Estates (RHE). Motor vehicles occasionally back up at the traffic signals along this road, and you may find yourself pedaling past them. RHE had a population of 8,067 in 2010. Although not quite as exclusive as Rolling Hills—despite the more exclusive sounding name—the

Bike Shop

The Bike Palace, 1600 S. Pacific Ave., San Pedro; (310) 832-1966; http://thebikepalace.com

Palos Verdes Drive South—The Unstable Road

The construction of Palos Verdes Drive South was completed during the summer of 1956. Less than two months later, offsets of 4 inches had been recorded. Ground motion slowed over the next month, but movements occur to this day, necessitating frequent repair of the road.

Palos Verdes Peninsula was once an island, before alluvial deposits from nearby mountains filled in the gap between the Los Angeles Basin. Uplifts that occurred along the Palos Verdes fault helped form the rugged peninsula landscape.

The road was built over an ancient landslide. The instability was further exacerbated when excavated sediment was dumped onto the upper hillsides and then watered, enabling the underlying clay to become lubricated. Homeowners in the Portuguese Bend area sued for damages as a result of the shoddy construction and won some $10 million. Development along the Bend is limited, however, primarily because of the instability but also to preserve its importance as a stopover on the Pacific Flyway and to retain the location's ecosystem. (*Note:* The name Portuguese Bend pertains to Portuguese whalers who whaled off the coast in this area during the mid-nineteenth century. *Passeio* means "tour" in Portuguese; hence the ride's title.)

city maintains a regal character with its extensive network of horse paths. One of those bridle trails parallels Palos Verdes Drive North for a distance.

After 3.0 miles in RHE, enter Palos Verdes Estates (PVE). With a population of 13,438 in 2010, PVE occupies the western side of the peninsula and has the most coastal development—and accessible coastline—of the peninsula cities. The city was master-planned by the legendary Frederick Law Olmsted. Palos Verdes Drive North makes a scenic passage through a forested neighborhood featuring numerous eucalyptus trees. After a rapid descent toward the coast, the road splits. Stay to the left and then carefully cross Palos Verdes Drive, merging with traffic coming from the right; you are now on Palos Verdes Drive West. After a short segment through a commercial district, the road begins to gradually curve around the western end of the peninsula. The ocean is below you and to the right in a series of coves, points, bays, and beaches. Through the heart of PVE, Palos Verdes Drive West travels along a wide boulevard with a wide, landscaped median. As the road is mostly downhill through here, slow down a bit to enjoy the scenery. After just under 18 miles, leave PVE and reenter RPV.

Like PVE, Rancho Palos Verdes (RPV) has an extensive coastline. Unlike PVE, though, RPV's coastline tends to be rugged and, in some places, unstable.

The road becomes Palos Verdes South as you curl to the left adjacent to the Point Vicente Interpretive Center (great for whale watching) and Point Vicente Lighthouse. The latter is on the National Register of Historic Places. As the road nears Portuguese Bend (community of RPV but also a geographical reference), you will notice the signs indicating that the terrain and the road are unstable (see sidebar). It is true—the ground along here moves at a measured average of 0.3 inch per day. The undulations in the road and occasionally damaged pavement are a direct result of the ground movement. Despite the instability, Portuguese Bend was once the site of an aquatic theme park, Marineland of the Pacific. The park operated from 1954 until 1987, when it moved to San Diego and became Sea World. The Greek freighter *Dominator* ran aground in Portuguese Bend during heavy fog in 1961. The wrecked ship became an attraction of its own, with some willing to hike down the cliffs to get a closer look. Some of the wreck remains, but most of it is gone.

Just beyond the dramatic Portuguese Bend on the right is the Trump National Golf Club. Despite the Trump name, it is a public course and is listed in *Golf Magazine*'s top 100. It is considered to be the most expensive golf course ever built, and because of the unstable ground, it occasionally has land shifts and landslides. At the intersection with Palos Verdes Drive East, close the Palos Verdes Peninsula loop 23.85 miles into the ride. Keep straight here, unless you are game for another lap. Enter San Pedro and after about 1.0 mile look for the left turn onto Western Avenue. Follow Western for about 1.0 mile and then move left for the turn onto West 9th Street. Turn left again onto Friendship Park Drive. This is the steepest grade of the ride (8.4%), skillfully placed at the end. The ride concludes at the top of the hill in Friendship Park.

MILES AND DIRECTIONS

0.0 Start at Friendship Park; exit the park and head down the hill (8.4% grade) on Friendship Park Drive.

0.35 Stop sign at West 9th Street; turn right.

0.4 Traffic signal at Western Avenue (SR 213); turn right.

1.45 Traffic signal at West 25th Street; turn right.

2.45 Leave Los Angeles and enter Rancho Palos Verdes; now on Palos Verdes Drive South.

2.95 Turn sharply to the right at Palos Verdes Drive East and start climbing (average 5.2% grade). The turn begins a counterclockwise loop around the Palos Verdes Peninsula.

4.9 Crest of Palos Verdes Drive East (elevation: 941 feet).

Passeio de Palos Verdes

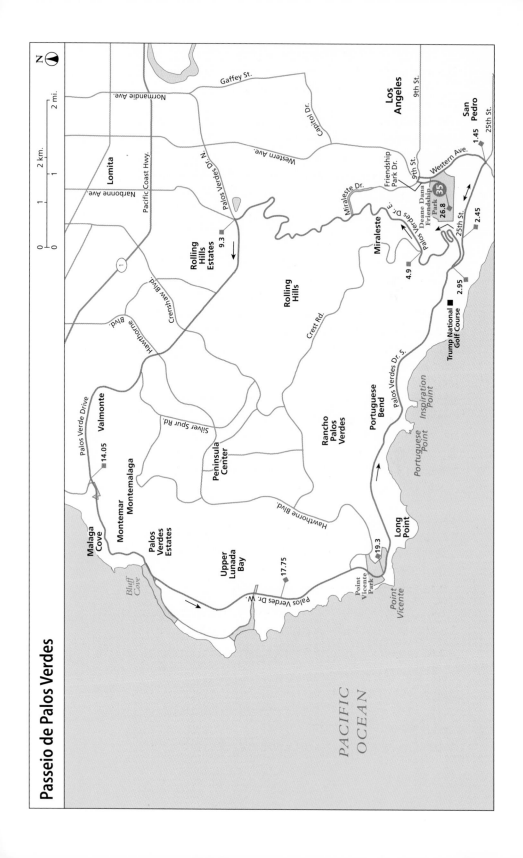

8.85 Leave Rancho Palos Verdes and enter Rolling Hills Estates.

9.3 Traffic signal at Palos Verdes Drive North; turn left.

12.3 Leave Rolling Hills Estates and enter Palos Verdes Estates.

13.95 Stay left at fork in Palos Verdes Drive North.

14.05 Stop sign at Palos Verdes Drive West; turn left and merge with traffic coming from the right. Move to the right when safe.

17.75 Leave Palos Verdes Estates and enter Rancho Palos Verdes.

19.3 Road becomes Palos Verdes Drive South, adjacent to Point Vicente Interpretive Center.

21.6 Low point of ride (159 feet) adjacent to Abalone Cove Shoreline Park.

23.85 End of counterclockwise loop at Palos Verdes Drive East; keep straight.

24.35 Leave Rancho Palos Verdes and enter Los Angeles (San Pedro); now on West 25th Street.

25.4 Traffic signal at Western Avenue (SR 213); turn left.

26.45 Traffic signal at West 9th Street; turn left.

26.5 Turn left at Friendship Park Drive; climb hill (8.4% grade).

26.8 End ride at top of hill in Friendship Park.

Rambla Piuma Pacifico

Start: Las Flores Creek Park, 3805 Las Flores Canyon Road, Malibu

Length: 18.7 miles (counterclockwise loop)

Riding time: 1.25 to 3.5 hours (my time: 1H36:38)

Terrain and surface: 100% paved roads

Elevation: Low: 4 feet across Malibu Lagoon on SR 1; high: 2,196 feet at Piuma Road and Costa del Sol Way

Traffic and hazards: The Pacific Coast Highway (PCH, or SR 1) was carrying 41,000 vehicles per day at Las Flores Canyon Road in 2013. Las Flores Canyon Road carried 1,610 vehicles per weekday near the park in 2011, Piuma Road carried 2,510 vehicles per Sunday near Malibu Canyon Road in 2009 (but only 655 vehicles per Sunday east of Monte Nido), and Malibu Canyon Road (CR N1) carried 23,290 vehicles per day south of Piuma Road in 2010. The tunnel along Malibu Canyon Road should be ridden with caution—a taillight is recommended.

Map: *The Thomas Guide—Street Guide: Los Angeles and Orange Counties* (any recent year), page 629

Getting there: By car—From central Los Angeles, head west on I-10 to SR 1 (Pacific Coast Highway) in Santa Monica. Continue north-northwestward into Malibu. Turn right at Las Flores Canyon Road; the park is on the left, just up the road. *Note:* The park has a very small parking lot.

　　By public transit—From central Los Angeles, ride the Metro Expo Line (light-rail) to the Culver City station. Transfer to Metro bus route 534, which travels to Malibu. Exit at SR 1 and Las Flores Canyon Road. Ride north on Las Flores Canyon to Las Flores Creek Park. Route 534 runs every 15 to 30 minutes on weekdays and Saturday and every 45 to 60 minutes on Sunday.

Starting point coordinates: N34.039906° / W118.637631°

36

THE RIDE

The Rambla Piuma Pacifico is a challenging loop that travels from the Malibu coast into the Santa Monica Mountains and then back down to the coast. In a distance of just 18.7 miles, the ride's elevation ranges from just 4 feet at Malibu Lagoon to 2,196 feet along Piuma Road in the mountains. The average gradient of the climbs ranges from 7% to 9%, so you are in for a workout. The rewards are the stunning views of the Pacific Ocean from high above, as well as the brisk ride along the PCH to conclude the ride. Start the ride at Las Flores Creek Park on Las Flores Canyon Road (0.25 mile north of the PCH), which had been open for less than a year as of this writing. The parking lot for the park was very small, and I was probably fortunate to find a legal space there. Turn left onto Las Flores Canyon Road and immediately begin climbing.

Malibu had a population of 12,645 as of 2010, stretched out over 19.8 almost-linear square miles that hug the coastline. The city's coastline is remarkably long, at some 27 miles. A series of beaches is strung along the coast, each of which is notable and popular. Nearly all the city's residents live along and within 1 mile of the ocean. The affluence of the city is evident in the city's residents, many of whom work in the entertainment industry (too many to list here). The city's oceanside lifestyle has been forever etched into the consciousness of TV, film, and video lovers, given the number that have used Malibu as a setting (see sidebar). The PCH is popular with cyclists, but the number of riders thins as you head inland because of the challenging, mountainous roads. In fact, the climb up Las Flores Canyon gets steeper as you leave the Malibu city limits (average grade 9.0%).

By the time you reach the stop sign at Rambla Pacifico at mile 3.15, you are already at 1,565 feet of elevation. Turn right here and continue to climb, now at an 8.1% grade. Once beyond Schueren Road (mile 3.75) you are on

---

Bike Shops

Helen's Cycles, 2501 Broadway, Santa Monica; (310) 829-1836; http://helenscycles.com

Cynergy Cycles, 2300 Santa Monica Blvd., Santa Monica; (310) 857-1500; http://cynergycycles.com

Bike Attack Santa Monica, 2400 Main St., Santa Monica; (310) 581-8014; www.bikeattack.com

Bike Effect, 910 Broadway #100, Santa Monica; (310) 393-4348; http://bikeeffect.com

Performance Bicycle, 501 Broadway, Santa Monica; (310) 451-9977; www.performancebike.com

A plucky rider wearing a "surfer's helmet" navigates the receptacles along the PCH in Malibu.

Piuma Road. Piuma continues to twist its way up the side of the mountain, with plenty of fantastic views of the ocean. Piuma finally crests at Costa del Sol Way, at 2,196 feet. From here the descent is gradual and then begins to plummet through a series of switchbacks. There is a view area in the middle of the first hairpin turn. The development in the valley below is Monte Nido, an unincorporated mountain community. Piuma scoots along the southern border of the community before terminating at Malibu Canyon Road. Turn left here and head toward the ocean.

Malibu Canyon Road is a fairly busy route to the coast (more than 20,000 vehicles per day) that has an adequate shoulder. Over the next 4.3 miles, Malibu Canyon descends from 475 to 203 feet at the PCH. In between, however, are numerous undulations, including a couple of moderate climbs. After 1.0 mile, Malibu Canyon Road enters a tunnel. The tunnel is dark, and a taillight is recommended for the short distance. I rode it without a taillight but was lucky—no motor vehicles entered the tunnel when I was inside. After a brisk climb out of the canyon, the road descends majestically into central Malibu, toward the ocean. The large green expanse of grass to your right is part of the landscaping of the Pepperdine University campus. This is a private university

Malibu's TV, Film, and Video Legacy

A staggering number of shows have been taped in Malibu, and still more are based in Malibu. *Gidget* and many of the 1960s surfing movies (more than one hundred!) were shot at Surfrider Beach and other Malibu beaches. In TV's *Two and a Half Men*, the show's characters live in Malibu. Miley Cyrus and her dad, Billy Ray, live in Malibu (fictionally) in the *Hannah Montana* TV series. English-Irish boy band One Direction's video for "What Makes You Beautiful" was shot on a beach in Malibu. In TV's *So Little Time*, twin sisters Mary-Kate and Ashley Olsen attend the fictional West Malibu High School. Numerous other song and show titles add to the legacy, including "Malibu" by Hole, "Down at Malibu Beach" by Jan and Dean, the film *Malibu's Most Wanted* (2003), and the TV teen drama *Malibu Shores* (1996). Probably the most famous Malibu scene was shot in 1968's *Planet of the Apes* (see Zoom Dume Zuma). The Malibu legacy may be best found, however, in like-named products, including Malibu Barbie, Malibu chicken, and the Chevy Malibu.

with a religious affiliation, which had 7,300 students in 2012. The university's alumni include politicians, actors, musicians, athletes, reporters, academicians, and others. The list of accomplished and successful graduates of the university is quite long! Two of the university's most famous current or former faculty members are Christopher Parkening (music; accomplished classical guitarist) and Ben Stein (actor, comedian, and speechwriter).

Turn left at the PCH and begin the fast coastal ride home. The ride starts off with a descent—from 203 feet at the turn to just 4 feet at the crossing of Malibu Lagoon. From there it is a false flat adjacent to Surfrider Beach, Carbon Beach, and then La Costa Beach back to Las Flores Canyon Road. The shoulder of the PCH is bound to be partially encroached upon by parked motor vehicles, many of whom belong to surfers. No problem—share the road! The left turn onto Las Fores Canyon Road is easy to miss (I went roaring past it!), so watch for the sign. The PCH was ridden in the time trial event of the 1932 Olympic Games (see sidebar with the Baldwin Hills Hahn-wind ride). The winner of that race averaged 25.2 miles per hour—can you?

MILES AND DIRECTIONS

0.0 Start at Las Flores Creek Park (elevation: 60 feet); exit the park, turn left, and head north on Las Flores Canyon Road. Begin climb at average 9.0% grade.

Rambla Piuma Pacifico

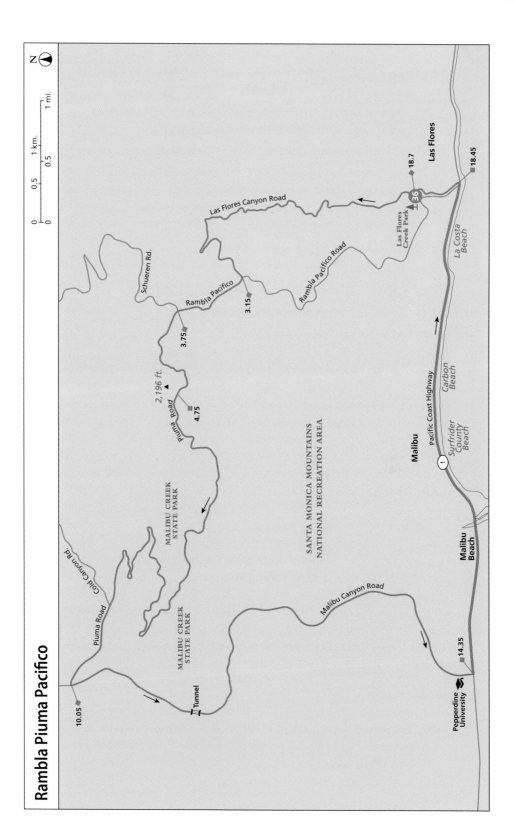

3.15 Stop sign at Rambla Pacifico (elevation: 1,565 feet); turn right and continue climbing at 8.1% grade.

3.75 Schueren Road on the right; keep straight, now on Piuma Road (elevation: 1,823 feet); climb at 7.2% grade from here.

4.75 High point of ride at Costa del Sol Way (2,196 feet); begin descent.

9.35 Cold Canyon Road intersection (keep straight on Piuma Road); now on border of Monte Nido community.

10.05 Stop sign at Malibu Canyon Road (CR N1); turn left (elevation: 475 feet).

10.95 Enter tunnel (taillight recommended).

11.05 Exit tunnel.

14.35 Traffic signal at PCH (SR 1); turn left (elevation: 203 feet).

18.45 Traffic signal at Las Flores Canyon Road; turn left.

18.7 End ride at Las Flores Creek Park.

Rondo Redondo Beach

Start: Veterans Park, 309 Esplanade, Redondo Beach

Length: 3.9 miles (clockwise loop)

Riding time: 12 to 40 minutes (my time: 16:31)

Terrain and surface: 100% paved (51% on roads and 49% on a bicycle path)

Elevation: Low: 21 feet along the Marvin Braude Bike Trail; high: 74 feet on Esplanade, south of Ruby Street

Traffic and hazards: Esplanade carried 5,970 vehicles per day in 2007. The connector from Paseo de la Playa to the Strand is a steep 17.4% downhill grade. Signs direct cyclists to walk their bikes.

Map: *The Thomas Guide—Street Guide: Los Angeles and Orange Counties* (any recent year), page 762

Getting there: By car—From central Los Angeles, head south on I-110 to SR 91 West. Continue straight onto Artesia Boulevard at the end of the freeway. Turn left onto the Pacific Coast Highway (SR 1) in Hermosa Beach and head south. Once in Redondo Beach, bear right onto Catalina Avenue. Veterans Park is just past Torrance Boulevard, on the right.

   By public transit—From central Los Angeles, ride the Metro Blue Line (light-rail) heading south. Transfer to Metro's Green Line (light-rail) at the Willowbrook/Rosa Parks station and head west. At the end of the line at the Redondo Beach station, transfer to Beach Cities Transit bus route 102 and head south to Redondo Beach Pier (end of the line). Exit here; Veterans Park overlooks the harbor and is accessible from George Freeth Way or Torrance Boulevard. Bus route 102 runs every 30 to 45 minutes, seven days per week.

Starting point coordinates: N33.836181° / W118.388822° (intersection adjacent to Veterans Park).

THE RIDE

The shortest road ride in the book, at just 3.9 miles, Rondo Redondo Beach is a loop course that uses the Marvin Braude Bike Trail and Esplanade. Although the Marvin Braude Bike Trail is 22 miles long, a break in the path that puts riders on city streets for a short segment in Redondo Beach made a good point at which to circle back to the beginning of the path to close the loop. Other rides in the book (see the South Bay Beach–Ballona Bike Tour and Topanga to Tuna to Tide rides) also use the Braude Trail. Nearly the entire ride is set in Redondo Beach, one of the L.A. region's eight or so beach cities. Redondo Beach had a population of 66,748 in 2010 and is best known for the Redondo Beach Pier (eateries, hotels, shops, ocean views), King Harbor (moorings and slips for private watercraft), and of course Redondo County Beach. David

Cyclists, surfers, and walkers (in the distance) share The Strand in Redondo Beach.

Bike Shops

Sprocket Cycles, 1018 S. Pacific Coast Hwy., Redondo Beach; (310) 540-1927; www.sprocketcycles.com

Corbins Redondo Bicycles, 607 S. Pacific Coast Hwy., Redondo Beach; (310) 543-3226; www.redondobicycle.com

Bill Ron's Bicycles, 807 Torrance Blvd., Redondo Beach; (310) 540-2080; www.billronbikes.com

Marina Bike Rentals, 505 N. Harbor Dr., Redondo Beach; (310) 374-9100; http://marinabikerentals.com

Hasselhoff's TV series *Baywatch* and the earlier TV series *Riptide* were filmed primarily in Redondo Beach. The city's natives and graduates or attendees of Redondo Union High School or Aviation High School include actress Demi Moore, pioneer aviator Charles Lindbergh, pro basketball star Paul Westphal, and musician-comedians Tom and Dick Smothers (*The Smothers Brothers Comedy Hour*).

Head south on Esplanade past some high-rise beachside residences that unfortunately block the view of the ocean. The view opens up, however, a few blocks later. Enjoy the ride along here, with the ocean below you and to your right, low-rise residences to your left, and the Palos Verdes Hills off in the distance. At the traffic circle, keep right onto Paseo de la Playa. The route enters the city of Torrance here. Although no more than about 0.5 mile of the ride passes through here, Torrance is actually the dominant South Bay city, with a population of 147,027 in 2012. The city may be best known as the American headquarters of Honda Motors and as the hometown of 1930s running star and World War II legend Louis Zamperini (1917–2014). Continue on Paseo de la Playa to Via Riviera. Turn right here and descend to the beach. The descent is on a steep (17.4% grade) path; signs direct cyclists to walk their bikes.

At the bottom of the path, turn right and head north on the Marvin Braude Bike Trail, otherwise known as The Strand. This is where the 22-mile-long path begins. The path is segregated into a pedestrian lane and two bike lanes (see photo). Bicyclists get the bulk of the path, but be alert to the occasional stray pedestrian, as well as to frequent crossings of the path. The operative words for safe cycling along The Strand may be "don't put your head down." The wide and alluring Redondo County Beach is to your left. To your right, steep staircases and ramps lead up and down the embankment, providing beach access.

After just under 2.0 miles, the path breaks to enter the Redondo Beach Pier area. Although the path continues north of here—cyclists are required to walk their bikes as directed by signs—leave the path by exiting to your right and then turning right onto George Freeth Way. George Freeth (1883–1919)

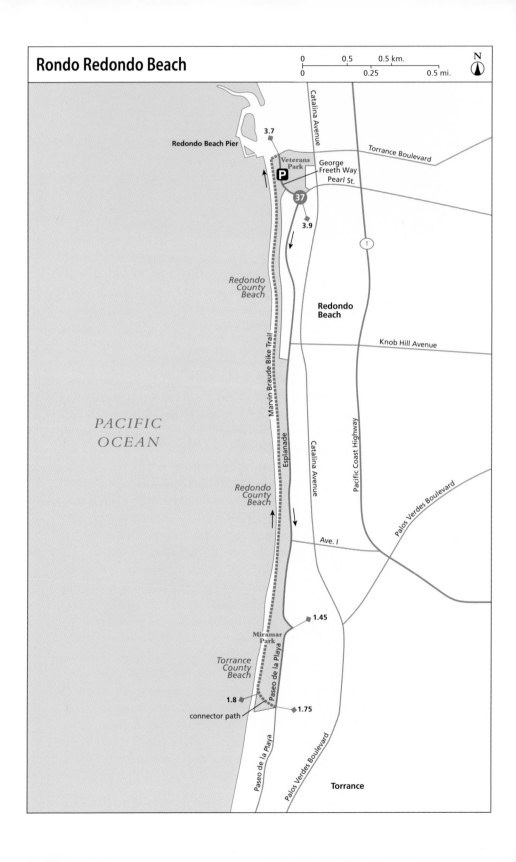

Rondo Redondo Beach

0   0.5   0.5 km.
0   0.25   0.5 mi.

N

PACIFIC OCEAN

Redondo Beach Pier

3.7

Veterans Park

George Freeth Way

Pearl St.

37

3.9

Redondo County Beach

Marvin Braude Bike Trail

Esplanade

Catalina Avenue

Redondo Beach

Torrance Boulevard

Catalina Avenue

Knob Hill Avenue

Pacific Coast Highway

1

Palos Verdes Boulevard

Ave. I

Redondo County Beach

1.45

Miramar Park

Torrance County Beach

Paseo de la Playa

1.8

connector path

1.75

Paseo de la Playa

Palos Verdes Boulevard

Torrance

is widely considered to be the "father" of modern surfing. End the ride at the intersection of George Freeth and Esplanade, adjacent to Veterans Park. Perhaps you have time for another lap?

MILES AND DIRECTIONS

0.0 Start at the intersection of George Freeth Way and Esplanade, on the southeast side of Veterans Park in Redondo Beach. Head south on Esplanade.

1.45 Yield at traffic circle at Paseo de la Playa; bear right. Enter the city of Torrance.

1.75 Stop sign at Via Riviera; turn right and enter parking lot. Continue onto steep (17.4% grade) downhill path to beach. Walk your bike down the hill.

1.8 Turn right onto Marvin Braude Bike Trail (this is where the path begins).

3.7 Break in path at entrance to Redondo Beach Pier area. Leave path by exiting to your right, and turn right onto George Freeth Way.

3.9 End ride at George Freeth Way and Esplanade, adjacent to Veterans Park.

South Bay Beach–Ballona Bike Tour

Start: Dockweiler State Beach, 12501 Vista del Mar, Playa del Rey

Length: 30.7 miles (clockwise loop)

Riding time: 1.5 to 4 hours (my time: 1H56:25)

Terrain and surface: 100% paved (51% on paved bike paths, 49% on roads)

Elevation: Low: 6 feet along Culver Boulevard, crossing the Ballona Wetlands in Del Rey; high: 123 feet at Highland Avenue and Seaview Court in Manhattan Beach

Traffic and hazards: Culver Boulevard carried 32,610 vehicles per day at Jefferson Boulevard in 2006; Jefferson Boulevard carried 24,665 vehicles per day at Centinela Avenue in 2004; Vista del Mar carried 24,240 vehicles per day at Imperial Highway in 2008.

Map: *The Thomas Guide—Street Guide: Los Angeles and Orange Counties* (any recent year), page 702

Getting there: By car—From central Los Angeles, head south on I-110 to I-105 West. At the end of the freeway, continue heading west onto the Imperial Highway. At Vista del Mar continue straight across and enter Dockweiler State Beach. Park here.

    By public transit—From central Los Angeles, ride Metro's Blue Line to the Willowbrook/Rosa Parks station. Transfer to the Metro Green Line, heading west. Exit at the Aviation/LAX station. Bus service along the Imperial Highway, heading westward toward the ocean, is limited to weekday commute periods only. Ride either Metro bus route 625 or LADOT Commuter Express route 438. At other times, ride to Dockweiler State Beach by heading west on Imperial Highway.

Starting point coordinates: N33.930642° / W118.436247°

THE RIDE

The South Bay Beach–Ballona Bike Tour is a narrow clockwise loop that incorporates the Marvin Braude Bike Trail, Ballona Creek Bike Path, and parallel roads as it passes through the L.A. communities of Playa del Rey and Del Rey and the cities of Culver City, El Segundo, Manhattan Beach, and Hermosa Beach. About 9 miles of the route is ridden oceanside along the beach bike path, with wonderful views of the Pacific. An additional 4 miles is on roads that parallel the beach, overlooking the ocean. With no serious climbs, the ride is a great outing—the full route may be great for the experienced rider, while any shortened version of the route would be suitable for novices, beginners, and kids.

From Dockweiler State Beach in Playa del Rey, head north on the Marvin Braude Bike Trail. The "official" starting point is directly opposite the intersection of Imperial Highway and Vista del Mar, at the main entrance to the beach. The beach is named in honor of Isidore B. Dockweiler (1867–1947), a prominent lawyer and politician who served in various capacities from the 1900s until the 1940s. Playa del Rey, literally "The King of Beaches," is an L.A. community having a population of 12,129 as of 2010. The hills in Playa del Rey are actually sand dunes, compacted over the years and now serving as the foundation for residential development. There are a number of mansions in the area, some of which are owned by notable personalities. Above and to your right as you head north on the Braude bike path is Los Angeles International Airport

Bike Shops

Spokes N Stuff, 9401 Vista Del Mar, Playa del Rey; (310) 306-7666; http://spokes-n-stuff.com/dockweiler_beach.html
Summit Ski and Cycle, 8419 Lincoln Blvd., Westchester; (310) 568-8357; www.summitskiandcycle.com

(LAX). You cannot really see the airport, as the ground level is above you, but you certainly that know it is there when a jet aircraft flies overhead!

The Marvin Braude path snakes its way along Dockweiler, gradually weaving its way northward. Be alert to other path users, especially to "crossers" (folks crossing the path to get to the beach). Marvin Braude (1920–2005) served on the Los Angeles City Council for thirty-two years and was a champion of bike paths, recreational uses, and smoking bans. When not wearing one of his famous polyester suits, he was an avid cyclist. After 2.5 miles the path curves to the right, adjacent to Ballona Creek. Cross over the Pacific Avenue Bridge here (no motor vehicles allowed) and turn right to continue on the Braude path. You are now riding on the north side of Ballona Creek. At mile 3.3 the Braude path turns to the left to continue northward to Venice and Santa Monica. Keep straight here—you are now on the Ballona Creek Bike Path.

Ballona Creek drains a 130-square-mile watershed within the Los Angeles Basin. The path is a pleasant jaunt next to the creek, although there was a rough and bumpy segment that needed repairs and improved maintenance. The path penetrates Culver City, finally ending after 6.0 miles with a tight switchback and ramp up to National Boulevard, adjacent to Syd Kronenthal Park. Upon arrival at National, bear left and continue following the path, which here is merely a sidewalk. At the signalized intersection with Jefferson Boulevard (the overhead structure is Metro's Expo Line), cross National and head south on Jefferson. You are now riding in the road, on the shoulder. Although you were in Culver City while on the Ballona Creek path, you are now in Los Angeles, on Jefferson in the Baldwin Village community. Baldwin Village is part of L.A.'s Crenshaw district and was once referred to as "The Jungle" because of some tropical foliage.

Reenter Culver City as Jefferson curves to the right, south of Rodeo Road. Culver City (population of 38,883 in 2010) is known for its media centers,

Cyclists lean into a bend along the Marvin Braude Bike Trail, north of Manhattan Beach Pier.

studios, and film production. Sony Pictures (formerly MGM Studios) is located here, as is National Public Radio (West) and the National Football League Network. Hal Roach Studios was formerly here, as were such centers as Desilu Productions and RKO Pictures. Films dating from the silent era to modern-day have been made in studios here—and sometimes spilling over onto city streets. Numerous TV shows have also been shot here. Some of the most notable productions have included the original *King Kong*, *The Wizard of Oz*, and *Gone with the Wind*. TV's *Green Hornet* series was shot here, as well—martial arts legend Bruce Lee, who played Kato, lived in Culver City during the series' production years (1966–67). While waxing nostalgic as you ride through Culver city, note that most of the old studio lots—including what was famously referred to as the "Back 40"—have since been redeveloped and replaced with residences.

Jefferson Boulevard gets a bit busier as you approach Sepulveda Boulevard—so busy, in fact, that traffic tends to slow down, actually making bicycling more manageable. Jefferson ends at Sepulveda; turn left here and head south. At Playa Street turn right to continue on the westerly segment of Jefferson Boulevard. After passing under the I-405 and SR 90 interchange complex at mile 12.7, leave Culver City and enter Del Rey (not to be confused with Playa del Rey), an L.A. community. Del Rey's population was 32,976 in 2008. Del Rey is known for being one of a number of L.A. region's communities with no majority race or ethnic group. Continue speeding along Jefferson as you head westward toward the ocean. The road is actually very gradually downhill through here. At Culver Boulevard, which is the end of Jefferson, turn left. Culver crosses the Ballona Wetlands (part of Ballona Creek's watershed and ecosystem), reaching the lowest point of the ride, just 6 feet above sea level. Reenter Playa del Rey just beyond the wetlands.

Culver curves to the left as you reach the beach and becomes Vista del Mar. You are now riding parallel to the ocean and the Marvin Braude Bike Trail, overlooking Dockweiler State Beach. Note the many fine residences in the hills to your left. Residential development ends as you enter the flight zone of LAX, to your left. Keep heading south on Vista del Mar; a number of beach users park along this road, so be watchful of pedestrians and opening car doors. At the traffic signal at Imperial Highway, you are back at the starting point at mile 18.3 of the ride. You can stop here or continue heading south on Vista del Mar. Enter El Segundo at mile 19.35 and then Manhattan Beach at mile 20.2. The high point of the entire ride comes at 34th Place (136 feet above sea level). You can catch some views of the ocean in between the somewhat dense housing development. Manhattan Beach (population 35,135 as of 2010) is the most northerly of a long string of beach cities. The string starts here and, interrupted only by the Palos Verdes Peninsula and San Pedro, continues into southern Orange County, well to the south of L.A. Manhattan Beach is known for its prime real estate, with more million-dollar homes sold here than in any other city in California during some years.

Since it is unlikely that you can afford to live here, just keep heading south through Manhattan Beach, now on Highland Avenue. As is the case with many L.A.-area cities, Manhattan Beach has been used extensively for filming. Dorothy (played by Renée Zellweger) in the film *Jerry Maguire* lived in Manhattan Beach. Also, somewhat oddly, the *CSI: Miami* beach scenes were shot in California, many in Manhattan Beach. A little-known fact is that much of the sand on Waikiki Beach in Honolulu was shipped across the Pacific from Manhattan Beach during the 1920s. Turn right onto Longfellow Avenue and head west toward the ocean, followed by a left onto Manhattan Avenue. Enter Hermosa Beach at mile 22.35.

Hermosa Beach had a population of 19,506 in 2010. Natives of the city include comedic actor Jack Black and 2004 Olympic water polo medalist Jacqueline Frank DeLuca. Manhattan veers to the right, becoming Greenwich Village, and then to the left, becoming (and actually joining) Hermosa Avenue. In the days of yesteryear, Hermosa Avenue featured an electric streetcar that was part of the region's "Red Cars" system. Continue on Hermosa to Herondo Street, a clever combination of "Hermosa" and "Redondo" to signify that you are at the border between these two cities. Turn right here onto the bike path; this is where the Marvin Braude Bike Trail resumes after a short break adjacent to the Redondo Beach Pier (see the Rondo Redondo Beach ride). The path turns to the right and heads north. As this is typically a busy segment, the speed limit is a casual 8 miles per hour. The Hermosa Beach Pier area is especially active at times, so use extra caution and courtesy when passing through. As you return to Manhattan Beach and near its pier, the path curves to the right and comes to a staircase. Walk your bike up the stairs and resume riding. Alternatively, you can turn right, off of the path, in advance of the staircase at one of the many connectors. Running parallel to the beachside path is another path that conveniently avoids the stairs.

Walk your bike through the Manhattan Beach Pier area. North of here the path features some long stretches with great ocean views to your left and industrial development (such as the huge Chevron Oil Refinery in El Segundo) to your right. There is also some great surf adjacent the El Porto neighborhood of Manhattan Beach, along El Segundo and Manhattan County Beaches. Continue northward on the path to Dockweiler State Beach. The ride ends on the bike path opposite Imperial Highway and the main entrance to the beach.

MILES AND DIRECTIONS

0.0 Start along the Marvin Braude Bike Trail at Dockweiler State Beach, opposite Vista del Mar and Imperial Highway in Playa del Rey. Head north on the path.

2.5 Path curves to the right.

2.6 Turn left and cross Pacific Avenue Bridge (over Ballona Creek).

2.65 Turn right at end of bridge and head northeast on Marvin Braude Bike Trail.

3.3 Junction; keep straight onto Ballona Creek Bike Path (Marvin Braude Bike Trail turns left and heads north).

9.3 Path switches back, climbing a ramp to National Boulevard.

9.35 Bear left at top of ramp and ride parallel to National Boulevard.

9.4 Traffic signal at northwest corner of National and Jefferson Boulevards in Culver City. Cross National and head south on Jefferson.

9.8 Leave Baldwin Village (L.A.) and enter Culver City.

12.0 Traffic signal at Sepulveda Boulevard; turn left onto Sepulveda (Jefferson resumes downstream of here).

12.4 Traffic signal at Playa Street; turn right to continue on Jefferson Boulevard.

12.7 Pass under I-405 and SR 90 (Marina). Leave Culver City and enter Los Angeles (Del Rey community).

15.35 Traffic signal at Culver Boulevard (end of Jefferson Boulevard); turn left here, onto Culver.

16.2 Traffic signal at Vista del Mar; turn left.

18.3 Traffic signal at Imperial Highway; keep straight on Vista del Mar. You are now adjacent to the starting point of the ride at Dockweiler State Beach. (**Option:** Stop here for a shorter ride.)

19.35 Traffic signal at Grand Avenue; keep straight on Vista del Mar. Leave Los Angeles and enter El Segundo.

20.2 Traffic signal at 45th Street; keep straight. Now on Highland Avenue, leave El Segundo and enter Manhattan Beach.

20.7 High point of ride (136 feet above sea level) at 34th Place.

22.35 Leave Manhattan Beach and enter Hermosa Beach.

22.45 Stop sign at Longfellow Avenue; turn right.

22.5 Traffic signal at Manhattan Avenue; turn left.

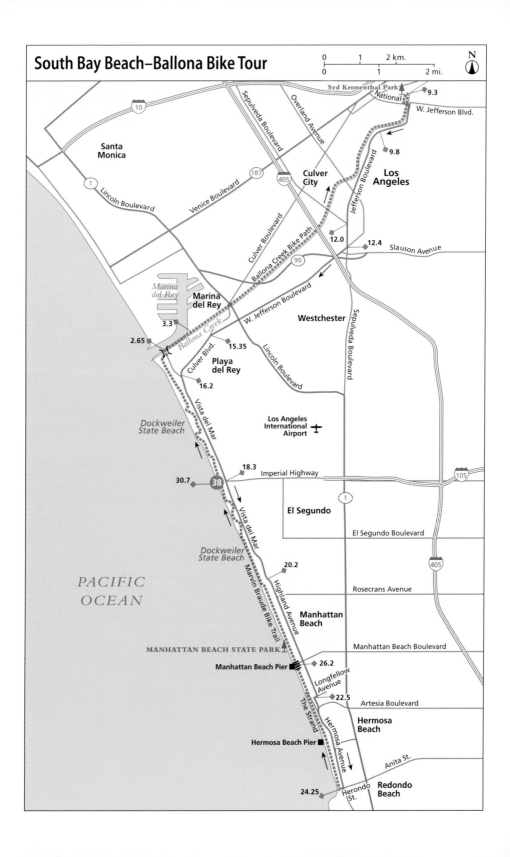

South Bay Beach–Ballona Bike Tour

22.7 Road veers to the right; now on Greenwich Village.

22.8 Road veers to the left; now on Hermosa Avenue.

24.25 Traffic signal at Herondo Street; turn right here onto bike path (Marvin Braude Bike Trail).

24.3 Bike path turns to the right and heads north.

25.0 Hermosa Beach Pier area; walk bike through here.

26.7 Manhattan Beach Pier area; walk bike through here.

30.7 End ride opposite Imperial Highway and Vista del Mar at Dockweiler State Beach.

Start: Topanga State Park, 580 Los Liones Dr., Pacific Palisades (Los Angeles)

Length: 16.75 miles (clockwise loop), including 0.66 mile of out-and-back at the start/finish

Riding time: 1.5 to 5 hours (my time: 2H16:54)

Terrain and surface: 63% dirt fire roads and trails; 37% paved roads

Elevation: Low: 66 feet at Los Liones Drive and Sunset Boulevard in Pacific Palisades; high: 2,048 feet on Temescal Ridge Trail at southern junction with Backbone Trail.

Traffic and hazards: Palisades Drive carried 13,495 vehicles per day near Sunset Boulevard in 2006; Sunset Boulevard carried 16,615 vehicles per day near Palisades Drive in 2006.

Map: *The Thomas Guide—Street Guide: Los Angeles and Orange Counties* (any recent year), page 630

Getting there: By car—From central Los Angeles, head west on I-10. Continue onto the Pacific Coast Highway (SR 1) at the end of I-10 in Santa Monica. Once in Pacific Palisades, turn right onto Sunset Boulevard. Turn left onto Los Liones Drive; head up the road and park in one of the Topanga State Park lots, on the right.

By public transit—From central Los Angeles, ride Metro bus route 2 or 302 westward along Sunset Boulevard. Exit in Pacific Palisades at Los Liones Drive; climb to the Los Liones trailhead to start the ride. Bus route 2 runs every 10 to 12 minutes on weekdays, every 13 to 35 minutes on Saturday, and every 17 to 42 minutes on Sunday. Routes 2 and 302 alternate during weekday commute periods.

Starting point coordinates: N34.044164° / W118.557842°

THE RIDE

The Topanga Puku Pawahe—translated from the Gabrielino/Tongva language as "Topanga One Six," in reference to the length of the ride—is a 16.75-mile mountain bike loop into the Santa Monica Mountains above Pacific Palisades in far western Los Angeles. The ride climbs from 66 to 2,048 feet (and back down, of course). Just under two-thirds of the route is on dirt fire roads, with the remainder on paved roads. About 0.75 mile of the ride is on a narrow singletrack. The ride starts at the Los Liones trailhead along Los Liones Drive in the Castellammare community of Pacific Palisades. This is about as close to Malibu as one can get without actually being in Malibu, which is immediately to the west. Castellammare is a part of the names of several communities in southern Italy; the name has been imported to this part of L.A., where many of the street names are Italian.

The Los Liones Trail heads into Topanga State Park, climbing into the Santa Monica Mountains. You are headed in the same direction as this trail but using a different route. Start by heading back down the hill on Los Liones (8.6% grade) to Sunset Boulevard. Out here you are at the far western, "quiet" end of Sunset Boulevard. East of here, though, Sunset Boulevard takes on a life of its own (see sidebar). Once on Sunset, turn left at the very next street, Paseo Miramar, and head up the 8.6% grade. The road winds its way through an attractive Castellammare neighborhood. At the 1.55-mile mark, now 625

Sunset Boulevard

Although the ride spends no more than 0.25 mile on Sunset Boulevard, the main segments of Sunset are to the east of here and warrant some attention. Sunset Boulevard is about 22 miles long, stretching from just west of downtown L.A. to the Pacific Ocean, generally following the base of the Santa Monica Mountains. The road does not necessarily make a great bike ride—there are segments with no shoulders (and traffic volumes can be heavy)—but is nonetheless worth exploring by car, on foot, or using public transit. The street has been immortalized in films such as *Sunset Boulevard* and *Sunset Strip*, and TV shows such as *Dan Raven* and *77 Sunset Strip* (the address was fictional).

The Sunset Strip is a 1.5-mile segment of the street through West Hollywood, famous for its nightclubs and colorful displays and long known as a hangout for the rich and famous of the entertainment industry. Although some of the glitz and glamour has faded, numerous "stars" reside in the hills overlooking the Strip. As for the fade, reality truly set in during July 2014, and again in September 2014, when water mains burst, flooding Sunset Boulevard and forcing its closure. About 20 million gallons of water spilled during the first flood. The ruptures called attention to L.A.'s aging infrastructure.

A dynamic duo approaches a junction along Temescal Fire Road in Topanga State Park.

feet above sea level, turn off Paseo Miramar (near its end) onto Topanga Fire Road. This is the beginning of the off-road portion of the route, through Topanga State Park. The park is part of the Santa Monica Mountains National Recreation Area (NRA). At 11,000 acres, located entirely within the city of Los Angeles, Topanga State Park is the largest US park completely contained within a city. You will see plenty of coastal sage scrub, California oak woodlands, and montane chaparral here.

Is there something wrong with your engine? You may feel as such, but this can be attributed to the gradient of Topanga Fire Road: 12.0% (average) for the next 1.25 miles. You will be at 1,477 feet of elevation before the grade finally eases. From this first crest, the fire road descends and climbs, descends and climbs, before finally descending to 1,331 feet adjacent to the Trippet Road trailhead at mile 6.25. The trailhead provides access from the Topanga community (see the Topanga to Tuna to Tide ride). The climbing resumes from here; reaching 1,677 feet by mile 7.45. Stay right at the fork to take Eagle Spring Fire Road (Backbone Trail heads off to the left but meets Eagle Spring Fire Road downstream). Eagle Spring Fire Road continues to climb, with a short, minor descent along the way, eventually reaching 2,006 feet at its junction with Backbone Trail and Temescal Fire Road.

Turn right at the junction onto Temescal Fire Road, which is also Backbone Trail. The two trails merge along this segment before splitting downstream.

Stay to the right at the next trail junction, then again at the next junction (mile 9.45). Here Backbone Trail heads off to the left; the trail to the right is now Temescal Ridge Trail. This is the high point of the entire ride (2,048 feet). Continue on Temescal Ridge Trail; stay to the left at the junction with Trailer Canyon Fire Road (mile 10.9) to remain on Temescal Ridge. At mile 11.2 the trail narrows, becoming singletrack along some segments amid the overgrowth. Singletrack trails are generally forbidden to mountain bikes within the Santa Monica NRA, but this trail is legal. The trail widens downstream. At mile 12.05 turn right for the steep (10.7%) descent down Split Rock Fire Road. (**Note:** Temescal Ridge Trail is off-limits to bikes beyond here.) The descent begins with a rough, eroded segment that may best be handled by dismounting and walking. Resume riding just beyond here. At mile 12.1 Split Rock descends into a series of concrete switchbacks. Follow these on down to the end of the trail, where it empties out onto a paved road.

Welcome to Palisades Highlands! You are now on Via Las Palmas (elevation: 1,546 feet), ready to continue descending. Palisades Highlands is a neighborhood within the larger Pacific Palisades community. The development of the Highlands was opposed by environmentalists, since access requires traversing Santa Ynez Canyon, which is within Topanga State Park. Obviously the developers won; the houses in this community typically start at $2 million. Turn right at the end of Via Las Palmas, onto Chastain Parkway. This road descends (8.8%) and curves to the left, eventually meeting Palisades Drive, which is the Highlands'

Bike Shop

Westside L.A. Bicycles Rentals, 700 Wilshire Blvd., Santa Monica; (310) 576-9900; www.downtownlabicycles.com/rentals.html.

main drag. Turn right here, now at mile 12.95, and continue to descend. Leave Palisades Highlands at mile 14.45 and enter the aforementioned Santa Ynez Canyon. The canyon separates the Highlands from the rest of Pacific Palisades and is generally undeveloped, with the steep walls of the surrounding mountains on either side of you.

Emerge from the canyon at mile 15.8, now at an elevation of just 185 feet. The 1900s-era film studio Inceville once occupied this area, with an extensive collection of sets and large production crews. Thomas H. Ince (1882–1924) built the studio, investing $35,000 in its facilities. Ince made about 600 films here, many of them epic Westerns, with cast members who lived on the studio property. The studio burned down around the same time as Ince's death, purportedly at the hands of William Randolph Hearst on board Hearst's yacht in a dispute over an actress. Turn right on Sunset Boulevard and descend to Los Liones Drive as you return to Castellammare. Turn right here for the final leg of the route. The ride ends at the parking area for Los Liones Trail. Castellam-mare is home to Getty Villa, one of two locations of the J. Paul Getty Museum. The villa contains some 44,000 Greek, Roman, and Etruscan antiquities and is highly recommended for a visit. The villa is located about 0.5 mile west of Los Liones, although it is best accessed from the Pacific Coast Highway.

MILES AND DIRECTIONS

0.0 Start at the Los Liones trailhead, on Los Liones Drive in Topanga State Park. Head southeast on Los Liones.

0.3 Traffic signal at Sunset Boulevard; turn left.

0.35 Turn left onto Paseo Miramar; begin climb (8.6% grade).

1.55 Leave Paseo Miramar; continue left onto Topanga Fire Road. Continue climbing, now at 12.0% grade.

2.85 Mid-climb crest (elevation: 1,477 feet); begin short descent followed by climbing at 5.8% grade.

3.65 Paseo Miramar Trail junction; keep straight on Topanga Fire Road.

6.25 Trippet Lane junction; keep straight on Topanga Fire Road (eastern portion), now at 1,331 feet.

7.45 Trail splits; bear right onto Eagle Spring Fire Road (elevation: 1,677 feet).

8.85 End of Eagle Spring Fire Road; junction with Temescal Fire Road and Backbone Trail (elevation: 2,006 feet).

9.35 Trail splits; stay to the right.

9.45 Junction; stay right, now on Temescal Ridge Trail (Backbone Trail continues to the left). High point of ride (2,048 feet).

10.9 Junction with Trail Canyon Fire Road; stay left on Temescal Ridge Trail.

11.2 Temescal Ridge Trail narrows (singletrack along some segments).

12.05 Turn right onto Split Rock Fire Road; begin descent at 10.7% grade.

12.1 Begin concrete (paved) switchbacks; continue descent.

12.25 Turn left onto Via Las Palmas (paved road) and enter Palisades Highlands neighborhood.

12.35 Stop at Chastain Parkway; turn right and continue descent (8.8% grade).

12.95 Stop at Palisades Drive; turn right.

14.45 Enter Santa Ynez Canyon.

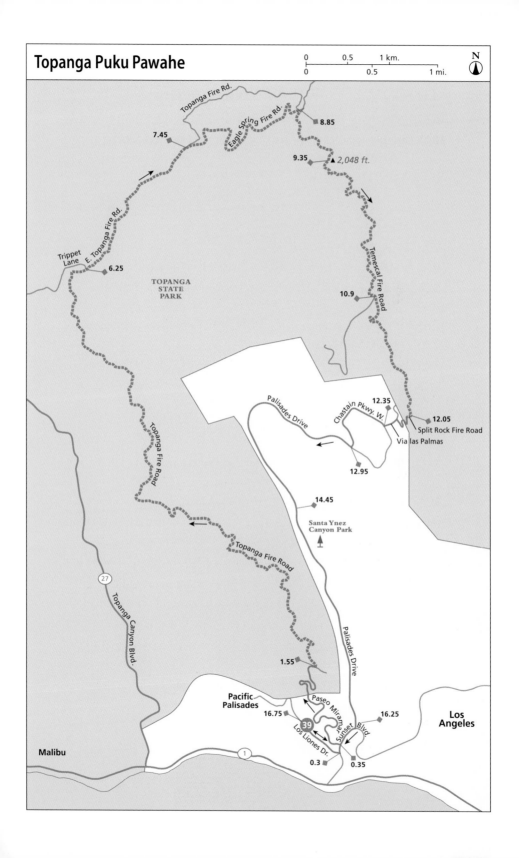

Topanga Puku Pawahe

15.8 Emerge from Santa Ynez Canyon; enter Castellammare community.

16.25 Traffic signal at Sunset Boulevard; turn right.

16.45 Traffic signal at Los Liones Drive; turn right.

16.75 End ride adjacent to the parking area for Los Liones trailhead (Topanga State Park).

Topanga to Tuna to Tide

Start: Mile 19.00 marker on the Marvin Braude Bike Trail, adjacent to Santa Monica State Beach near the Pacific Coast Highway (PCH/SR 1) and California Incline, Santa Monica

Length: 38.2 miles (figure-8 route plus an out-and-back segment)

Riding time: 2 to 6 hours (my time: 2H39:22)

Terrain and surface: 100% paved (85% paved roads; 15% paved bike path)

Elevation: Low: 13 feet, along the Marvin Braude Bike Trail in Santa Monica; high: 1,834 feet at Tuna Canyon Road and Saddle Peak Road in the Fernwood community of Topanga.

Traffic and hazards: 63,000 vehicles per day on SR 1 east of Sunset Boulevard in 2013; 16,900 vehicles per day on SR 27 at Old Topanga Canyon Road in 2013; 4,150 vehicles per day on Old Topanga Canyon Road west of SR 27 in 2009; 2,170 vehicles per day on Fernwood Pacific Drive west of SR 27 in 2009; 550 vehicles per day on Tuna Canyon Road at Saddle Peak Road in 2013. There are no traffic controls along the PCH at the left turn from Tuna Canyon Road, so use extra caution in making this maneuver.

Map: *The Thomas Guide—Street Guide: Los Angeles and Orange Counties* (any recent year), page 671

Getting there: By car—From central Los Angeles, head west on I-10. Continue onto PCH/SR 1. Near California Incline, an access to downtown Santa Monica, look for an entrance to a parking area for Santa Monica State Beach, on your left, north of the Santa Monica Pier. Any of the parking lots along here would be fine.

    By public transit—From central Los Angeles, ride Metro's Expo Line (light-rail) to the Culver City station. Transfer to Metro bus route 534 to Santa Monica. The bus runs every 10 to 30 minutes on weekdays and every 25 to 55 minutes on weekends and holidays. The travel time from Santa Monica is between 65 and 75 minutes. Ask the driver about where to exit for Santa Monica State Beach.

Starting point coordinates: N34.016850° / W118.504328°

THE RIDE

"Topanga to Tuna to Tide" refers to three of the route's main features: Topanga Canyon Boulevard, Old Topanga Canyon Road, and the community of Topanga; Tuna Canyon Road; and the tide, since the ride starts and finishes along the beach. The route is one of the most scenic in this book; but it is not easy, with three significant climbs and one steep descent along the way. It is a 38.2-mile figure-8 route with two loops crisscrossing in Fernwood, plus an out-and-back segment along the beach. With oceanfront and mountain riding, a quiet back road, and spectacular ocean views, this may be the consummate L.A. bike ride!

Start the ride along the Marvin Braude Bike Trail in Santa Monica, adjacent to Santa Monica State Beach. The official starting point is the painted mile 19.00 marker along the path. The marker is near a public restroom facility, behind the parking lot that is just to the north of the Santa Monica Pier (not the Pier's parking lot). Once on the bike path, head northwest. The path is essentially flat, running parallel to Santa Monica State Beach and then Will Rogers State Beach; PCH/SR 1 is to your right. This is the low point of the ride, dipping to just 13 feet above sea level. Enjoy the beach and ocean views.

The path ends after 3.3 miles. Enter the adjacent parking area and ride parallel to PCH/SR 1; at the marked crosswalk, turn right and then safely cross over PCH/SR 1. From here ride westward along PCH/SR 1 on the shoulder. Although the highway is busy (63,000 vehicles per day east of Sunset Boulevard), there is a shoulder. This is a popular cycling route. The highway passes the Pacific Palisades community of L.A., including the exclusive Castellammare neighborhood (and Getty Villa), before entered an unincorporated area. After 2.3 miles of riding along PCH/SR1, turn right onto Topanga Canyon Boulevard (SR 27).

Bike Shops

Helen's Cycles, 2501 Broadway, Santa Monica; (310) 829-1836; http://helenscycles.com

Cynergy Cycles, 2300 Santa Monica Blvd., Santa Monica; (310) 857-1500; http://cynergycycles.com

Bike Attack Santa Monica, 2400 Main St., Santa Monica; (310) 581-8014; www.bikeattack.com

Bike Effect, 910 Broadway #100, Santa Monica; (310) 393-4348; http://bikeeffect.com

Performance Bicycle, 501 Broadway, Santa Monica; (310) 451-9977; www.performancebike.com

Consummate SoCal: palm trees, sand, and beachgoers along Marvin Braude Bike Trail at Will Rogers Beach

You are now heading northward into Topanga State Park. The shoulder width varies, but it is mostly narrow. Stay to the right—traffic volumes, though much lighter than on PCH/SR1, are still in the 17,000-per-day range. The highway climbs, gradually at first and then a bit steeper, before easing as you ride on into Fernwood. Your elevation is in the 750-foot range. This community is part of the larger community of Topanga, which occupies the developed areas within Topanga Canyon. Topanga had a population of 8,289 in 2010. The community is renowned as a bohemian enclave, attracting a variety of artists, musicians, filmmakers, poets, and others seeking to pursue their craft in a nearly rural setting. Notables such as Pete Seeger, Woody Guthrie, Arlo Guthrie, Neil Young, Emmylou Harris, Linda Ronstadt (once seen hitchhiking barefoot in the canyon, carrying a guitar), Etta James, and others have lived and/or performed here.

As you shoot on through Fernwood (you will return here later), keeping your eyes and ears open for the sights and sounds of Topanga, bear left onto Old Topanga Canyon Road at mile 10.2 of the ride. I am not certain about the history, but this was probably the main canyon road before the state highway was built—although the road did not seem that old, and the state highway seemed just as twisty and winding! It is a gradual climb to the first real crest of this ride (1,528 feet). Just beyond the peak, the road enters the city of

Santa Monica Pier

Although the Topanga to Tuna to Tide ride starts and finishes about 0.5 mile north of Santa Monica Pier, a side trip there is highly recommended. Pacific Park—an amusement area featuring rides, carnival games, and even a trapeze school—occupies part of the pier. The solar-powered Ferris wheel (the only such one in the world) is a landmark, as is the Blue Streak Racer wooden roller coaster. The pier was completed in 1909 and is actually two side-by-side piers that are joined. The carousel (with calliope!), which dates from 1922, is housed inside the Santa Monica Logoff Hippodrome, which itself is on the National Register of Historic Places. The La Monica Ballroom, a popular dance hall that could accommodate 5,000 guests, was located on the pier from 1924 to 1963.

As is the case with many other L.A.-area landmarks and communities, the Santa Monica Pier has been the backdrop for numerous shoots. These include *The Sting* (1973), which featured the Hippodrome and carousel; *Ruthless People* (1985; the film's final scene), *Terminator: The Sarah Connor Chronicles*; TV's *24* (one of the characters gets shot at and dies under the pier) and *The Amazing Race* (the pier was the starting line one year); multiple episodes of the TV series *Touch*, *Private Practice*, and *Drop Dead Diva*; and many others. The video for legendary songstress Selena's "Bidi Bidi Bom Bom" was shot at the pier in 1994; and in the film *2012* the pier is lost forever, sinking into the ocean during a massive earthquake. (Just kidding! The pier was rebuilt after the film.)

Calabasas. After a brisk 1.55-mile descent, turn right onto Mulholland Highway. At Mulholland Drive (not to be confused with the highway), turn right again. You are now in the Woodland Hills community of L.A., having ridden to the north side of the Santa Monica Mountains. Turn right at Topanga Canyon Boulevard (SR 27) for the return to Topanga. The highway climbs in a series of switchbacks, many offering great views, to a peak of 1,504 feet. From there it is a rapid and thrilling descent into Topanga Canyon. Hollywood crews have enjoyed filming chase scenes on this road. Once in "central" Fernwood, keep riding past the Old Topanga Canyon Road intersection. After 0.5 mile, look for the Fernwood Pacific Drive intersection, on the right.

Turn right onto Fernwood Pacific Drive and begin the climb (average 5.8% grade) into the hills. The average grade kicks up to 7.8% as you near Rocky Ledge Drive, where the road name changes to Tuna Canyon Road. The road crests at mile 28.4 (elevation: 1,834 feet), the highest point of the ride, at the intersection with Saddle Peak Road. The residences up here are spectacular, as is the view of the Pacific. Keep straight on Tuna Canyon—the road plunges toward the ocean, dropping from 1,834 to 22 feet above sea level in just 3.4 miles (10.1% grade). The road is thankfully one way over nearly the entire distance, so you can claim the entire road while navigating your bike down the tricky and steep hill. When looking ahead at the ocean, at times you may feel as though the road is headed for the water's edge! The grade eases as you near PCH/SR 1, although the last 0.5 mile or so is narrow and rough. Some road repair work is definitely needed (the rough segment is actually in the city of Malibu).

Carefully make a left turn onto PCH/SR 1, watching for traffic from both ways, and head east toward Santa Monica. You are 31.8 miles into the ride and have just under 6.5 miles to go. To your right is Las Tunas County Beach, followed by Topanga County Beach and then Will Rogers State Beach as you return to Pacific Palisades. Opposite Seaview Drive, on your left, look for the entrance to a beach parking lot on your right. Ride through the lot, parallel to PCH/SR 1, and then veer off onto the Marvin Braude Bike Trail. The final 3.3 miles of the ride are forgiving, flat, and extremely scenic along Will Rogers and Santa Monica State Beaches. The ride ends at the mile 19.00 marker along the path, north of the Santa Monica Pier (see sidebar).

MILES AND DIRECTIONS

0.0 Start at mile 19.00 along the Marvin Braude Bike Trail, adjacent to Santa Monica State Beach in Santa Monica near where California Incline meets PCH/SR 1. Head north on path.

3.3 End of bike path. Turn left and ride along parking access road; then turn right into crosswalk to cross PCH/SR 1.

3.4 Turn left onto PCH/SR 1 and head west.

5.7 Traffic signal at Topanga Canyon Boulevard (SR 27); turn right.

10.2 Bear left onto Old Topanga Canyon Road in the Fernwood community (elevation: 756 feet).

14.35 Crest of Old Topanga Canyon Road (1,528 feet) at Calabasas Peak Mountainway; begin descent (5.6% grade) and enter city of Calabasas.

15.9 Stop sign at Mulholland Highway; turn right.

17.6 Traffic signal at Mulholland Drive; turn right and enter Los Angeles (Woodland Hills).

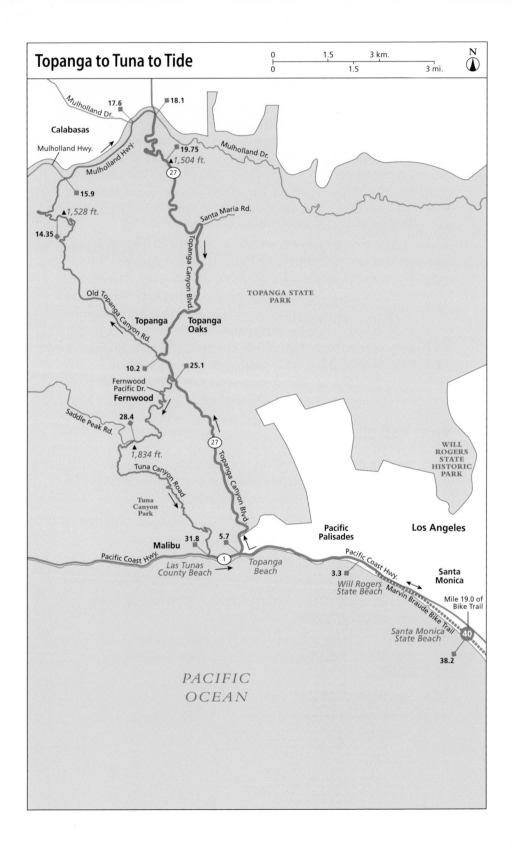

Topanga to Tuna to Tide

0   1.5   3 km.

0   1.5   3 mi.

N

Mulholland Dr.

17.6

18.1

Calabasas

Mulholland Hwy.

Mulholland Dr.

Mulholland Hwy.

19.75
▲1,504 ft.

27

15.9

Santa Maria Rd.

▲1,528 ft.

14.35

TOPANGA STATE PARK

Old Topanga Canyon Rd.

Topanga Canyon Blvd.

Topanga

Topanga Oaks

10.2

25.1

Fernwood Pacific Dr.

Fernwood

Saddle Peak Rd.

28.4

▲
1,834 ft.

27

Tuna Canyon Road

Topanga Canyon Blvd.

Tuna Canyon Park

Malibu

31.8

5.7

Pacific Palisades

Los Angeles

Pacific Coast Hwy.

1

Pacific Coast Hwy.

WILL ROGERS STATE HISTORIC PARK

Las Tunas County Beach

Topanga Beach

3.3

Santa Monica

Will Rogers State Beach

Marvin Braude Bike Trail

Mile 19.0 of Bike Trail

40

Santa Monica State Beach

38.2

PACIFIC OCEAN

18.1 Traffic signal at Topanga Canyon Boulevard (SR 27); turn right and begin climb (5.3% grade).

19.75 Crest of Topanga Canyon Boulevard (1,504 feet) at Summit-to-Summit Mountainway; begin descent. You're now in Topanga community.

25.1 Turn right onto Fernwood Pacific Drive, in Fernwood community; begin climb (5.8% average grade).

27.5 Keep straight at Rocky Ledge Road intersection; now on Tuna Canyon Road (elevation: 1,467 feet; average grade 7.8%).

28.4 High point of ride (1,834 feet) at Tuna Canyon and Saddle Peak Roads; begin steep descent (10.1% grade).

31.8 Stop sign at PCH/SR 1; turn left.

34.8 Leave PCH/SR 1 at Will Rogers State Beach, adjacent to Seaview Drive; ride through parking area, parallel to PCH/SR 1.

34.9 Veer right onto Marvin Braude Bike Trail.

38.2 End ride at mile 19.00 mark along Marvin Braude Bike Trail.

Start: Sara Wan Trailhead, Corral Canyon Park, 25623 Pacific Coast Hwy., Malibu (parking fee)

Length: 33.1 miles (counterclockwise loop plus a short out-and-back segment)

Riding time: 1.75 to 5 hours (my time: 2H24:10)

Terrain and surface: 100% paved roads

Elevation: Low: 19 feet on the Pacific Coast Highway (PCH/SR1) in Point Dume; high: 2,122 feet at Latigo Canyon Road and Castro Mountainway

Traffic and hazards: There were 29,500 vehicles per day on PCH/SR 1 at Kanan Dume Road (CR N9) in 2013; 1,050 vehicles per day on SR 23 south of Mulholland Highway in 2013; 585 vehicles per day on Latigo Canyon Road east of Kanan Dume in 2009; 8,775 vehicles per day on Kanan Dume Road south of Mulholland Highway in 2009; 1,860 vehicles per day on Mulholland west of Kanan Dume in 2009; 615 vehicles per day on Mulholland east of Westlake Boulevard in 2009.

Map: *The Thomas Guide—Street Guide: Los Angeles and Orange Counties* (any recent year), page 628

Getting there: By car—From central Los Angeles, head west on I-10. At the end of I-10, continue onto PCH/SR 1 to Malibu. Look for the Sara Wan Trailhead for Corral Canyon Park on the right side of the highway, a little over 1 mile west of Pepperdine University and Malibu Bluffs State Park (and immediately adjacent to Malibu Seafood).

By public transit—From central Los Angeles, ride Metro's Expo Line (light-rail) to the Culver City station. Transfer to Metro bus route 534 and continue into Malibu. Exit at the Sara Wan Trailhead. The bus runs every 10 to 30 minutes on weekdays and every 25 to 55 minutes on weekends and holidays. The travel time from Culver City is between 65 and 75 minutes.

Starting point coordinates: N34.033597° W118.734794°

THE RIDE

Zoom Dume Zuma is a moderately challenging 33.1-mile ride; just under 40% of the distance is along the flat to rolling coastline, and 60% is in the Santa Monica Mountains, overlooking the ocean. The minimum elevation is near sea level; the maximum elevation is 2,122 feet. There are no steep climbs, but there is one extended climb and a few shorter ones. The title refers to two prominent Malibu landmarks: Point Dume and Zuma Beach. Just under half the ride is in the city of Malibu; the other half is in unincorporated areas of Los Angeles County, high above Malibu. The ride starts from the Sara Wan Trailhead for Corral Canyon Park, located along the Pacific Coast Highway (SR 1, or PCH) adjacent to Puerco Beach and Dan Blocker County Beach. The parking lot for the trailhead (fee) is next to Malibu Seafood, a popular eatery.

Exit the parking lot and turn right, watching for traffic; head west on PCH/ SR1. The best, up-close views of the ocean of the entire ride are along this stretch. Dan Blocker (1928–1972), namesake of the adjacent beach, is best remembered for his portrayal of "Hoss" during the long-running TV series *Bonanza*. After 1.85 miles along PCH/SR1, in which the highway climbs to 112 feet, turn right onto Latigo Canyon Road. The road leaves Malibu as it

Point Dume in Film

When riding past Point Dume on the Pacific Coast Highway, you may somehow recognize the promontory. That may be because the formation has appeared in several films and TV shows. The promontory is a long bluff that extends into the Pacific Ocean—a natural boundary to Santa Monica Bay, which lies to the south. In *Iron Man*, Tony Stark lives in a mansion that is located on the bluff, on the edge of a cliff. In reality the mansion never existed, even as a temporary structure, because of strict prohibitions on construction in the area. Hollywood film techs got around this by digitally imposing a 3-D model of the house on the promontory.

In the pilot episode of TV's *I Dream of Jeannie,* Point Dume is the South Pacific Island on which Tony Nelson's space capsule washes ashore, after which he discovers and releases Jeannie from her bottle. In the original *Planet of the Apes* (1968), Taylor (Charlton Heston) and Nova (Linda Harrison) ride their horses along Point Dume State Beach to discover the ruins of the Statue of Liberty, which was actually a papier-mâché model. Thankfully, the thermonuclear war that destroyed most of humanity in that film has not yet occurred, allowing you to enjoy some fabulous cycling in Malibu!

With the ocean "behind the cars and buildings," Malibu's busy Pacific Coast Highway is a rite of passage for cyclists.

climbs steadily (average grade 5.3%) into the Santa Monica Mountains. Traffic volumes are surprisingly light, although residences are scattered about the mountainside along the side roads. Enjoy the magnificent views of the Pacific Ocean as the road twists and turns its way into the mountains. After 7.0 miles Latigo Canyon reaches its first crest (2,084 feet) at Blackton Drive. The road descends for 1.1 miles to Newton Canyon Road (1,786 feet) before the climb (same gradient) resumes. Latigo Canyon finally crests at Castro Mountainway, the high point of the ride (2,122 feet), after 9.25 miles. From here the road descends rapidly (7.9% grade) to Kanan Dume Road.

Turn right at Kanan Dume Road and head north to Mulholland Highway. Turn left onto Mulholland and head west. This road is discussed (and ridden) in other rides in this book, making it the backbone of numerous routes extending from Malibu in the west and to the hills above Hollywood in the east. After 1.0 mile the road splits, with Mulholland Highway veering to the right and Encinal Canyon Road heading left. Stay on Mulholland. The road climbs and then descends to Westlake Highway (mile 16.0 of the ride). Turn left here to continue on Mulholland Highway. After a short climb and false flat, the road splits, with Mulholland Highway turning right and Decker Canyon Road continuing straight. This time, keep straight onto Decker Canyon Road (SR 23). Enjoy the views of the ocean as you ride along this lightly traveled state highway. At South Foose Road, at mile 19.3, the highway starts to descend precipitously. Over the next 3.3 miles, the highway drops from 1,532 feet at South Foose to 98 feet at PCH/SR1. The average grade on the descent is 8.2%, although there are some steeper segments and some spectacular hairpin turns that you can see from above.

Keep your wits about you, and stay on the right side of the road as you spiral down the highway. At the bottom, where there is good sight distance, turn left onto PCH/SR1. This begins a long, 10.5-mile trek back to Sara Wan Trailhead along the coastal highway. The highway is not flat, but rolls gradually. This segment of PCH/SR1 was part of the 1932 Olympic Games' 100 km cycling time trial. The top rider, an Italian, averaged 25.2 miles per hour for the Moorpark to Santa Monica trip. Although he was riding a 1930s-era bicycle, he did not have to worry about traffic signals and modern-day traffic levels!

Bike Shop

The Bicycle Shop, 940 North Ventura Rd., Oxnard; (805) 308-2453; http://vcbicycles.com

PCH/SR1 scorches past beach after beach—El Pescador, Robert H. Meyer, La Piedra, El Matador, Lechuza, and Zuma—before turning away from the ocean in the Point Dume area. Looking to the right as PCH/SR1 curves to the left, you can see the Point Dume promontory. You may even recognize it (see sidebar). The highway makes a nifty climb (4.9% grade) from 19 to 215 feet above sea level in the Point Dume area before entering a series of false flats and gradual undulations. From here it is just over 3.0 miles to Latigo Canyon Road to close the loop, and then another 1.9 miles to the Sara Wan Trailhead to end the ride. **Note:** The entrance to the trailhead will be on the opposite side of PCH/SR1, and there are no provisions for a left turn. Exercise caution in crossing the highway here or, perhaps more safely, at the traffic signal at Cold Canyon Road, west of the trailhead.

MILES AND DIRECTIONS

0.0 Start from the Sara Wan Trailhead (Corral Canyon Park) at 25623 Pacific Coast Hwy. Head west on PCH/SR 1.

1.85 Turn right onto Latigo Canyon Road; begin climb (average 5.3% grade).

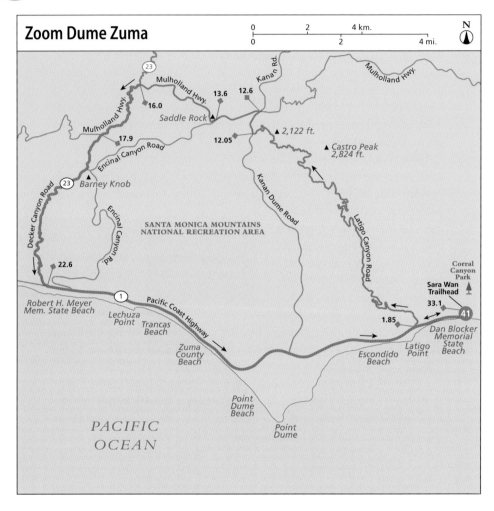

Zoom Dume Zuma

Map scale: 0–4 km / 0–4 mi.

N

- **Mulholland Hwy.** (23)
- 16.0
- Saddle Rock
- 13.6 12.6
- Kanan Rd.
- Mulholland Hwy.
- Mulholland Hwy.
- 17.9
- Encinal Canyon Road
- 12.05
- ▲ 2,122 ft.
- ▲ Castro Peak 2,824 ft.
- (23) ▲ Barney Knob
- Decker Canyon Road
- Encinal Canyon Rd.
- **SANTA MONICA MOUNTAINS NATIONAL RECREATION AREA**
- Kanan Dume Road
- Latigo Canyon Road
- Corral Canyon Park
- **Sara Wan Trailhead** ♁
- 22.6
- (1)
- Pacific Coast Highway
- Robert H. Meyer Mem. State Beach
- Lechuza Point
- Trancas Beach
- Zuma County Beach
- 33.1
- 1.85
- (41)
- Dan Blocker Memorial State Beach
- Escondido Beach
- Latigo Point
- Point Dume Beach
- Point Dume
- *PACIFIC OCEAN*

8.85 First crest of Latigo Canyon Road (elevation: 2,084 feet), at Blackton Drive; begin descent and then resume climbing.

11.1 High point of entire ride (2,122 feet) at Latigo Canyon Road and Castro Mountainway; begin twisting descent (7.9% grade).

12.05 Stop sign at Kanan Dume Road (CR N9); turn right.

12.6 Turn left onto Mulholland Highway.

13.6 Bear right at the split in the road to remain on Mulholland Highway. (Encinal Canyon Road heads off to the left.)

16.0 Stop sign at Westlake Highway; turn left to continue on Mulholland Highway.

17.9 Keep straight at fork in road; now on Decker Canyon Road (SR 23). (Mulholland Highway continues to the right.)

19.3 Keep straight at South Foose Road; begin descent at 8.2% average grade (road drops from 1,532 to 98 feet at PCH/SR 1).

22.6 Stop sign at PCH/SR 1; turn left. It is 10.5 miles from here to the end of the ride.

33.1 End ride at Sara Wan Trailhead (on opposite side of highway).

Zuma Trancas Calayas

Start: Malibu Equestrian Park, 6225 Merritt Dr., Malibu

Length: 12.85 miles (clockwise loop)

Riding time: 1.75 to 6 hours (my time: 2H28:37)

Terrain and surface: 77% on dirt fire roads and trails; 23% on paved roads

Elevation: Low: 19 feet on the Pacific Coast Highway (PCH/SR 1) near Point Dume; high: 1,812 feet at Zuma Ridge Mountainway and Zuma Edison Road

Traffic and hazards: PCH/SR 1 was carrying 16,700 vehicles per day in the Point Dume area in 2013. Most of the ride is on park fire roads and trails (no motor vehicles) and quiet residential streets.

Map: *The Thomas Guide—Street Guide: Los Angeles and Orange Counties* (any recent year), page 667

Getting there: By car—From central Los Angeles, take I-10 West. At the end of the freeway in Santa Monica, continue onto PCH/SR 1, heading north and then westward. Continue into Malibu. After passing Point Dume, look for and turn right onto Morning View Drive, followed by a right turn onto Merritt Drive. After rounding the sweeping curve and heading up the hill, look for Malibu Equestrian Park, on the left. Enter and park in the large paved lot.

By public transit—From central Los Angeles, ride Metro's Expo Line (light-rail) to the Culver City station. Transfer to Metro bus route 534 and continue into Malibu. Exit Metro bus route 534 at PCH/SR 1 and Morning View Drive in Malibu. Ride up Morning View Drive and then turn right onto Merritt Drive. Continue up the hill to Malibu Equestrian Park. The bus runs every 10 to 30 minutes on weekdays and every 25 to 55 minutes on weekends and holidays. Expect the bus to take 75 to 90 minutes.

Starting point coordinates: N34.023372° / W118.823250°

THE RIDE

Save the best for letter "Z"? Well, "Zuma" means "abundance" in Chumash, so Zuma! Zuma Trancas Calayas is certainly one of the best off-road rides in this book and definitely among the most challenging. Although the route is in the Santa Monica Mountains, which are not nearly as tall and daunting as the San Gabriels, the ride features an unusual double climb—there are two summits rather than just one. The first climb elevates from 116 to 1,812 feet, while the second rises from 732 to 1,710 feet, for a net of 2,674 feet. Only two other rides in this book (the Mounts Lowe and Wilson Expedition and the White Saddle Challenge) have a greater net elevation differential. The terrain is forgiving, with generally good, graded dirt fire roads with minimal erosion and a moderate number of rocks.

Start the ride at Malibu Equestrian Park in Malibu (Malibu Park neighborhood). The park is a public horse facility that has two riding arenas. Your horse

On Zuma Edison Road, overlooking Zuma Canyon with the Pacific Ocean in the distance

Zuma Trancas Calayas

is your bicycle, so leave the park via the access road and turn left onto Merritt Drive. The road climbs at a 5.1% grade to the Busch Drive intersection; bear left and climb at a 6.9% grade to the end of the road. From here (note the parking area), continue past the gate and onto Zuma Ridge Mountainway (also known as Zuma Ridge Trail). This fire road climbs at an average grade of 11.2% for the next 1.0 mile. A few switchbacks let you enjoy the view of the Pacific, but the climb is otherwise relentless and steep. Get some short relief at mile 2.0, where the grade eases (to 9.4%) at the Chumash Indian Trail junction (elevation: 1,017 feet). Continue up the climb on Zuma Ridge. Trancas Edison Road is on the left at mile 3.5, followed shortly by Zuma Edison Road at mile 3.6. This is the high point of the entire road (1,812 feet). Turn right for the descent into Zuma Canyon.

The Zuma Canyon descent is steep (10.8% grade) and curvy, so enjoy it while keeping solid control of your bicycle. Zuma Edison Road (a dirt fire road) descends into the woodlands of the canyon, with portions completely shaded. At the bottom of the canyon (elevation: 732 feet), the road makes a hairpin turn in preparation for the climb up the opposite side. This climb (11.1% grade) is just as steep, if not steeper, than the Zuma Ridge climb. Your orientation is now southward, toward the ocean, giving you constant views of the Pacific. After 1.65 miles the road makes a hairpin curve to reorient northward. You are now at just over 1,700 feet. Just beyond the curve at mile 7.45, turn right onto Zuma Canyon Connector Trail. This is truly a

Bike Shop

The Bicycle Shop, 940 North Ventura Rd., Oxnard; (805) 308-2453; http://vcbicycles .com

"trail," much narrower than the "roads" you have been riding. Begin descending at a 9.0% grade. You can pick up the noises of vehicles traveling along Kanan Dume Road, which is to your left and below you. The sounds let you know that you are always near civilization.

Watch out for rocks along the trail as you rapidly descend. Keep straight at the Canyon View Trail and Ocean View Trail junctions, which come in rapid succession near the 9.5-mile mark of the ride. Either of these trails would be an excellent way to return to the starting point—if bicycles weren't prohibited. The alternative is to keep straight on Kanan Edison Road, which continues steeply downhill (14.1% grade). Watch out for some trail erosion. At the fork, bear right onto an unnamed trail that skirts the edge of a small open space. At the end of the trail, turn left onto a paved water tank access road. At the bottom of this road, turn right onto Cavalleri Drive. You are now riding through one of Malibu's many pleasant neighborhoods. At the fork at mile 10.25, bear left to continue on Cavalleri. Turn right at the stop sign at PCH/SR 1 and head westward on the highway. This is the busiest road of the ride but is nonetheless popular with cyclists. This is also the low point of the ride, as the ocean and several successive beaches are to your left. Turn right at Morning View Drive and make the short but stiff climb (8.7% grade) to Merritt Drive. Turn right here and follow the road as it makes a long curve to the left. Look for the entrance to Malibu Equestrian Park on the left. Turn here and travel along the park access road to the parking area to end the ride.

MILES AND DIRECTIONS

0.0 Start in the Malibu Equestrian Park parking area and head toward the exit on the park access road.

0.1 Stop at Merritt Drive; turn left and begin climb (5.1% grade).

0.45 Stop sign at Busch Drive; turn left and continue climbing (6.9% grade).

1.0 End of Busch Drive; continue past gate onto Zuma Ridge Mountainway (unpaved; also called Zuma Ridge Trail). Climb at 11.2% grade.

2.0 Keep straight at junction with Chumash Indian Trail, now at 1,017 feet of elevation. Continue climbing at 9.4% grade.

3.5 Keep straight at junction with Trancas Edison Road (unpaved).

3.6 Junction with Zuma Edison Road (unpaved); turn right. High point of ride (1,812 feet); begin descent into Zuma Canyon (10.8% grade).

5.5 Bottom of Zuma Canyon. After hairpin curve (elevation: 732 feet), begin climbing up the other side of the canyon (11.1% grade).

7.15 Hairpin curve at 1,701 feet; grade eases.

7.45 Junction with Zuma Canyon Connector Trail (elevation: 1,710 feet); turn right on the narrower trail. Begin descent (9.0% grade).

8.2 Merge with Kanan Edison Road (dirt trail), now on Kanan Edison; continue descending on 9.1% grade.

9.45 Keep straight at junction with Canyon View Trail.

9.55 Keep straight at junction with Ocean View Trail; steep descent (14.1% grade).

9.8 Bear right at split in trail, now on unnamed access trail.

9.85 Turn right onto water tank access road.

9.95 Stop at Cavalleri Road; turn left.

10.25 Bear left at split in road to continue on Cavalleri.

10.8 Stop sign at PCH/SR 1; turn right.

12.35 Traffic signal at Morning View Drive (elevation: 20 feet); turn right and climb hill (8.7% grade).

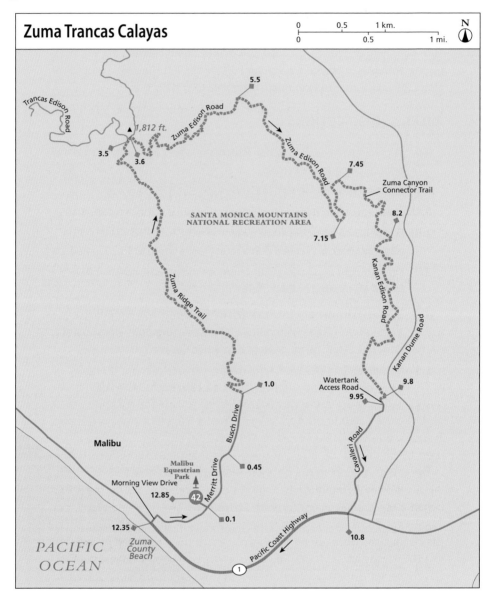

Zuma Trancas Calayas

0   0.5   1 km.
0   0.5   1 mi.

N

Trancas Edison Road

▲ 1,812 ft.

3.5

3.6

5.5

Zuma Edison Road

Zuma Edison Road

7.45

Zuma Canyon
Connector Trail

8.2

7.15

SANTA MONICA MOUNTAINS
NATIONAL RECREATION AREA

Zuma Ridge Trail

Kanan Edison Road

Kanan Dume Road

1.0

Watertank
Access Road
9.95

9.8

Busch Drive

Cavalleri Road

Malibu

Malibu
Equestrian
Park
Morning View Drive

12.85   42

Merritt Drive

0.45

0.1

12.35

10.8

Zuma
County
Beach

Pacific Coast Highway

1

PACIFIC
OCEAN

12.4 Turn right onto Merritt Drive; grade of climb eases.

12.75 Entrance to Malibu Equestrian Park on the left; turn left.

12.85 End ride at end of park access road, adjacent to large parking area.

Best Catalina Island Rides

As the song says, Santa Catalina Island lies 26 miles across the sea from the mainland. The words to the 1960 Four Preps song say a lot. The distance is accurate, and the island is indeed a destination. No Los Angeles–area bicycling book would be complete without including some riding on this lightly developed island. The island is one of the eight Channel Islands located in the Pacific Ocean off the California coast. Five of the eight islands are part of Channel Islands National Park; Santa Catalina is not. At 75 square miles, Catalina is the third-largest of the Channel Islands and the only one with a permanent population; 88% of the island is under the protection and controls of the Santa Catalina Island Conservancy (www.catalinaconservancy.org). Most of the development on the island is concentrated in busy Avalon, an incorporated city that is home to 90% of the island's 4,096 residents. Outside Avalon, a permit is needed to explore the island's back roads. Well worth the fee (see the conservancy's website for permit details), in my opinion. Avalon is definitely worth exploring: romantic venues, restaurants, gift shops, boating, fishing, diving, dolphins, scenery, and plenty of other activities. But the real treat is to bicycle around town and then head away from the city to see the backcountry.

The original inhabitants of Catalina were the Gabrielino-Tongva tribe, of which there may have been 2,500 on the island at one time. Spanish explorers "discovered" Catalina in the sixteenth and seventeenth centuries. The arrival of the Spaniards led to the decline of the Native Americans, mainly because of the introduction of new diseases. Without any real control, the island was used by hunters (seals, otters, whales), smugglers (pirates enjoyed hiding in the coves), herders, and even miners. Once folks such as George Shatto, William Wrigley Jr., and the Bannings got their hands on Catalina, the island began a transformation into a resort destination. During World War II, the island was closed and used strictly for military use. In 1972 Chicano activists claimed the island under the flag of Mexico (they departed peacefully). In 1981 actress Natalie Wood drowned in the waters off Catalina; the case was reopened thirty years later on the basis of new information. Outside of these "hiccups"—tragic events; major fires in 1915, 2007, and 2011; and even a tsunami in 2011—Catalina has remained a popular tourism spot. During the decades of and prior to the Natalie Wood incident, the island was very popular among the Hollywood elite. Stars such as Errol Flynn, Perry Como, Charlie Chaplin, Paulette Goddard, George Harrison, and many others could be seen cavorting and enjoying Avalon and its offerings.

Today Catalina's appeal is perhaps more oriented toward the general public. It is expensive, for sure—the combination of round-trip ferry fare plus one night's lodging might cost a minimum of $200. A conservancy permit, island bus fare, extra charge for bicycle portage, and—oh, yes—food bump the cost up to at least $300 for one person. So plan in advance and save up; the trip is worthwhile. Catalina Express ferry boats were departing from terminals in San Pedro, Long Beach, Newport Beach, and Dana Point as of this writing. (Visit http://catalinaexpress.com for rates and reservations.) There was no scheduled commercial air service (although there has been in the past). This book features one road and two mountain bike rides, all of them leaving from or near Avalon. You should be able to do at least two of the rides—and maybe all three—during a two-day, one-night excursion to the island. The routes do not venture out to the western end of the island, but an extended trip there would certainly be worthwhile. ***Note:*** Even with a conservancy permit, bicycles are restricted to specific trails and dirt roads. Follow the rules, and make some memories!

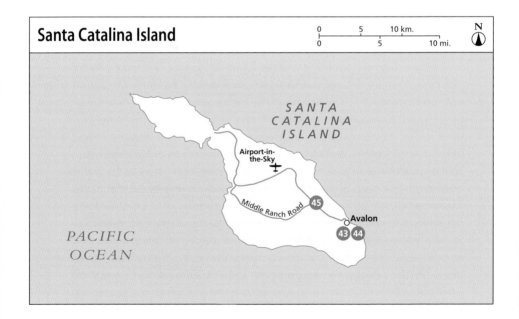

Catalina East End Eco-Ride

Start: Intersection of Crescent and Clarissa Avenues, Avalon, Santa Catalina Island

Length: 13.3 miles (clockwise loop)

Riding time: 1.5 to 4 hours (my time: 1H55:48)

Terrain and surface: 62% on dirt roads; 23% on good paved roads; 15% on partially or poorly paved roads

Elevation: Low: 12 feet on Crescent Avenue in Avalon; high: 1,630 feet along East End Road

Traffic and hazards: The descent of Old Stage Road is narrow, winding and bumpy. Be alert to oncoming traffic.

Map: Green Planet Maps, *Santa Catalina Island*

Getting there: Take ferry to Catalina Island; the starting point is to the northeast of the ferry terminal (Cabrillo Mole) in central Avalon.

Starting point coordinates: N33.342892° / W118.324503°

THE RIDE

The Catalina East End Eco-Ride is an extremely scenic, somewhat challenging tour of Santa Catalina Island's east end. Avalon is situated near Catalina's east end, so the ride starts and ends in town, taking you high into the mountains that overlook Avalon Bay. Although there are paved road segments at the beginning and end, most of the ride is off-road. Be sure to have a Freewheeler Bike Pass properly displayed on your mountain bike before leaving town. The permit validates (and pays for) your use of Catalina's backcountry dirt roads, as explained in the section introduction. Start on the east end of Avalon at Crescent and Clarissa Avenues. You may have had to walk your bike on Crescent Avenue to get there (no riding allowed on Crescent adjacent Middle and South Beaches). Crescent immediately curves to the left, becoming Pebbly Beach Road.

Pebbly Beach Road quickly leaves town, heading southeastward on a coastal route that takes you past Cabrillo Mole (ferry terminal), Lover's

On Catalina's East End Road, looking out over the Palisades and the blue Pacific

Cove, Abalone Point, and Pebbly Beach. Past these points of interest, the environment begins to look highly industrial. Near the end of the road is a power-generating station and a helipad. The road turns sharply to the right, becoming Wrigley Road. Wrigley climbs abruptly (7.9% grade); this is the beginning of your trek into the mountains of Catalina's east end. At the 1.95-mile mark, 0.65 mile up Wrigley, leave the road via the trailhead on your left. This is the start of Renton Mines Road (dirt) and also the start of the Trans-Catalina Trail, which runs from the east to the west end of the island, covering some 37 miles. Renton Mines climbs steadily at a grade of 7.1% to 7.5%; the surface is quite rocky at the lower elevations but gets smoother as you climb. Stay on the main dirt road at the first hairpin turn; you are now on East End Road. The view is toward the east—Jewfish Point and of course the Pacific Ocean, which is a magical blue on sunny days.

The next hairpin turn, at mile 4.95 (elevation: 1,523 feet), is at the far southeastern corner of the island—below you are Seal Rocks and the expansive Pacific. You are now headed in a westerly direction, with views of Binnacle Rock, the Palisades, and the Catalina coastline to your left and the city

Best Bike Rides Los Angeles

of Avalon to your right. The scenery is breathtaking—even riders who want to break the course record will be inclined to stop for some photo shoots! After cresting at 1,630 feet at mile 5.65, East End Road descends, with a few undulations thrown in. For a stretch the appearance is that you are headed toward the ocean—a great illusion. East End Road reaches a low point (1,099 feet) at the junction with Garden to Sky Trail. This trail leads down to Avalon Canyon, offering a shortcut back to Avalon. Tempting, but the trail is actually off-limits to bicycles.

From this junction, East End road climbs at a steep 11.2% grade to a junction with Hermit Gulch and Lone Tree Roads (elevation: 1,512 feet). The road changes its name; you are now on Divide Road (dirt). From here, for the next 1.9 miles, the road remains within 100 feet of the 1,512-foot elevation. Divide Road remains along a high ridge, with Avalon Canyon to the east and Grand Canyon to the west, which serves as a dividing line between the eastern and middle sections of the island. Divide Road ends at Airport Road (elevation: 1,431 feet) 10.25 miles into the ride. Make a sharp right and begin the Airport Road descent. As suggested by its name, this partially paved road leads to Catalina's Airport-in-the-Sky, which is west of here. Where Airport Road's surface changes to pavement (although it was in poor condition when I rode it), the road name changes to Old Stage Road. The downhill along

Bike Shop

Brown's Bikes, 107 Pebbly Beach Rd., Avalon; (310) 510-0986; www.catalina biking.com

here is narrow, winding, and rough—be alert to oncoming motor vehicles (mostly minibuses heading to the airport, and ecotour jeeps).

Leave Old Stage Road at Hogsback Gate; this barrier separates the free, public roads of the Avalon area from the dirt and rough backcountry roads of Catalina's interior. Negotiate the gate and then turn left onto Chimes Tower Road. This steep road (9.4% grade) continues the descent. As you round the curve, you may hear an adventurer yipping (maybe even screaming) as he or she rides the zip line in the adjacent canyon to your left. Chimes Tower Road continues to drop while rounding the bend, offering a spectacular view of Avalon and the bay. It is definitely worth another stop for a photograph. The Deagan Chimes Tower is on the left as you descend. The tower chimes a melodic tune every 15 minutes between 8 a.m. and 4 p.m. Just down the road from the tower is the Zane Grey Pueblo Hotel, on the right. Built in 1926, this was once the famous Western novelist's home. Farther down the hill, turn left at the split in the road onto Vieudelou Avenue. Grab the brakes on this steep hill—a stop sign awaits at the next intersection. Turn left onto Marilla Avenue. The oldest house in Avalon is located on the corner; it is a survivor of

Santa Catalina Island Conservancy

The Santa Catalina Island Conservancy (www.catalinaconservancy .org) was established in 1972 following gifts from the William Wrigley Jr. family (son Philip K. Wrigley and daughter Dorothy Wrigley Offield). The gifts granted 88% of the land to the nonprofit conservancy to preserve and act as stewards of Catalina's unspoiled interior. Despite its size (75 square miles), Catalina Island is home to a number of indigenous species, including the Catalina Island fox, the Catalina quail, Beuwick's wren, Catalina grass, Catalina Island buckwheat, Catalina bedstraw, and several others. In addition, Catalina provides a habitat for a number of classic species, including bison and the California bald eagle.

The interior is protected but is nonetheless accessible to the general public upon paying a conservancy membership fee (see website for current rates). The basic membership is for a full year, but there are other membership options available. To be able to do this ride—and have access to the majesty and beauty of Catalina—I highly recommend becoming a conservancy member! Day-use permits for bicycling are not available.

a 1915 fire that destroyed nearly every structure between here and the water. Descend Marilla (12.1% grade) to Crescent Avenue, once again keeping your hands near the brakes. Turn right onto Crescent and ride 1 block to Metropole Avenue to conclude the ride. To get back to the starting point, walk along Crescent (no riding) to Clarissa Avenue.

MILES AND DIRECTIONS

0.0 Start at the intersection of Crescent and Clarissa Avenues in central Avalon. Head east, away from town.

0.05 Road curves to the left, becoming Pebbly Beach Drive.

1.3 Sharp curve to the right; now on Wrigley Road. Begin climbing (7.9% grade).

1.95 Leave Wrigley Road at trailhead to the left; now on Renton Mine Road (unpaved). Continue climbing (7.1% grade).

3.15 Hairpin turn; stay on main trail, now on East End Road (unpaved). Continue climbing (7.5% grade).

4.95 Hairpin curve to the right; stay on main trail. Still on East End Road, oriented westward (elevation: 1,523 feet).

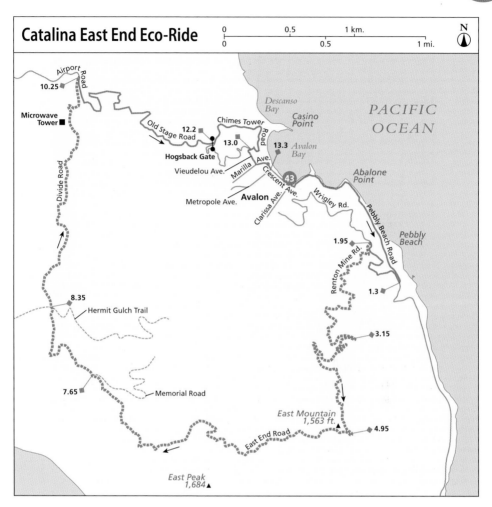

Catalina East End Eco-Ride

5.65 High point of ride (1,630 feet); begin gradual descent (average 5.0% grade).

7.65 Keep straight at junction with Garden to Sky Trail, also referred to as Memorial Road (elevation: 1,099 feet). Begin climbing (11.2% grade).

8.35 Keep straight at junction with Hermit Gulch Trail, followed by Lone Tree Road (elevation: 1,512 feet), now on Divide Road (unpaved).

10.25 End of Divide Road; turn sharply right onto Airport Road (partially paved; elevation: 1,431 feet), with a downhill grade of 9.5%.

11.45 End of Airport Road; keep straight onto Old Stage Road. Road is paved but in poor condition (elevation: 832 feet); continue descent (8.4% grade).

12.2 Hogsback Gate, at end of Old Stage Road. Proceed past gate and turn left onto Chimes Tower Road (one way); descend at 9.4% grade.

13.0 Bear left at fork in the road onto Vieudelou Avenue; continue descent (10.2% grade).

13.15 Stop sign at Marilla Avenue; turn left and descend (12.1% grade).

13.25 Stop sign at Crescent Avenue; turn right.

13.3 End ride at intersection of Crescent and Metropole Avenues in central Avalon.

In & Around Avalon Road Tour

Start: Intersection of Crescent and Clarissa Avenues, central Avalon, Santa Catalina Island

Length: 10.6 miles (clockwise loop, including two out-and-back segments)

Riding time: 45 minutes to 2.5 hours (my time: 1H04:32)

Terrain and surface: 100% paved

Elevation: Low: 12 feet on Crescent Avenue in central Avalon; high: 497 feet at Old Stage and Chimes Tower Roads

Traffic and hazards: The descent of Old Stage Road is narrow, winding and bumpy. Be alert to oncoming traffic.

Map: Green Planet Maps, *Santa Catalina Island*

Getting there: Take ferry to Catalina Island; the starting point is to the northeast of the ferry terminal (Cabrillo Mole) in central Avalon.

Starting point coordinates: N33.342892° / W118.324503°

THE RIDE

The In & Around Avalon Tour is a road ride that is essentially a grand tour of Avalon and its immediate environs. Although 88% of Santa Catalina Island is owned by the Santa Catalina Island Conservancy—and to see it, one must purchase a membership—it is possible to get in a decent road ride in "non-protected" Avalon on its public roads. This ride, therefore, is a less costly, more leisurely option for those not up to attacking Catalina's rugged interior. The tour is not easy to ride fast because of the narrow and sometimes steep streets, the levels of vehicular and pedestrian activities, the numerous points of interest, and the sheer scenery. Avalon is Catalina Island's only incorporated

> ### Bike Shop
> **Brown's Bikes,** 107 Pebbly Beach Rd., Avalon; (310) 510-0986; www.catalina biking.com

city; its 3,686 residents (as of 2010) represent 90% of the island's population. The population swells, of course, with the daily influx of visitors.

The ride starts off similarly to the Catalina East End Eco-Ride: From the intersection of Crescent and Clarissa Avenues in central Avalon, head east along the shoreline on Pebbly Beach Road. After the sharp turn adjacent to the power generating station, climb Wrigley Road to its crest (411 feet). Enjoy the view of the city and the ocean from up here. Wrigley then descends, passing the Inn on Mount Ada (hugely popular tourist stop, as well as a bed-and-breakfast). Watch out for oncoming traffic on the twisting descent.

The Wrigley Road descent practically brings you back down to sea level. Turn left onto Clemente Avenue. At the next big intersection, turn left onto Avalon Canyon Road. This road climbs gently (4.4% grade) to the Wrigley Memorial and Botanical Gardens, passing the Catalina Island Golf Course, a skate park, athletic fields, a nature center, and a campground. Be sure to stay to the left at the two forks in the road. The entrance to the Wrigley Memorial (elevation: of 337 feet) is 1.2 miles up the canyon. Turn around here and enjoy the descent back down the canyon.

William Wrigley Jr.

Although the Banning family, headed by Phineas Banning, can be attributed with starting the momentum toward establishing Avalon as a tourist destination, it was William Wrigley Jr. (1861–1932) who invested the heaviest in the concept. In fact, Wrigley invested in the entire island, effectively owning it after purchasing the Santa Catalina Island Company in 1919. Among Wrigley's many contributions were the founding of Pebbly Beach quarry, which provided island residents jobs as well as materials for buildings, and the construction of the Avalon Casino. He also established a plant to produce Catalina tile using mud and clay found on the island; tile pieces and Catalina pottery are now collectors' items.

The Wrigley Company (Wrigley's gum, Life Savers candy) never had any facilities on the island, however. As Wrigley owned the Chicago Cubs baseball team, Catalina Island served as the team's spring training home from 1921 until 1951. After his death, Wrigley's ashes were interred at the Wrigley Memorial and Botanic Garden. The ashes have since been moved to Forest Lawn Memorial Park in Glendale, California, but the memorial remains. To further his legacy, the Wrigley family established the Santa Catalina Island Conservancy in 1972 to protect the island's native habitats and pristine wilderness.

Cyclists keep pace with an electric cart on Crescent Avenue near Middle Beach in Avalon.

Upon returning to Tremont Street, make a sharp left onto Country Club Drive. This is the beginning of a ride along Avalon's hilly southwest perimeter. The roads out here are narrow, winding, and undulating; residences line the streets. At the end of Country Club, turn left onto East Whittley Avenue, followed shortly by another left onto Las Lomas Drive. Keep straight where Las Lomas turns, and continue onto Camino del Monte. This road makes a hairpin turn to the right and then climbs gradually to an intersection with Old Stage Road (also known as Stagecoach Road and Isthmus Road). Hang a sharp left here and begin climbing. The road is one way uphill, twisting and curving at a 9.4% grade. At the crest, to your left is Hogsback Gate. Passage beyond the gate requires a permit from the conservancy.

Keep straight here (this is the high point of the ride; elevation: 497 feet) onto Chimes Tower Road. (This portion of the ride duplicates a portion of the Catalina East End Eco-Ride.) Descend Chimes Tower, followed by a left turn onto Vieudelou Avenue and then a left turn onto Marilla Avenue. At the bottom of Marilla, turn left onto Crescent Avenue. Stay to the right and head west on Casino Way. This road takes you toward Avalon's most recognized landmark, the Avalon Casino. Along the way, Casino Way passes the Tuna Club, a fishermen's club that has existed since 1898 (the present structure was a rebuild after the 1915 fire). The Casino was built in 1927 and houses a movie theater, ballroom, and museum. Despite the name, it is not a gambling facility. Continue past the Casino—you are now on St. Catherine Way, also called Descanso Canyon Road. Descanso Beach is to your right; this area was once the site of the Hancock Banning home (the Banning family contributed to the development of Avalon as a tourist center, starting in the late nineteenth century). Continue along the road as it gradually climbs to 207 feet, affording a fabulous view of Descanso Bay. Turn around at the secured entry to the Hamilton Cove Condominiums. Return along Descanso Bay Road, St. Catherine Way, and Casino Way to central Avalon. The ride ends at the intersection of Crescent and Metropole Avenues.

MILES AND DIRECTIONS

0.0 Start at the intersection of Crescent and Clarissa Avenues in central Avalon. Head east, away from town.

0.05 Road curves to the left, becoming Pebbly Beach Road.

1.3 Sharp curve to the right; now on Wrigley Road. Begin climbing (7.9% grade).

2.25 Crest of Wrigley (elevation: 411 feet); begin descent (7.7% grade).

3.2 Stop sign at Clemente Avenue (elevation: 23 feet); turn left.

3.3 Clemente curves to the right; now on Tremont Street.

3.4 Turn left onto Avalon Canyon Road.

3.55 Road splits; stay to the left to remain on Avalon Canyon.

3.85 Road splits; stay to the left to remain on Avalon Canyon.

4.65 Gate at entrance to Wrigley Botanical Garden; turn around here (elevation: 337 feet).

5.85 Stop sign at Tremont Street; turn sharply to the left, now on Country Club Drive.

5.9 Stay to the left to remain on Country Club; climb an average grade of 5.4%.

6.4 Stop sign at East Whittley Avenue; turn left.

6.5 Stop sign at Las Lomas Drive; turn left.

6.6 Keep straight at intersection; now on Camino del Monte.

In & Around Avalon Road Tour

7.0 Road splits; turn left, now on Old Stage Road (one way uphill). Begin climb (9.4% grade).

7.6 Crest adjacent to Hogsback Gate (high point of ride; elevation: 497 feet). Keep straight onto Chimes Tower Road (one way downhill at 9.4% grade).

8.3 Turn left onto Vieudelou Avenue; continue descent (10.2% grade).

8.45 Stop sign at Marilla Avenue; turn left. Steep descent (12.1% grade).

8.55 Stop sign at Crescent Avenue; turn left and stay to the right, now on Casino Way.

8.85 Pass the casino, on the right; now on St. Catherine Way (also called Descanso Canyon Road).

9.55 Security booth at entrance to Hamilton Cove Condominiums; turn around here.

10.25 Keep straight at casino; now on Casino Way.

10.55 Keep straight upon returning to central Avalon; now on Crescent Avenue.

10.6 End ride at Metropole Avenue.

Middle Catalina Traverse

Start: Middle Ranch Junction, Middle Ranch and Airport Roads, Santa Catalina Island

Length: 20.0 miles (clockwise loop)

Riding time: 1.5 to 4.5 hours (my time: 2H06:20)

Terrain and surface: 77% on dirt roads; 23% on a paved road with damaged pavement

Elevation: Low: 94 feet on Middle Ranch Road near Cottonwood Beach; high: 1,573 feet at entrance to Airport-in-the-Sky

Traffic and hazards: Watch out for dust clouds kicked up by passing motor vehicles, of which there may be a handful. Also watch out for bison near the roadway!

Map: Green Planet Maps, *Santa Catalina Island*

Getting there: Take the ferry to Catalina Island. Once on the island, proceed to Island Tour Plaza, located between Catalina and Summer Avenues, just south of 3rd Street. Walk here from the Cabrillo Mole ferry terminal via Pebbly Beach Road, Crescent Avenue, and then Catalina Avenue to the plaza. Hop on the airport shuttle bus to Avalon (fare plus extra charge for bicycle) to the Airport-in-the-Sky; call (310) 510-0143 for schedule. Exit at Middle Ranch and Airport Roads.

Starting point coordinates: N33.365911° / W118.374233°

THE RIDE

The Middle Catalina Traverse takes place entirely within Catalina Island's interior, in its "midsection" (west of Avalon and east of Two Harbors, Catalina's other town). About three-fourths of the ride is on dirt roads; the remaining quarter is on Airport Road. The latter is paved, but the surface was in poor condition when I rode it during the summer of 2014. The dirt roads are wide and generally in good condition. Motor vehicle activity is light; airport shuttle buses use Airport Road, along with the occasional maintenance vehicle. Maintenance vehicles and ecotour jeeps also use the dirt roads. The ride starts at

Middle Ranch Road, descending toward the ocean and overlooking Cottonwood Beach

the intersection of Airport and Middle Ranch Roads. Although one can ride here from Avalon, I would recommend taking the airport shuttle bus to Middle Ranch Road and starting the ride from there. This will save your energy for the main course. Also, you may find yourself riding (the bus, that is) with other cycling enthusiasts (the point-to-point ride from the airport back to Avalon is popular).

From Middle Ranch Junction, head west-southwest on Middle Ranch Road. The road actually makes a long sweeping curve, eventually heading west. It is essentially all downhill, making this a pleasant, breezy start to a reasonably challenging ride. Enter Middle Ranch at mile 4.8; stay on Middle Ranch Road. A native plant nursery is located here. Farther ahead, well off to the left, is Thompson's Reservoir. This 100-million-gallon lake provides water for Avalon via a 12-mile-long pipeline system. Still farther ahead, adjacent to the junction with Old Eagle's Nest Trail, is Eagle's Nest Lodge. This was formerly a stop for stagecoach travelers; later it became a hunting lodge and then an outpost for the US military. Until 1994 the lodge was simply a tourist stop. That year, a heavy storm washed out roads, causing some damage. The lodge has remained closed since then, but restoration efforts were being made as of this writing.

Stay to the right at the next junction—a dirt road leading to Ben Weston Beach and Campground—to remain on Middle Ranch Road. At the next junction (Ben Weston Junction) bear left to remain on Middle Ranch. You are now 8.3 miles into the ride. The ride's low point, just 94 feet above sea level, comes after a descent into a wash crossing. To your left is Cottonwood Beach. The beaches on this side of Catalina Island can be accessed only by dirt road, as

Catalina's Bison

The bison you see roaming around Catalina's backcountry are not natives but were shipped in by filmmaker William Farnum, ostensibly for 1924's *The Vanishing American*, an adaptation of a Zane Grey novel. His crew brought fourteen bison to the island for the shooting of the silent film. When filming was done, the crew found that rounding up to the bison was no easy task. They decided to leave the bison behind. Later, after finally rounding up the hard-to-find film, it was observed that there were no bison in the movie—and scenes from the film did not resemble Catalina's backcountry. Researchers have suggested that the bison were actually brought over for a different film altogether, such as 1925's *The Thundering Herd* (a silent film that probably features a buffalo stampede), although this film has been lost. Another candidate is 1923's *The Covered Wagon*, although the bison in that film were purportedly shot (and several literally *were* shot) on Antelope Island in Utah.

By 1934 the number of bison had increased to nineteen; an additional thirty were brought in from Colorado. The herd has grown to as high as 600, but the Santa Catalina Island Conservancy works toward holding the total at 150. When the bison herd gets too large, some are shipped to buffalo ranches, while others are destined for the butcher. Keeping the herd size under control is critical, and fencing and other interventions have kept the bison away from populated centers. In 1978, however, a rogue bison was seen walking along Avalon's beach. He left the beach, walked up Sumner Street, and ended up on a golf course. By then, local police were attempting to corral him, using a blaring siren to frighten the bison toward an opening that would lead him back to the island's interior. After missing the opening some eight times, the bison finally got the message and darted away. The rogue bison had probably been ostracized by his herd after being challenged by a younger bull.

you are doing, or by boat. The climb from the low point is at an 8.3% grade. The gradient eases as you reach Little Harbor Overlook. The harbor, which is quite scenic from this vantage point, offers anchorage for boats as well as a campground. Continue heading northeasterly at the junction with Little Harbor Road, which heads toward the harbor. You are now on Rancho Escondido Road. From the overlook (elevation: 309 feet) it is a gradual climb to a false crest (648 feet) before descending to the New Escondido Vineyards and Wrigley Ranch House (elevation: 500 feet) at mile 11.6. Bison (please see sidebar) are frequently sighted along this road.

From here Rancho Escondido Road climbs steadily, at an average grade of 5.5%, for the next 3.7 miles. The high point of the ride (1,573 feet) is reached at the entrance to Airport-in-the-Sky. As you near the airport, in addition to seeing some aircraft activity, you'll note that the road begins to climb in switchbacks. Although the airport may seem so close that you can almost touch the aircraft, the distance is extended by the twists in the road. Upon reaching the airport, you may want to take a short break—there are lavatories,

Bike Shop

Brown's Bikes, 107 Pebbly Beach Rd., Avalon; (310) 510-0986; www.catalinabiking .com

water, and an eatery (Runway Café, also known as DC-3 Gifts & Grill). The airport was completed in 1946; construction was delayed during World War II to deter enemy aircraft from using the new runway. Although the airport did not have any scheduled commercial flights as of this writing, United Airlines regularly flew aircraft here during the 1940s and 1950s. That heyday has passed, but the popularity of private, civilian aircraft has continued to increase. Once you are done here, turn right onto the paved Airport Road and head east.

Although Airport Road is paved, the surface was in poor condition when I rode it. The road is much more suited to a sturdy mountain bike than a sleek road bike. Airport Road is generally downhill to Black Jack Junction (elevation: 1,370 feet), at mile 17.3 of the ride. Black Jack Mountain, to your right, reaches up to 2,006 feet; it is exceeded only by Mount Orizaba (elevation: 2,097 feet) among Catalina Island's highest points. From here Airport Road undulates, with fast downhills and sharp uphills. The net elevation remains about the same, however. You should be able to catch views of the Pacific to your left. The ride ends at Middle Ranch Junction. From here you can wait for an airport shuttle to take you back into town. Alternatively, if you are game you can ride the (net downhill) 5.05 miles from here to Avalon.

Middle Catalina Traverse

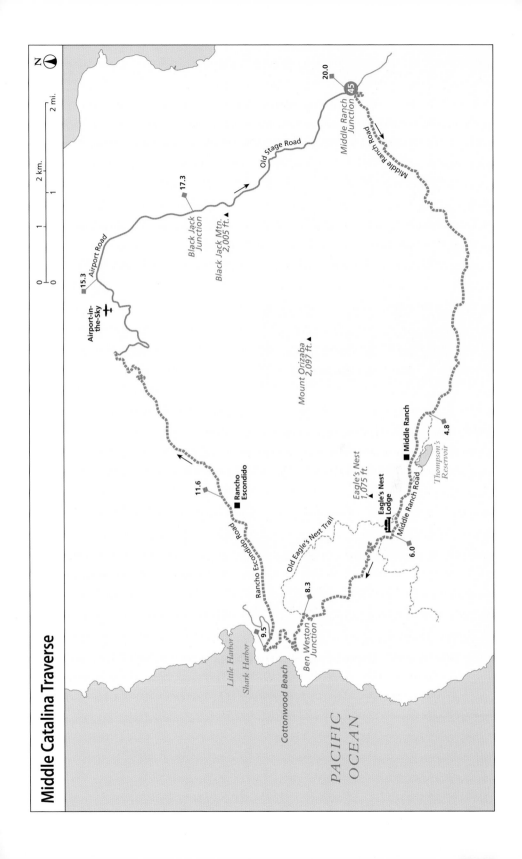

N

2 mi.
2 km.

Airport-in-the-Sky

Airport Road

15.3

Black Jack Junction
17.3

Black Jack Mtn.
2,005 ft. ▲

Old Stage Road

20.0
45

Middle Ranch Junction

Middle Ranch Road

Mount Orizaba
2,097 ft. ▲

11.6
■ Rancho Escondido

Rancho Escondido Road

Old Eagle's Nest Trail

Eagle's Nest
1,075 ft. ▲

Eagle's Nest Lodge

■ Middle Ranch

4.8

Thompson's Reservoir

Middle Ranch Road

6.0

9.5

8.3
Ben Weston Junction

Little Harbor
Shark Harbor
Cottonwood Beach

PACIFIC OCEAN

0.0 Start at Middle Ranch Junction, at the intersection of Airport and Middle Ranch Roads (on Airport Road between Avalon and Airport-in-the Sky). Head west-southwest on Middle Ranch Road (elevation: 1,367 feet).

4.8 Enter Middle Ranch, adjacent to Cape Canyon Road junction; stay on Middle Ranch Road.

6.0 Remain on Middle Ranch Road at junction with Old Eagle's Nest Trail.

8.3 Remain on Middle Ranch Road at Ben Weston Junction.

9.05 Low point of ride (94 feet) at hairpin curve near Cottonwood Beach. Climb (8.3% grade) to Little Harbor Overlook from here (elevation: 309 feet).

9.5 Little Harbor Overlook and junction with Little Harbor Road; stay to the right, now on Rancho Escondido Road. Gradual climb from here.

11.25 "False" crest (elevation: 648 feet) along Rancho Escondido Road; a short descent from here.

11.6 Keep straight at junction adjacent to New Escondido Vineyards and Wrigley Ranch House (elevation: 500 feet). Begin climb at average 5.5% grade.

15.3 Turn right onto Airport Road (paved, poor condition) adjacent to Airport-in-the-Sky. High point of ride (elevation: 1,573 feet); begin gradual downhill.

17.3 Remain on Airport Road at Black Jack Junction (elevation: 1,370 feet).

20.0 End ride at Middle Ranch Junction. (**Option:** Ride back to Avalon via Airport Road, Old Stage Road, Chimes Tower Road, Vieudelou Avenue, and Marilla Avenue—5.05 extra miles.)

Ride Log

Ride	No.	Miles	Bike	Region	Elev. Change
Ahwingna Pahe Mahar	20	3.65	mtn	NE	641 ft.
Azusadora 39 Classic	21	32.7	road	NE	2,753 ft.
Baldwin Hills Hahn-wind	31	3.35	mtn	W/SW	227 ft.
Beverly Hills Brevet	32	11.3	road	W/SW	960 ft.
Big Tujunga Canyon Epic	9	36.2	road	N/NW	2,346 ft.
Catalina East End Eco-Ride	43	13.3	mtn	Catalina	1,618 ft.
Cheeseboro-Comado Canyons Chug	10	10.7	mtn	N/NW	812 ft.
Circuito de Calabasas	11	23.6	road	N/NW	913 ft.
Crankin' Franklin Canyon	33	6.05	mtn	W/SW	538 ft.
Emerald Necklace Cruise	22	35.5	road	NE	617 ft.
Ernest Debs MASH Ride	1	8.0	mtn	central/SE	459 ft.
Glendora Mountain Trails Traverse	23	6.3	mtn	NE	924 ft.
Glendora Ridge Stage	24	39.4	road	NE	3,648 ft.
Hahamongna Watershed Shred	25	8.7	mtn	NE	1,200 ft.
Hollywood Ride of Fame	2	20.8	road	central/SE	815 ft.
In & Around Avalon Road Tour	44	10.6	road	Catalina	485 ft
Josephine Peak Hill Climb	12	8.0	mtn	N/NW	1,867 ft.
L.A. River Ramble & Echo Park Challenge	3	17.6	road	central/SE	415 ft.
Little Old Ride through Pasadena	26	17.5	road	NE	787 ft.
Malibulldog MASH 4077 Tour	34	16.65	mtn	W/SW	1,947 ft.
Middle Catalina Traverse	45	20.0	mtn	Catalina	1,479 ft.
Mission Point: Weldon Canyon	13	11.2	mtn	N/NW	1,463 ft.
Mounts Lowe and Wilson Expedition	27	24.7	mtn	NE	4,444 ft.
OC North Coast Promenade	4	19.0	road	central/SE	28 ft.

Ride	No.	Miles	Bike	Region	Elev. Change
The Oliver Twist	14	8.4	mtn	N/NW	951 ft.
Passeio de Palos Verdes	35	26.8	road	W/SW	782 ft.
Rambla Piuma Pacifico	36	18.7	road	W/SW	2,192 ft.
Ride Up over Mulholland	15	17.3	mtn	N/NW	928 ft.
Rondo Redondo Beach	37	3.9	road	W/SW	53 ft.
Ruta del Placerita Tujunga	16	31.95	road	N/NW	1,682 ft.
Santa Anita Canyon Call	28	9.4	road	NE	1,529 ft.
Schabarum Scramble	29	9.5	mtn	NE	865 ft.
South Bay Beach–Ballona Bike Tour	38	30.7	road	W/SW	117 ft.
South Central Urban Experience	5	23.1	road	central/SE	96 ft.
Topanga Puku Pawahe	39	16.75	mtn	W/SW	1,982 ft.
Topanga to Tuna to Tide	40	38.2	road	W/SW	1,821 ft.
Tour of the Lower San Gabriel Valley	6	39.0	road	central/SE	1,004 ft.
Verdugo Mountains Panorama Ride	17	13.8	mtn	N/NW	2,201 ft.
Verdugo Mountains Perimeter Ride	18	21.7	road	N/NW	1,173 ft.
Vuelta Tres Rios de Los Angeles	7	49.9	road	central/SE	229 ft.
Way of the Wilson and May Canyons	19	15.2	mtn	N/NW	2,240 ft.
White Saddle Challenge	30	17.0	mtn	NE	3,070 ft.
Whittier–Workman Hill Workout	8	9.85	mtn	central/SE	967 ft.
Zoom Dume Zuma	41	33.1	road	W/SW	2,103 ft.
Zuma Trancas Calayas	42	12.85	mtn	W/SW	1,793 ft.

References

Alleman, Richard. *Hollywood: The Movie Lover's Guide—The Ultimate Insider Tour of Movie L.A.* New York: Harper and Row, 1985.

Arcadia Historical Society. *Images of America: Arcadia.* Charleston, SC: Arcadia Publishing, 2008.

Bates, Colleen Dunn, ed. *Hometown Pasadena: The Insider's Guide.* Pasadena, CA: Prospect Park Books, 2006.

Bishop, Greg, Joe Oesterle, and Mike Marinacci. *Weird California: Your Travel Guide to California, Local Legendary & Best Kept Secrets.* New York: Sterling Publishing Co., Inc., 2009.

Boston, John, and the Santa Clarita Valley Historical Society. *Images of America: Santa Clarita Valley.* Charleston, SC: Arcadia Publishing, 2009.

Brady, Patrick. *Bicycling Los Angeles County: A Guide to Great Road Bike Rides.* Birmingham, AL: Menasha Ridge Press, 2007.

Brundige, Don and Sharron. *Cycling Los Angeles,* 2nd edition. El Cajon, CA: Sunbelt Publications, 2007.

Bullock, Paul. *Watts: The Aftermath.* New York: Grove Press, Inc., 1969.

California Coastal Commission. *California Coastal Access Guide.* Berkeley, CA: University of California Press, 1991.

Cannon, Lou. *Official Negligence: How Rodney King and the Riots Changed Los Angeles and the LAPD.* Boulder, CO: Westview Press, 1999.

Carcamo, Cindy. "Huntington Beach Settles Surf City USA Lawsuit," *Orange County Register,* Jan. 22, 2008.

Carlberg, Marvin, and Chris Epting. *Huntington Beach.* Charleston, SC: Arcadia Publishing, 2009.

Cerro, Julie Logo. *Images of America: Culver City.* Charleston, SC: Arcadia Publishing, 2004.

Cerro, Julie Lugo, and Marc Wanamaker. *Images of America: Movie Studios of Culver City.* Charleston, SC: Arcadia Publishing, 2011.

Clark, Ginger Garnett. *Images of America: Rancho Palos Verdes.* Charleston, SC: Arcadia Publishing, 2009.

Conyers, Patrick, Cedar Phillips, and the Pasadena Museum of History. *Images of America: Pasadena—1940–2008.* Charleston, SC: Arcadia Publishing, 2009.

Cornejo, Jeffrey Lawrence Jr. *Images of America: Azusa.* Charleston, SC: Arcadia Publishing, 2007.

Dedek, Peter. *Hip to the Trip: A Cultural History of Route 66.* Albuquerque, NM: University of New Mexico Press, 2007.

Deener, Andrew. *Venice: A Contested Bohemia in Los Angeles.* Chicago: University of Chicago Press, 2012.

Denham, T. D. "California's Cycle-Way," *Good Roads,* Nov. 1901.

Dennis, Jan. *Images of America: Manhattan Beach.* Charleston, SC: Arcadia Publishing, 2001.

Denton, Brad, and Kristine Denton. *The Outdoor Guide to the Palos Verdes Peninsula.* San Diego: Sunbelt Publications, 2007.

Deverell, William, and Greg Hise (eds.). *A Companion to Los Angeles.* Malden, MA: Wiley-Blackwell, 2010.

Diffrient, David Scott. *TV Milestones Series: M*A*S*H.* Detroit, MI: Wayne State University Press, 2008.

Dreyson, Mark. "Marketing National Identity: The Olympic Games of 1932 and American Culture," *OLYMPIKA: The International Journal of Olympic Studies,* Volume IV, 1995, pp. 23-48.

Droz, Robert V. "U.S. 66: In the Beginning," *U.S. Highways: U.S. 1 to U.S 830.* Self-published, Dec. 10, 2006.

Eberts, Mike. *Griffith Park: A Centennial History.* Los Angeles: Historical Society of Southern California, 1996.

Ehrenreich, Ben. "The End—Features," *Los Angeles Magazine,* Nov. 1, 2010.

Elrick, Ted. *Images of America: Los Angeles River.* Charleston, SC: Arcadia Publishing, 2007.

Epting, Chris, *Huntington Beach: Images of America.* Chicago: Arcadia Publishing, 2001.

Fox, Richard. *enCYCLEpedia Southern California: The Best Easy Scenic Bike Rides.* Westcliffe, CO: Westcliffe Publications, 2014.

Garate, Donald T. *Juan Bautista de Anza: Basque Explorer in the New World, 1693–1740.* Reno, NV: University of Nevada Press, 2003.

Garcia, Courtney. "Out with Kodak, In with Dolby at Home of Oscars," Reuters, Jun. 11, 2012.

Gish, Judy. "Highway 39: Caltrans vs. Mother Nature," *Inside Seven.* Los Angeles, CA: California Department of Transportation–District 07, October 2008.

Goldstone, Bud, and Arloa Paquin Goldstone. *The Los Angeles Watts Towers.* Los Angeles, CA: J. Paul Getty Museum and Getty Conservation Institute, 1997.

Gottfried, Ted. *Earvin Magic Johnson: Champion and Crusader.* New York, NY: F. Watts, 2001.

Gottlieb, Robert. *Reinventing Los Angeles: Nature and Community in the Global City.* Cambridge, MA: M.I.T. Press, 2007.

Gray, Madison. "The L.A. Riots: 15 Years after Rodney King," *Time,* Apr. 25, 2007.

Gumprecht, Blake. *The Los Angeles River: Its Life, Death, and Possible Rebirth.* Baltimore, MD: Johns Hopkins University Press, 2001.

Hall, Clarence, Jr. *Introduction to the Geology of Southern California and its Native Plants.* Los Angeles, CA: University of California Press, 2007.

Harris, James. *Santa Monica Pier: A Century on the Last Great Pleasure Pier.* Los Angeles, CA; Angel City Press, 2009.

Hawthorne, Christopher. "Ambitious Goal for L.A. River: Continuous 51-Mile Path by 2020," *Los Angeles Times,* July 23, 2013.

Hein, Frank J., and Carlos de la Rosa. *Wild Catalina Island: Natural Secrets and Ecological Triumphs.* Charleston, SC: Natural History Press, 2013.

Home, Gerald. *Fire This Time: The Watts Uprising and the 1960s.* Charlottesville, VA: University of Virginia Press, 1995.

Hough, Susan E. *Finding Fault in California: An Earthquake Tourist's Guide.* Missoula, CA: Mountain Press, 2004.

Isaac, Jim, and Tom Herrera. *San Pedro: Then and Now.* Charleston, SC: Arcadia Publishing, 2011.

International Olympic Committee. "The Games of the Xth Olympiad: Official Report." Xth Olympiad Committee of the Games of Los Angeles. Los Angeles, CA, 1933.

Koon, Stacey C., and Robert Deitz. *Presumed Guilty: The Tragedy of the Rodney King Affair.* Washington, DC: Regnery Gateway, 1992.

Kotkin, Joel. "Let L.A. be L.A." *City Journal,* 22(3), Summer 2012.

"Kramer First Name Put in Walk of Fame," *Los Angeles Times,* Mar. 29, 1960, p. 15.

Krintz, Jennifer. *Images of America: Redondo Beach Pier.* Charleston, SC: Arcadia Publishing, 2011.

Larson, Tom, and Miles Finney. "Rebuilding South Central Los Angeles: Myths, Realities, and Opportunities," Working Paper. Los Angeles: School of Business and Economics, California State University, no date.

Lawler, Mike, and Robert Newcombe. *Images of America: La Crescenta.* Charleston, SC: Arcadia Publishing, 2005.

Lawler, Mike. "Treasures of the Valley: La Crescenta Motel as a Movie Location," *Crescenta Valley Weekly,* Apr. 26, 2012.

Linton, Joe. *Down By the Los Angeles River: Friends of the Los Angeles River's Official Guide.* Berkeley, CA: Wilderness Press, 2005.

Lockeretz, David. *Nobody Hikes in L.A.: The Guidebook.* Edgemont, SD: Trail Head Enterprises, 2010.

Loomis, Jan. *Images of America: Pacific Palisades.* Charleston, SC: Arcadia Publishing, 2009.

Lopez, Ronald William. *The Battle for Chavez Ravine: Public Policy and Chicano Community Resistance in Post-War Los Angeles, 1945–1962.* Berkeley, CA: University of California, 1999.

Lund, Ann Scheid. *Historic Pasadena: An Illustrated History.* Pasadena, CA: Pasadena Historical Museum, 1999.

Mallan, Chicki. *Guide to Catalina and California's Channel Islands,* 5th edition. Paradise, CA: Pine Press, 1996.

Marcus, Ben, and Marc Wanamaker. *Images of America: Malibu.* Charleston, SC: Arcadia Publishing, 2011.

Martin, Hugo. "Over 50 Years, Walk of Fame Turned Hollywood into Destination," *Los Angeles Times,* Feb. 8, 2010.

Mathews, Tom, et al. "The Siege of L.A.", *Newsweek,* May 1992.

Maxwell, Pat, Bob Rhein, and Jerry Roberts. *Catalina A to Z: A Glossary Guide to California's Island Jewel.* Charleston, SC: The History Press, 2014.

Maynard, John Arthur. *Venice West: The Beat Generation in Southern California.* New Brunswick, NJ: Rutgers University Press, 1991.

Medved, Harry, and Bruce Akiyama. *Hollywood Escapes: The Moviegoer's Guide to Southern California's Great Outdoors.* New York, NY: St. Martin's Press, 2006.

Messer, Steve, Jim Hasenauer, and Mark Langton. *Where to Bike Los Angeles Mountain Biking: Best Mountain Biking around Los Angeles.* Where to Bike (BA Press), 2012.

Messinger, Cheryl, and Terran McGinnis. *Images of America: Marineland.* Charleston, SC: Arcadia Publishing, 2011.

Miller, Michael. "Sunset Annexed, Group Plans Appeal," *Huntington Beach Independent,* Aug. 25, 2011, pp. A1 & A10.

Moffat, Susan. "Pedaling His Bikeway Plan," *Los Angeles Times,* Aug. 29, 1995, p. 2.

Montoya, Carina Monica. *Pacific Coast Highway in Los Angeles County.* Charleston, SC: The History Press, 2014.

Morgan, Diane. *The Buddhist Experience in North America.* Westport, CT: Greenwood Press, 2004.

Mulholland, Catherine. *William Mulholland and the Rise of Los Angeles.* Los Angeles, CA: University of California Press, 2000.

Normark, Don. *Chavez Ravine, 1949: A Los Angeles Story.* San Francisco, CA: Chronicle Books, LLC, 1999.

Ockun, Dave. "Hollywood, California: Hollywood History and Information," Nov. 16, 2010; www.abouthollywood.com/hollywood-neighborhoods/hollywood-california-history-and-information, retrieved on May 29, 2014.

Ostertag, Rhonda, and George Ostertag. *California State Parks: A Complete Recreation Guide,* 2nd edition. Seattle, WA: The Mountaineers Books, 2001.

Owens, Caitlin, James Queally, and Emily Alpert Reyes. "UCLA-Area Water Main Break Spews Millions of Gallons," *Los Angeles Times,* Jul. 29, 2014.

Patris, Michael, Steve Crise, and the Mount Lowe Preservation Society. *Mount Lowe Railway.* Charleston, SC: Arcadia Publishing, 2012.

Perkins, Maggi. *Images of America: Newhall.* Charleston, SC: Arcadia Publishing, 2010.

Pollack, Alan, Kim Stephens, and E. J. Stephens. *Legendary Locals of the Santa Clarita Valley.* Charleston, SC: Arcadia Publishing, 2012.

Phillips, John. *Images of America: Palos Verdes Estates.* Charleston, SC: Arcadia Publishing, 2010.

Pierloni, Allen. "The Question Remains: Which City Is Surf City?" *Sacramento Bee,* May 14, 2007.

Pomeroy, Elizabeth. *Images of America: Pasadena—A Natural History.* Charleston, SC: Arcadia Publishing, 2007.

Pool, Bob. "Getting the Slant on L.A.'s Steepest Streets," *Los Angeles Times,* Aug. 21, 2003.

Randall, Laura. *60 Hikes within 60 Miles: Los Angeles, Including Ventura and Orange Counties.* Birmingham, AL: Menasha Ridge Press, 2009.

Randall, Laura. *Peaceful Places Los Angeles: 110 Tranquil Sites in the City of Angels and Neighboring Communities.* Birmingham, AL: Menasha Ridge Press, 2010.

Reyes, Emily Alpert. "Water Main Break Repaired on Sunset Boulevard; Street May Reopen Soon," *Los Angeles Times,* Sept. 27, 2014.

Riddle, Jon, and Sarah Amelar. *Where to Bike Los Angeles: Best Biking in City and Suburbs.* Where to Bike (BA Press), 2012.

Riedel, Allen, and Monique Riedel. *Best Hikes Near Los Angeles.* Guilford, CT: Globe Pequot/FalconGuides, 2011.

Robinson, John H. *Trails of the Angeles: 100 Hikes in the San Gabriels,* 9th edition. Birmingham, AL: Wilderness Press, 2013.

Sanburn, Josh. "Top 11 Zoo Escapes," *Time,* Mar. 30, 2011.

Sapp, Methea Katherine. *America's Natural Places: Pacific and West.* Santa Barbara, CA: Greenwood Publishing Group, 2010.

Saxena, K. R., and V. M. Sharma. *Dams: Incidents and Accidents,* Leiden. The Netherlands: A. A. Balkema Publishers, 2005.

Schad, Jerry. *101 Hikes in Southern California.* Berkeley, CA: Wilderness Press, 2005.

Schad, Jerry. *Afoot and Afield Los Angeles: A Comprehensive Hiking Guide,* 3rd edition. Berkeley, CA: Wilderness Press, 2010.

Seims, Charles. *Mt. Lowe, The Railway in the Clouds.* San Marino, CA: Golden West Books, 1976.

Sherwood, Wayne E. "Pier into the Past," *Huntington Beach Magazine,* Vol. 1, No. 2, Oct. 2003.

Stephens, E. J., and Marc Wanamaker. *Griffith Park: Images of America.* Charleston, SC: Arcadia Publishing, 2011.

Thomson, David. *The Whole Equation: A History of Hollywood.* New York, NY: Vintage Books, 2006.

Turner, Michelle L., and the Pasadena Museum of History. *Images of America: The Rose Bowl.* Charleston, SC: Arcadia Publishing, 2010.

Vitti, Jim. *Chicago Cubs: Baseball on Catalina Island.* Charleston, SC: Arcadia Publishing, 2010.

Vonder Linden, Karl. "The Portuguese Bend Landslide," *Engineering Geology,* Vol. 27, Issues 1–4, Dec. 1989, pp. 301–373.

Wallechinsky, David, and Jaime Loucky, *The Complete Book of the Olympics: 2008 Edition.* London, England: Aurum Press, 2008.

Wanamaker, Marc. *Images of America: Hollywood: 1940–2008.* Charleston, SC: Arcadia Publishing, 2009.

_____. *Images of America: Beverly Hills, 1930-2005.* Charleston, SC: Arcadia Publishing, 2006.

_____. *Images of America: Early Beverly Hills.* Charleston, SC: Arcadia Publishing, 2005.

Warshaw, Matt. *History of Surfing.* San Francisco, CA: Chronicle Books, 2010.

Water Conservation Authority. *Emerald Necklace Implementation Plan—Phase I: Initial Study.* Azusa, CA: ECORP Consulting, Mar. 2013.

Williams, Gregory Paul. *The Story of Hollywood: An Illustrated History.* Los Angeles, CA: BL Press, 2006.

Winning, Robert. *Short Bike Rides In and Around Los Angeles,* 2nd edition. Guilford, CT: Globe Pequot/FalconGuides, 1998.

Wood, Daniel B. "L.A.'s Darkest Days," *Christian Science Monitor,* Apr. 29, 2002.

WEBSITES

Article on hiking above Lake View Terrace (www.everytrail.com).

California State Parks websites (www.parks.ca.gov) on Bolsa Chica State Beach, Dockweiler State Beach, Huntington State Beach, Kenneth Hahn State Recreation Area, Malibu Creek State Park, Malibu Lagoon State Beach, Placerita Canyon State Park, Point Dume State Beach, Robert H. Meyer Memorial State Beach, Santa Monica State Beach, Sunset State Beach, Topanga State Park, Watts Towers of Simon Rodia State Historic Park, Will Rogers State Beach.

City of Hope (www.cityofhope.org), accessed on Oct. 5, 2014.

Ernest R. Debs Regional Park, Los Angeles (www.debspark.org), accessed on Jan. 10, 2014.